~sity of

business
Information
Technology

Timothy Cleary

Higher Colleges of Technology
Dubai UAE
Formerly University College Suffolk

FINANCIAL TIMES
PITMAN PUBLISHING

I would like to dedicate this book to my loving Irish parents.

Semper Fidelis

FINANCIAL TIMES MANAGEMENT
128 Long Acre, London WC2E 9AN
Tel: +44 (0)171 447 2000
Fax: +44 (0)171 240 5771
Website: www.ftmanagement.com

A Division of Financial Times Professional Limited

First published in Great Britain in 1998

© Financial Times Professional Limited 1998

The right of Timothy Cleary to be identified as Author of
this Work has been asserted by him in accordance with the
Copyright, Designs and Patents Act 1988.

ISBN 0 273 63410 0

British Library Cataloguing in Publication Data
A CIP catalogue record for this book can be obtained from the British Library.

10 9 8 7 6 5 4 3 2 1

Typeset by Land & Unwin (Data Sciences) Ltd, Northampton
Printed and bound in Great Britain by Bell and Bain Ltd, Glasgow

The Publishers' policy is to use paper manufactured from sustainable forests.

Contents

Preface

First of all I would like to thank my family, especially my brother Mark as it was he who got me going on the book in the first place. My mother and father and my other five brothers and sisters did their bit to hasten the process by always wanting to know when I was actually going to finish the book whilst my Uncle Jack pacified me with long phone calls on those odd occasions when I thought I was going to pack it in.

Secondly I would like to thank my Editor at Pitman, namely John Cushion. He was critical to the completion of this book and I am indebted to him.

I would also like to thank the following list of friends and colleagues from my former place of study, the University of Manchester Institute of Science and Technology and my former place of work, University College Suffolk. The list also contains the names of people who were there for me when I needed them most. Sue Busby, Nick Velonis, Chris Thorpe, Julia Egorova, Diane Keeble Allen, Paul Jones, Geoff Poole, Shirley Marshall, Riff Ali, Ashan Razvi, Dr Michael Gregory, Dr Ron Impey, Sue Jolliffe, John Kennedy, Kulvinder Kang, Mark McChrystal, Charlie Duffy, Paul and Kate O'Donnell, Rod Burrell, Jerry Chitty, Natasha Butalova, Dr George Passalidis, Julian Drew, Rick Williams, Martyn Gowers, Dr James Brown, Stuart Pask, Alex McGuigan, Dr Tony Manyani, Pat Heathcote, Chris Manning and John McDermot.

Finally I would like to say thank you to my current employers, colleagues and students at the Higher Colleges of Technology in Dubai in the United Arab Emirates. Their professionalism is second to none and the civility and demeanour with which I have been treated has been over and beyond anything I might have expected.

May you, the reader, find this book, God willing, a useful one.

Timothy James Cleary

Acknowledgments

I would like to thank the following organisations who provided me with so much useful information:

Advanced Micro Devices (AMD); America Online; American Megatrends Inc.; American Telephone & Telegraph (AT & T); Apple Corporation; Artisoft Ltd; Borland; British Telecom; Canon; Central Point Software; Commodore; Compaq; Compuserve; Computer Associates; Cray Computers; Cybertec Ltd; Cyrix; Digital Equipment Corporation (DEC); Disctronics; Epson; Hewlett Packard; Hitachi Corporation; Informix; Intel; IBM; International Computers Ltd (ICL); Ionica; Kodak; Lotus; Mercury; Microsoft; Motorola; Netscape Communications; Nintendo; Novell; Oracle; Phillips; Psion; Quattro; S&S International; Sage; Santa Cruz Operation (SCO); Sony; Storacall Voice Systems; Sun Microsystems; Symantec Corporation; Tetra; Triangle Software International; Unisys; Xerox.

1

Business computing technology

1.1 INTRODUCTION

The main objective of this chapter is to provide both an overview of the impact and substance of contemporary business technology as well as a general perception of the direction of business computing.

Section 1.2 considers the manner in which new technology is operating in the contemporary global commercial environment whilst section 1.3 is an examination of the vexed question of computing standards and the concept of computing technology interoperability. Finally section 1.4 deals with the ever-changing fortunes and trends within the computing industry.

1.2 THE INFORMATION AGE

The commercial backdrop of the early 1980s is believed to have been the start of what is now commonly referred to as the "Information Age". Although there is no precise explanation as to what the term Information Age actually means, it is frequently acknowledged as being that term used to describe the manner in which the current global business environment is enveloped within a plethora of information, the vast majority of which is being generated by contemporary new technology.

The Information Age also appears to be a term which recognises the current era as the time whereby most countries around the world have deemed new technology as the leading force in modern economic growth and who have as a consequence begun to evolve into what is commonly thought of as the post-industrial state. In other words, countries, many of which had previously evolved from an agrarian-based economy to that of one based on heavy industry, were, and are, gradually moving towards an information-driven trading environment. This is not to say that those countries have lost their substantial agricultural/manufacturing industry, natural resources or whatever else was their original source(s) of prosperity, but simply a recognition that the prime vein of wealth and business leadership within these countries is now embedded in a computerised information-centred setting.

Consider for example the downloading of information services or software applications across the Internet (see 14.1). In the past, the providers of the information/software would have to produce, in a physical form of one sort or another, a copy of the required information/software for each individual user. Nowadays the provider simply installs one copy of the software/information on their particular Internet site. Users then wishing to access the information/software simply dial up the site and read it accordingly. The point is, it does not matter whether it is accessed by one user or ten million. The cost of production and delivery to the provider are as much for the first user as they are for the last. Such a change in the costs of supply is revolutionary to say the least and the idea that the planet is at the point of entering a commercial digitised environment relatively free from the constraint of allocating scarce resources due to the possibility of an infinite and readily available rearrangement of binary coded data is rapidly dawning on business and governments across the world.

In this respect, the 1990s has experienced an incredible transformation in the manner in which commercial functions and decisions are conducted. However, this current precipitous growth in the use of Information Technology (IT) in the business and domestic environment is primarily due to the collective crystallisation of the relatively recent and significant technological advances which have been made in the computing and communication industries.

Critical features of these advances include increased miniaturisation and the ability of manufacturers to produce sophisticated electronic/computer components with cost-effective mass-production techniques. The staggering gains that have been made in this regard can be measured by the arrival of the astounding array of goods and services that are available to industry and individual alike. In addition to the incredible advances in microelectronics, developers have succeeded in producing intricate complementary software applications in order to take full advantage of an ever-improving hardware situation.

As a result of these gains, computers and computer-controlled devices are tackling ever more complex tasks with an ever-increasing cost advantage and so providing the very platform that has enabled the new technologies to become as widespread as they have. What is more, commercial acumen has taken full advantage of this technological progress, a fact which is reflected in the business and home environment of the late 1990s as domestic and small business users access powerful desktop computers which supply far greater processing power than the huge expensive commercial computers of the mid to late 1980s. The users of these computers are also operating a whole new range of intelligent graphic-enhanced software systems such as new sophisticated multimedia style communication applications, many of which are allowing users to present, store, analyse, transmit and receive data and information with unparalleled effect. Business and domestic IT users in the late 1990s are also beginning to realise that computing and telecommunication technologies are no longer developing in isolation but are gradually merging in an increasingly innovative and intriguing manner.

1.2.1 Technological convergence

A good macro example of technological convergence is encapsulated in the telecommunication industry's' increasing reliance on computing technology, a trend which is depicted in the arrival of a new generation of automated switchboards, voice mail systems and high technology call centres. Further technological improvements, such as that which has occurred in computer networks, has fuelled the development of other advanced communication systems. These include products such as digital mobile phones, video conferencing and e-mail, all of which are allowing business users to make those informed critical decisions which are so necessary for commercial success. The concept of converging technologies has also reached the clutter of the general office as independent peripheral devices such as faxes, printers, scanners and modems are merged into intelligent multifunction machines, the likes of which are capable of performing a whole range of ancillary tasks.

However the arrival of all this sophisticated equipment cannot be viewed in mechanistic isolation. Other non-technical factors which have enabled increasing progress in the use and substance of IT in the business environment centre on the quality of employee education and the current tide of global deregulation legislation.

1.2.2 The digital business environment

In the mid 1990s governments across the world instituted a gush of legislation privatising and liberalising their computing and telecommunication industries and markets. As a consequence, users, individual and commercial, are not only experiencing an upsurge in the quality of various computing and communication services but are also benefiting from an accommodating reduction in relative operational costs as increased competition introduces more realistic pricing structures.

With respect to the employees in a digital business environment, it is a fact of life that modern organisations using significant levels of IT require workers that are well educated, mobile and mentally prepared to adapt to an ever-evolving setting. Facilitating such flexibility has meant that numerous governments have had to indulge in strenuous employment deregulation as well as pumping money into huge training programmes.

Unfortunately, despite these efforts, commercial organisations every-where are discovering that critical and necessary talents are still in short supply. This is so despite the huge pool of redundant unskilled and semi-skilled employees found in countries across the world. Such workers were, until relatively recently, the backbone of the majority of the world's indus-trialised work forces. However transforming these workers into employees that are equipped with appropriate high tech expertise has proved to be problematical to say the least.

Conversely, in a global cost-conscious economy, employers are also using IT to maximise efficiency by scheduling their workers to provide their skills only as and when they are needed. As a consequence, even those workers that have the necessary skills are facing reduced opportunities as part-time/short-term employment becomes the norm. What is more, IT is not only affecting the terms and conditions of modern employment but even the location of the actual workplace. Telecottages and teleworking (see 14.3) means that vast swathes of the working population no longer need to commute to expensive office complexes in order to perform their duties. Instead, employers have discovered that workers, given the right equip-ment, can complete their work routines from the comfort of their own homes/localities. In addition suitably furnished mobile employees known as nomad workers can also operate with the minimum of infrastructure. For example, sales representatives can roam across the country from customer to customer selling or providing various goods and services without ever having to return to their employer's head office. Such workers could and do employ laptop computers providing all the necessary paperwork so that they can bill their customer as well as provide a useful multimedia type application enabling users to sell their products/services. Top of the range wireless-linked laptop computers enable such workers to relay the results of their activities as and when needed as well as receive any necessary incoming information from their employer.

In the final analysis IT has enabled business users/organisations to raise productivity levels, decrease the lead times for the impact of their decisions, accelerate production cycles and generally compete in a far more cogent and effective manner in the new global economy. However, critical physical limitations in the form of the restricted transmission bandwidth of the various computing and communication links currently installed across the globe means that many prospective services either are on hold or, because of the narrow user base, enjoy slow take-up rates. Even so the late 1990s is experiencing a massive growth in the use of high-speed modems, ISDN telephone lines, hybrid fibre/coaxial cable and various wireless technologies, all of which promise to deliver the very capacity needed to supply VOD (Video on Demand), etc. It is expected that improvements in such technology will enable business users to have greater access to, and control of, those services available from external sources such as the Internet as well as to gain greater internal control of their particular organisation's activities. It is also expected that such control will be exercised in an integrated and seamless manner. For example, voice and data communication systems based on state of the art satellite technology can make dramatic improvements in the delivery of sophisticated global mobile computer telephony services. Connecting such services to wireless computers/ phones operating intelligent user friendly software can provide users with the pinnacle in communication and processing capabilities.

1.3 COMPUTING STANDARDS

The computing industry of the late 1990s is commonly recognised as being a lucrative and vigorous business. Companies involved in the computing industry are perceived to operate within a fiercely competitive environment. The fact that top software companies have started the practice of giving away certain types of expensive blue-chip software in order to attract customers to their product line goes some way in highlighting the intensity within this sector of commerce.

One theme which embodies the relentless conflict within the computing industry is that of computing standards. Unfortunately, computing standards are crucial for users and developers alike, and an inappropriate choice of computing technology can prove disastrous. Having said this, computing standards are, due to ever-advancing technology, in a continuous state of flux and choosing the most advantageous standard(s) usually comes down to informed timing.

Computing standards fall into two broad categories. The first consists of those standards which are regulated by numerous official bodies. For example, there is the American National Standards Institute (ANSI), an organisation specialising in the regulation of computing languages. Another significant body is the International Standards Organisation (ISO). It specialises in the regulation of communication systems. Organisations such as ANSI and the ISO are highly respected international bodies and are usually independent of particular commercial interests.

The second type of computing standard usually refers to those unofficial standards which have been established by individual developers/organisations. A good example is IBM's Systems Application Architecture (SAA), which was a policy commitment by IBM to bring a concerted programming environment, uniform user interface, and a seamless application platform across all its product range from the PC through to the mainframe.

In the past most major computing companies concentrated on producing proprietary systems. The significance of proprietary systems was that they were usually incompatible with the technology of rival companies. As a result, users were usually severely restricted in their choice of equipment, as they were, more often than not, locked into the technology which was supplied by the original vendor. In addition users of proprietary systems also discovered that they were hostage to the whims and fortunes of the technology's vendor who could increase prices and discontinue services as and when the need arose.

The fact is computing vendors were and are only too aware of their own capital investment and are consequently very cagey at the possibility of empowering competitors' standardisation and compatibility. They know that a proprietary system gives them a captive user base which is an asset in its own right.

However, the arrival of the Open Systems concept (see 1.3.1) as well as other factors such as changing technology and increased competition, all meant that computer developers had to come to terms with the idea of producing products which would co-operate with those of their rivals. Even industry giants such as IBM were destined to be incapable of dictating computing standards. This was to prove especially so with the arrival of the de facto PC (Personal Computer) standard, a standard which currently accounts for something like 90% of the world's computers.

The arrival of the PC meant that major hardware and software developers across the globe have had to concur on a wide range of product protocols and standards so as to enable a myriad of computing products to integrate and interoperate. Without such agreement, the PC could not have taken the market share that it did and has. What is more, the success of the PC resulted in a general acceptance by the computing industry that real growth and profit would only be achieved by companies producing computer hardware/software products which were capable of working not only with those produced by their own organisation and partners but also those of their adversaries.

As a consequence the early to mid 1990s in the computing industry was a period of technological rationalisation as developers and users moved towards an Open Systems environment. For example, hardware manufacturers began to turn their attention to the production of computers known as cross-platforms. These computers differ from proprietary-based systems in that they are capable of operating the software designed for other computers as well as that of their own systems. Such interoperation of software was further fuelled in the late 1990s with the arrival of the Java (see 9.8.1) programming language, a computing language enabling developers to produce computing applications capable of running on almost any computer.

1.3.1 The Open Systems concept

The original Open Systems concept was a result of a corporate strategy pursued in the 1980s by the North American corporation, Sun Microsystems. The company promoted its workstation computers as machines capable of being 'plugged and played' across the product lines of hundreds of different producers. The strategy minimised Sun Microsystem's research and development costs by using readily available 'parts/components' and propelled the advance of their own products by enabling competitors to develop similar systems so creating platform markets into which they could supply.

However, the Open Systems concept is now recognised as being a term embracing a general strategic approach by the whole of the computing and communications industry. The main attraction of the Open Systems concept is that it promises users and developers an interchangeable component approach. Technology, therefore, which claims to operate within an Open Systems type environment suggests that users can, for example, procure distinct units of computing hardware/software from many different vendors, confident that they will work in a fully co-ordinated system.

Despite its appeal, a 'pure' Open Systems environment, in other words a situation in which every piece of hardware and software is designed to be capable of interoperating with every other piece of hardware and software, is, for the foreseeable future, an unrealistic dream to say the least. Two major hurdles in the way of such a possibility are:

(a) The technological limits of current software and hardware.

(b) The continuing failure of vendors/developers to agree on common standards in so many areas of computing and communications technology.

Nonetheless as has already been mentioned, there are computing/communication markets which are, in effect, operating inside what might be thought of as a de facto Open Systems environment. A working concept of a de facto Open Systems within a computing/communication context appears to centre on two major underlying principles. These are user independence and software transparency.

1.3.2 User independence

In the microcomputer market, user independence is not such a predicament. The reason for this, strange as it may seem, is because the current market is dominated by a handful of microprocessor standards. Two of the biggest are Intel and the PowerPC. (The PowerPC is a microprocessor range originally developed by a consortium made up of Motorola, IBM and Apple.) The combined global market share of these two standards in 1997 stood at about 80% of the PC market.

The point is that this dominance has resulted in developers producing a vast range of compatible software and hardware capable of operating with either the Intel or PowerPC architecture or indeed both. As a result of this development the purchaser is free to choose from a wide range of autonomous suppliers and is not hostage to the original vendors.

However, user independence in this regard is much less certain in the upper end of the computer market. The rivalry between mainframe, minicomputer, workstation and PC server computer manufacturers and software developers is much more savage and complex. The reason for this is that many developers in this sector have huge vested interests in what can be described as *mission critical* technology. This is a term used to describe those systems which, as a rule, provide users, the majority of whom tend to be of a corporate calibre, with a very secure and dependable processing environment. The main reason that these systems are so reliable is that they are usually based on mature mainframe/minicomputer technology. As a result, computer developers are, as has already been explained, often reluctant to indulge in standardisation in case they empower their rivals to produce cheaper clone technology, an event which would undermine their customer base.

1.3.3 Software transparency

Software transparency is concerned with two main features: the uniformity of the software and the seamless manner in which it operates.

Uniformity

In the early years of software development, many updated software applications often bore no resemblance to previous generations of the same product. In addition, they were, more often than not, not only incompatible with other software products but also incompatible with previous generations of the same application. In other words, users were unable to read and use files created by other applications or earlier versions of the same product. Such incompatibility usually caused great upheaval in the client base as users were forced to adapt to the changes. In order therefore to retain and attract customers, software developers realised the necessity of carrying certain critical 'features' and 'commands' through the generations of their software products so reducing the user's learning curve. In addition developers also recognised that it was necessary that their products were to be backwardly and outwardly compatible with the data created from previous versions of the product as well as data created by other applications.

A good example of successful uniformity is that which was originally instigated on the mass market by Microsoft's Windows environment. Windows-oriented applications have provided the obvious advantage of enabling users to employ known skills gained from using other similar applications as well as enabling users to access valuable data already keyed in by other applications.

Seamless interfacing

Seamless interfacing in an Open Systems environment is usually concerned with those programs that protect users from that unnecessary detail needed to interface with other computers/applications. A good example of seamless interfacing includes emulation programs enabling PCs to simulate the commands of a dedicated mainframe/minicomputer terminal. Another good example of a seamless interfacing type program is the current Web browser software (see 9.10.1(l)). The advantage of this software is that it enables users to traverse all the various computer systems currently linked up to the World Wide Web (WWW) without the need to enter laborious complex text commands.

1.3.4 Adoption

Because of their bitter experiences, such as loss of market share due to cheaper alternatives, major computing developers of every type have, to varying degrees, adopted the concept of Open Systems. However, the individual organisational adoption policies tend to be, due to natural competitive tactics, a movable feast. In other words, computing and communication companies adopt Open Systems as and when it is profitable for them to do so.

The contemporary adoption of Open Systems can be seen amongst those developers involved in producing expensive Critical Mission Software (CMS). Software applications which are generally classed as CMS usually refer to a class of industry-standard software which is considered to be both robust and extremely reliable. However, these CMS applications were, until very recently, usually proprietary in nature and were, more often than not, usually only capable of running on the larger more expensive computers.

However, software developers, in line with the general trend towards Open Systems, have started to produce portable, scaleable versions of their CMS products. By revamping proprietary CMS applications in 'shrink package' versions capable of operating on a wide variety of non-mainframe computers such as workstations and PCs, software developers discovered that they could stem customer drift to other emerging economic applications/systems.

Another major reason for developers adopting an Open Systems approach hinges on their need to share the now enormous research and development (R&D) costs, the size of which can be crippling even for mighty corporations such as IBM or Microsoft. However, as necessary R&D becomes increasingly expensive so the computing industry appears to be being reduced to a series of corporate alliances as leading companies combine to fund costly research projects to produce those products and services that will provide them with the necessary competitive edge.

Such alliances have, understandably, attracted considerable criticism as many observers believe that they can prove detrimental in that they can produce monopolistic technological fronts, thus coercing other competitors to conform to those technological standards in order to sell their particular goods/services, as well as reducing opportunities for new entrants to the industry.

1.4 THE COMPUTING INDUSTRY

To date, the modern computing industry is considered to have experienced three major stages of development. The first stage started with the mainframe and minicomputer whilst the second stage centred on the PC/desktop computer. In the third and current stage, the computing industry is perceived as advancing various types of computer networking technologies.

Contemporary computing technology is also going through a dramatic reclassification process due to the major technological advances which have occurred since the first two stages. For example there has been a certain blurring of differentiation between the various classes of computer configurations. The reason for this confusion in machine genus is evidenced by the nature of the components and architecture of numerous modern mainframe/minicomputers, many of which are now remarkably similar to their cheaper PC/workstation counterparts.

1.4.1 Previous developments

The initial thrust of each stage of the computer industry's development can be mirrored in the fortunes of the companies that helped bring them about.

In the 1960s and 1970s the computing industry was well and truly dominated by IBM. Other major industry players, such as the Digital Equipment Corporation (DEC), Cray Computers and International Computers Ltd (ICL), cornered significant sections of the computing market but never really came anywhere near to challenging IBM's overall global leadership. In 1984, when IBM was considered by many to be at the peak of its power, it set the record for the largest earnings ever made by any corporation when it declared a profit of $16.6 billion. However despite this success, the mid 1980s was to prove to be a critical turning point in IBM's fortunes. In 1981 IBM had launched its illustrious PC, which is believed to have been originally formulated as IBM's answer to Apple's microcomputers. Unfortunately even the market leaders appear to have been unaware of the total significance of this machine, a machine which was to herald a seismic shift of power within the computing industry.

As a result of intelligent leadership, upstart companies, such as Microsoft and Intel, were able to join the computing power brokers. Their success centred around their ability to take full advantage of the new emerging PC technologies. Products such as friendly graphic-enriched software and powerful low-cost microprocessors, both of which began to emerge with PC development, enabled these new companies to not only grab existing markets but create new ones. In contrast, established companies such as IBM itself appear to have concentrated on their more mature products/systems the bulk of which resided in the mainframe and minicomputer sector.

From the mid 1980s to the mid 1990s PC/desktop-oriented companies such as Microsoft, Intel, Compaq, Sun Microsystems, Novell and Hewlett Packard were to experience staggering rates of growth as users became conscious of powerful PC/desktop computers capable of performing a wide range of functions for a fraction of the price demanded by the conventional mainframe/minicomputer suppliers.

Microsoft in particular was able to amass a fortune from sales generated by its PC operating system software (see Chapter 4) whilst Intel supplied the bulk of PC microchips. Both organisations also had the business foresight to invest in a range of successful PC products/applications. By the mid 1990s Microsoft was universally recognised as the world's leading PC software developer and Intel the world's foremost supplier of microprocessors. Compaq became the largest producer of PCs whilst Novell developed Netware, the world's most widely used local area network operating system. Estimates suggest that during the early to mid 1990s Netware was operating on somewhere between 70% and 80% of PC LANs.

Unfortunately the early PCs were highly susceptible to various software crashes and operating breakdowns. As a consequence of these early failures, corporate management viewed them with a certain degree of justified suspicion. Nevertheless, one desktop-based computer which did meet their strict performance criteria was Sun Microsystem's mid-range Unix-driven workstations. The significance of the workstation was that it provided users with a robust reliable cost-effective computer technology that satisfied certain critical processing requirements which were above that of the ordinary PC but for a price far less than that of the conventional contemporary minicomputer. By 1992 Sun Microsystems was generating over $4 billion in hardware and software sales, the bulk of which flowed from its Unix workstation products.

Nevertheless, despite all this success in the PC/desktop computer market, IBM, the inventor of the PC and the world's biggest computer company, was undergoing a fraughtful transition which culminated in 1993 when it recorded a deficit of almost $8 billion. This loss, in stark contrast to the heady days of 1984, was the biggest ever loss in corporate history. In spite of this setback, IBM went through a successful restructuring process and has since returned to its profit-making ways. At the time of writing the company appeared to have refocused on the PC/desktop market although it is still heavily involved with mainframe/minicomputer technology.

This is not, however, to denigrate mainframe technology, a technology which has, despite its maturity, certain critical attributes which make it invaluable to those corporate users requiring large-scale processing facilities. Nevertheless, IBM is no longer the unrivalled computer giant that it once was and at the beginning of 1997 some Wall Street analysts considered Microsoft to be of a greater stock value.

1.4.2 Contemporary forces

Contemporary computing developers of the late 1990s are currently engaged in a new battleground. This new battleground concerns the provision of various trading, information and entertainment services across different communication/computing networks. Because of the need to link computers, telephones and TVs to reach these external sources the late 1990s is witnessing an intensification in rivalry between various terrestrial/cable TV networks, telephone companies and satellite providers as to who will supply appropriate services such as Video On Demand, shopping, banking, Internet access, etc. As a result, multifunction desktop computers combining the attributes of a PC, TV and phone are beginning to become more commonplace as users begin to take advantage of the new wave of telephone/videoconferencing services which are starting to emerge on networks such as the Internet.

Cable TV companies have become significant players in the provision of such services because of the nature of the cabling of their customer base. Unlike the majority of the world's telephone subscribers, cable TV subscribers are invariably connected via optical fibres which provide the bandwidth necessary to supply the user with process-hungry applications such as VOD.

However, telephone companies across the world are gradually replacing their older systems/installations with advanced cabling technologies/wireless connections. In addition, the world's communication giants appear to be entering a new era of co-operation and merger activity with their erstwhile competitors. They also have an extra advantage in that, unlike the cable TV companies who are only connected to restricted sections of the population, telephone companies are linked to everyone. TV and telephone companies also have the added advantage that they already have a charging infrastructure set up with this customer base. As a consequence computing companies such as IBM, Lotus, Microsoft and Novell are also beginning to engage in numerous local and global alliances with various cable TV/telephone companies so that they can secure a firm business route for the charging and delivery of the various services on offer.

The late 1990s is also witnessing a new struggle for computer hardware/software standards as a result of the surging demand posed by the Internet. Microsoft currently has a commanding lead in the Small Medium Enterprise (SME)/domestic PC operating system market and is making significant inroads into the corporate market with programs such as Windows NT. However, Microsoft is facing fierce competition as it and other developers race to supply users with a secure and flexible Internet interface. As a consequence Microsoft is beginning to make large investments in Internet technology.

One company which has sprung from nowhere and which has become a market leader in Internet Web browser applications is Netscape Communications. Its main product is the Netscape browser, which at the beginning of 1997 was estimated to have a user base of 40 million.

Another interesting product to consider is Sun Microsystem's Java, a programming language that is proving extremely popular amongst software developers. The significance of Java is that it is extremely flexible, it enables fast application development and sits comfortably on the Internet server computers. As a result of its Internet friendly architecture, many software developers are switching to the new Java environment so that they can access a wider market for their particular applications/products.

On the hardware front, 1996 saw Oracle, one of the world's foremost database corporations, present the Network Computer (NC), a machine which some observers have described as a low-cost Internet terminal. The significance of the NC is that it appears to have established the principle that users can be provided with the latest computing technology without having to constantly totally re-upgrade their own equipment. Although it is still early days the NC has caught the eye of the corporate sector and it is expected that the late 1990s will result in a major assault by the NC on the PC market.

On the domestic front other manufacturers have started to produce NetPCs which are supposed to be a hybrid of a PC and a NC but it should be said this is somewhat of a moot point.

1.5 CONCLUSION

Organisations and individuals operating in the modern business environment depend on good information and the best way of manipulating and extracting this information is through the medium of new technology. What is more, many observers believe that it is the accelerating technological convergence of the 1990s which is the driving ethos facilitating the development of those machines and systems that are enabling the global business community to produce and deliver an unprecedented range of high quality goods and services.

However the actual nature and substance of new technology is in a constant state of flux. The fortunes of manufacturers and developers appear to rise and fall with every new innovation, a fact which makes the choice of equipment standards problematical for user and investor alike. In any event, new technology does appear to be on an ever-upward performance curve and ultimately it is predicted that users will be able to access devices that will provide instant communication, as well as numerous information and entertainment services supplying totally refreshed data that embodies what is occurring externally, across the globe or internally, within business, at that particular instant.

2

Large-scale computer systems

2.1 INTRODUCTION

The main objective of this chapter is to consider some of the various developments and components which have contributed to contemporary large-scale computer systems. Smaller-scale desktop computer systems and peripheral devices will be dealt with in the next chapter.

However it should be noted that whilst this chapter deals with computers that are generally substantially more expensive and larger than the computers in the next chapter, the fact is that the overwhelming majority of computers have a common technological core. As a consequence of this commonality it should also be noted that many of the respective technological developments which have occurred at the various levels of computing technology have the tendency to permeate throughout computer systems of every type.

Section 2.2 starts the chapter with a discussion on the concept of digital technology. Sections 2.3 and 2.4 are a brief examination of the metamorphosis of corporate computers and the development of the computer processor (see below), both of which will give the reader an insight into the rapid pace of change within the computer industry.

Sections 2.5 to 2.9 cover the three main classes of large-scale computer systems, namely the mainframe, minicomputer and workstation. These sections seek to explain some of the perplexities of current computer hardware with due reflection on the recent past as well as consideration of future trends. Finally, section 2.10 considers the concept of rightsizing, a new strategy employed by organisations seeking to rationalise the deployment of their computer resources.

2.2 DIGITAL TECHNOLOGY

Before embarking on an examination of the various forms of computing/IT technology it is useful to consider what is actually meant by the term digital technology.

Digital technology concerns the system whereby physical variables are converted into number values, which, when processed, recreate the original information which the physical variables represent. These variables include human speech, photos, music, film and so forth. In contrast that technology which uses physical variables to directly represent and process information is called *analogue technology*.

In order to compare these two technologies it is useful to consider the old vinyl playing record which is an analogue device as opposed to the conventional compact disc (CD) which is a digital device. It should be pointed out that whilst most major western music producers no longer manufacture vinyl records, there is still, at the time of writing, a vibrant vinyl record market for both consumers and producers across the globe.

With a vinyl record, sound is represented by varying the height and width of the tracks on the record's surface. There are two points to note. Firstly, as time progresses the sound quality of the vinyl record gradually deteriorates through sheer wear and tear of the record's tracks. Secondly other than actual playback there isn't a great deal the listener can do with a vinyl record. For example, the user cannot edit the record or guarantee exact duplication of the record's sound on another analogue device.

In contrast a compact disc (CD) stores data such as sound, pictures, etc. in a numeric pattern of bits (see 3.6.2). This pattern is constructed through a series of laser cuts on the surface of the CD. When it comes to reading the data from the CD, it is the numeric value of the data stored on the CD which determines the actual composition of the data as opposed to the CD's physical contours.

This means, in fact, that the sound signals which are analogue waveforms had to be converted into digital form. This is done by devices called analogue-to-digital converters. The analogue waveform is sampled at close intervals and at each sample point the amplitude, or height, is measured which is then converted into a binary number consisting of ones and zeroes (see figure 2.1). It is this series of binary numbers which represents the original waveform in digital form and which can be stored on a CD or indeed transmitted along any digital communication link. There are, in fact, several methods of performing this conversion but figure 2.1 illustrates the simplified general principle.

It might be helpful at this juncture to point out that digital technology on which computers are based operate physically by treating the ones and

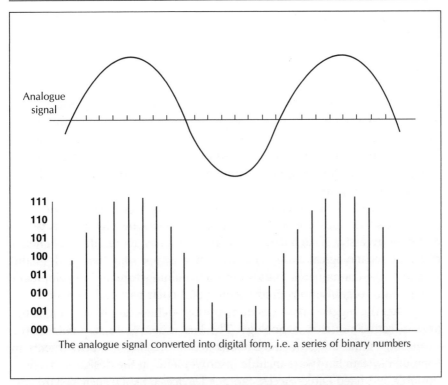

Fig 2.1 The basic principle of analogue-to-digital conversion

zeroes as a series of higher voltages for the ones and lower voltages for the ones so that a clear distinction is made. At a simpler level, binary numbers can be transmitted by using ON/OFF switches to correspond to one/zero.

Because of this physical independence, digital sound recordings, video, photos, etc. can be reconstituted without fear of degradation. What this means in effect is that all that digital technology devices require to replicate the original information is the numeric value of the initial source of data.

Another advantage of this physical independence is the fact that digital technology means that blocks of information stored in numeric format can be shuffled and manipulated almost at will. As a result, digital technology means that digitised data can be effectively deployed and edited without any great difficulty.

2.3 EVOLVING MACHINES

A favourite phrase of the developers and users of new computing technology in the late 1980s and early 1990s was *downsizing*. The phrase was a recognition of the migratory trend by corporate type customers from con-

17

temporary larger expensive computers to the new agile equipment configurations. It was also a recognition of the fact that, despite their shrinking size, new computers were, and are, constantly outperforming previous generations of hardware.

This apparent perpetual improvement in computing technology is, a direct result of radical changes in *computer architecture* most of which have led to its continued miniaturisation. Computer architecture concerns the organisation of a computer system's internal and external hardware. In turn, this organisation refers to the structure and relationship between the different parts of the computer system and the mode in which data flows through the computer.

The point is, a computer is not a single technological entity but a co-ordinated system of components. These components are physically separate and their diversity is such that each component has, more often than not, a different technological base. This diversity is not only reflected in the nature of the components but also in their manufacture and development as numerous organisations produce their particular part of the system.

To date, the biggest advances in computer architecture have been in the area of semiconductor technology. The best example in this field is the evolution of the microprocessor. Other recent significant enhancements in computer system hardware include improvements in the design and use of portable and fixed Direct Access Storage Devices (DASD) such as hard and floppy disks, both magnetic and optical, as well as improvements in areas such as computer memory and the general layout of a computer system. At the time of writing, developers are paying particular attention to those technologies which enable computers to internetwork and communicate with other computers.

However, despite the general trend of improvement, computer developers have discovered, and are continuing to discover, that the technology they are currently using has various limits. These limits normally concern issues such as data storage space, data transfer rates or processing speeds. Nevertheless, the computing industry has shown remarkable adaptability when confronted with physical performance barriers of this type and appears to possess an innate ability to switch technologies in order to move forward and so propel the computer's ever-upward performance curve. This ability is no more clearly apparent than in the evolution of the processor.

2.4 GENESIS OF THE PROCESSOR

A processor is a device inside a computer which has been designed to perform various operations on the inputted data. A microprocessor is the creation on a single chip of a computer's complete central processing unit (CPU) which performs and controls the execution of program instructions.

2.4.1 Valves and transistors

Before the arrival of the microchip there was the transistor and before this was the valve. The valve, otherwise known as the vacuum valve, was the basic on/off switch (a good example of simple 'bit' representation) in an electronic circuit. These valves were made of metal and glass and had to be heated. As such they were vulnerable and needed to be constantly replaced. The first industrial/commercial computers that appeared in the late 1940s used tens of thousands of them, a very expensive exercise. Not surprisingly a cheaper and more efficient solution was sought. The remedy arrived with the transistor invented at AT&T's Bell Laboratories in America in the 1950s. Unlike the valve, the transistor proved to be a robust gadget. Transistors were made from semiconducting materials such as silicon and germanium and acted as switching devices in the same way as valves but needed significantly less energy.

Transistors could be linked together on printed circuit boards and the subsequent economies were quickly felt. Within a very short space of time the valve was redundant. Interestingly so was people's knowledge. Transistor technology was totally different in nature from valve technology and there are notorious case studies of electrical manufacturers dismissing whole work forces because of their desperate need to switch to those with the necessary skills so that they could compete.

However, interestingly in the early 1990s, long after valve technology had ceased to be a serious part of the Western electronic/computer industry, military analysts were dumbfounded when they discovered that critical components in high-class military planes in the former USSR were built using miniature valve technology.

2.4.2 Chip technology

As transistor technology evolved so the idea of the integrated circuit began to emerge, the essence of which is the miniaturisation of transistors and their circuits into a minute space. The consequence of this miniaturisation was to reduce the distance that the transistors' various signals had to travel. This in turn meant that the processing power and speed of a circuit rose dramatically and by concentrating these circuits into a small chip of silicon eventually resulted in manufacturers producing what is now commonly referred to as the *microchip*.

By the mid 1960s the first commercial industrial microchips had arrived.

They were to prove sturdy, reliable and cheap. More importantly because of their size they proved to be all pervasive, turning up absolutely everywhere.

We can gain an insight into the rapid development of microchip technology by examining computers such as the International Computers Ltd (ICL) 2903 mainframe which was launched in 1973. This mainframe computer employed state of the art technology and as with other contemporary systems the computer used silicon memory chips. Each chip supported 1000 miniaturised transistor circuits/switches. However twenty years later computer scientists were producing microprocessors less than half an inch square containing millions of transistors on a line surface area the same thickness as that of an ordinary human hair.

Because of these advances there has been a radical shift in the way computers are now evaluated. Until relatively recently users used size as a means of estimating the power of a computer. However, the astounding advance in microchip technology has led to a reappraisal of using the appearance/scale of computers as a rough rule of thumb in order to estimate equipment performance. The fact is that a relatively inexpensive PC of the late 1990s can outperform a million pound plus mainframe system of the early 1970s.

A famous remark by the Intel chairman Gordon Moore that the number of transistors that could be put on a silicon chip would double every two years without a corresponding increase in production costs goes some way to explaining the exponential development of the microchip and the resulting improvement in cost/price performance of modern computers/ electronic goods.

2.5 MODERN MAINFRAMES

As has already been stated, the classification of computers into various categories is not as clear-cut as it once was. For example, contemporary multi-million dollar mainframe computers are now being built using the same microprocessors as found inside PCs and other desktop computers. However the computing community, for various reasons, continues to use terms such as mainframe, minicomputer, workstation and PC/desktop. The point is, these terms are still useful so long as they are used in context. In other words, so long as the user employs the terms relative to the technology concerned, then broad categories such as mainframe and minicomputer, etc. can still convey the purpose and power of the computer systems under discussion.

In computing, a mainframe is a label used to describe an extensive general-purpose computer serving a major section of an organisation or institution. Until the arrival of the silicon chip, mainframe computers were power-hungry machines with only basic processing capabilities. With the introduction of silicon chip technology, mainframe computers started to perform a host of new but nonetheless essential processing duties, and organisations that had never used a computer before realised that these machines were becoming an essential part of the corporate scene.

As silicon processor technology improved, mainframe computer designers were provided with new tools. These tools enabled these designers to develop systems straight onto silicon chips instead of having to use ready-made purpose-produced chips. This was a revolution in its day and allowed designers to advance in an original and inventive manner. The result was the development of a new breed of mainframe computers which were infinitely more powerful and flexible than their predecessors.

2.5.1 Conventional mainframe architecture

Mainframe computers that have been produced by the major manufacturers have been of widely different architectures. Modern mainframes are still bulky machines although their overall size and environmental needs have radically altered. Because of their enormous energy consumption they are either air cooled or water cooled. In recent years most of these mainframes have been modular in concept. The idea is that extra memory can be increased through the addition of extra circuit/memory boards to the main circuit board or that extra processing power can be obtained by purchasing more expensive subsystems.

Other critical features usually include:

(a) Concurrent operating systems

Concurrent operating systems facilitate smooth internetworking (see 5.9) with other computer systems by allowing users to execute proprietary and non-proprietary applications simultaneously.

(b) Compatible architecture integration

Compatible architecture integration usually means that the mainframe computer integrates seamlessly with other computers in a particular manufacturer's product range. This integration enables painless communication between different types of computers. A good example would be the transfer and sharing of data and applications between a PC and a mainframe both manufactured by the same company.

Compatible architecture integration is also concerned with mainframe computers made by different manufacturers but with a similar architecture.

At the time of writing, IBM is the global leader in the manufacture and delivery of mainframe systems. In the late 1990s IBM was estimated to be supplying approximately 80% of the world's mainframe market.

However, the computer company Amdahl has made considerable profits by becoming the largest manufacturer of IBM mainframe compatibles. Other major mainframe suppliers which supply machines that conform to IBM's Enterprise System Architecture (ESA) mainframe architecture include Hitachi Data Systems and Comparex. Such compatibility has been of certain advantage to end users, for whilst they may be committed to IBM's proprietary architecture, the employment of this standard by other manufacturers has generated competition and enabled users to play one supplier off against another.

(c) Operational communication links

Modern mainframes have sophisticated connecting modems which enable users to employ Remote Support Facility (RSF) and Remote Operation Facility (ROF) communication links. These links empower specialist personnel to operate and access a widely dispersed system such as a network from a central site.

(d) Concurrent power maintenance (CPM)

CPM devices are mandatory for mainframe systems. Their task is to facilitate the replacement of a failed power supply during system operation.

(e) Data security

Because of the huge data store employed by computer mainframes it is critical that the hardware has good data security features (see Chapter 7). Modern mainframes are supplied with powerful cryptographic utilities to ensure that data is shielded from outsiders. Other data security measures include support packages protecting information in transmission over communication lines and sophisticated password access systems.

Many mainframe computers also include operating systems that contain options to use multiple disk drives to provide backup disks known as disk mirroring. This is known as Redundant Array of Inexpensive Disks (RAID) technology, whereby data can be spread across several drives at once.

2.5.2 Mainframe processing

The main traditional advantage of mainframe computers has been their ability to process vast batches of data and to handle multiple programs all at the same time. They have carried out these operations by employing concepts such as multiple processors, time sharing and parallel processing.

(a) Multiple processors

Modern mainframes have multiple processors that deal with various tasks. One processor may be involved in the delivery of data to the various input/output (I/O) devices such as terminals or off-site backup storage whilst another processor could be devoted to controlling the flow of data to the computer's CPU.

(b) Time sharing

This is where multiple programs can operate on the same processor. What happens is that each program is allocated a small time slot. In fact this time slot or 'slice' is so minuscule and the computer processor so quick that many programs and users can be supported all at the same time without any detrimental effect. The computer simply switches between the time slices at great speed. Having said this, heavy data traffic will of course have a detrimental effect on the computer's response time.

(c) Parallel computing

Until recently, the majority of all types of computers were equipped with processors that operated sequentially. In other words program instructions are executed by the computer one after the other in turn. The significance of this is that as the volume of data is increased so response time decreases.

A solution that has found favour with computer hardware and software manufacturers is to employ an array of processors operating in parallel. This type of architecture is known as parallel processing or concurrent computing. The idea is that individual processors deal with a certain part of a particular task so enabling them to 'work' at the same time as they drive towards a required result. Parallel-designed computers have gained favour with manufacturers of every type of computer and their success has been such that it is the major reason why it is so much more difficult to classify what a particular computer actually is. Consider, for example, Parallel Sysplex as outlined below.

2.5.3 Parallel Sysplex

At the time of writing, IBM has introduced a new mainframe technology called Parallel Sysplex. Built with a combination of CMOS (complementary metal oxide semiconductor) microprocessors plus conventional mainframe technology, Parallel Sysplex systems operate premium CMS applications which enables users to fuse the processing power of dozens if not hundreds of CPUs within a mainframe or chain of mainframes. The result of such fusion means that the user is employing what appears to be an exceptionally powerful single computer system. With this type of design, mainframe managers can lessen the possibility of a system failure in the event of individual or groups of CPUs overloading by simply arranging the tasks in hand to be transferred to other CPUs. In addition, because of this ability to link CPUs almost at will, mainframe computer systems can, within reason, be upgraded to whatever processing capacity is required by simply adding more CPUs.

2.6 SUPERCOMPUTERS

There is an elite and very expensive group of mainframe computers known as Supercomputers. Supercomputers provide users with a vast amount of raw processing power for calculations and logical operations. Manufacturers that have excelled in the production of these extravagantly expensive computers are IBM and Cray Supercomputers.

Because of their sheer processing power and speed they have been used principally for scientific and engineering projects. Furthermore, with the advent of ever more sophisticated commercial applications these computers are now beginning to appear in commercial use. Their disadvantage is their horrendous expense and whilst they are unquestionably important they are relatively rare.

At the end of 1996 IBM displayed a $US 53 million supercomputer which was constructed using 7,264 Pentium Pro microprocessors. The significance of the computer was that it was capable of operating at 1.06 Teraflops. Its initial purpose was to simulate nuclear explosions.

2.7 OUTLOOK FOR MAINFRAME TECHNOLOGY

The ever-increasing trend of miniaturisation within computing technology has not gone unnoticed by the corporate business community. Most major organisations are only too aware that any necessary large-scale processing requirements can often be met using equipment such as moderately priced PC and minicomputer client/server networks as opposed to relatively expensive centralised mainframe systems. (In a *client/server network*, tasks are distributed between the client computer, in effect the user's terminal, and the server or host, which provides the necessary service.)

However, an automatic migration by users to these smaller systems is not so simple. The reason for this is that the future of mainframe technology not only centres on the long-term changing economics of the processing capabilities of computers but also on the nature of the potential user's requirements. For example, as large-scale computing applications have become more sophisticated so there is evidence to suggest that many corporate users are employing mainframe computers to process even more data. This is especially so with those users, such as ISPs (Internet Service Providers), employing new multimedia type database applications to enable the supply of external services such as VOD. In addition, the arrival of technologies such as the Network Computer (NC), the main purpose of which is to enable end users to fully access the latest applications from central computer systems and networks such as the Internet without the need to be constantly totally upgraded, has fuelled a resurging demand in the mainframe computer.

The continued popularity of the mainframe is in part evidenced by the fact that two of IBM's flagship mainframe computer systems, namely the S/390 and the ES/9000, have experienced a massive surge in sales in the mid to late 1990s. The reality is that contemporary mainframes are designed to handle huge volumes of data/transactions with incredible reliability. As a result mainframes fulfil the need of those corporate users who require total confidence in their computer system's day-to-day operations. Unfortunately such reliability of operation is not, for various reasons, always available on other less-expensive systems and is most probably the major reason for the continued resistance by large-scale corporate customers to possible alternatives to their mainframe configurations. This is not to say that many mainframe users would not switch to other more economically priced/sized systems if it was in their interest to do so. In fact, continued improvements in computing technology suggest that the drift by medium-sized mainstream corporate users to smaller computer systems appears to be an almost unavoidable event.

What is more, computer developers are continuing to invest in mainframe technology and thus making it even more attractive for many large-scale users to stay with mainframe-centred systems. For example, until relatively recently most mainframes would only operate under the control of specifically designed operating systems (OSs). However, this proved to be a major disadvantage for those users wishing to co-ordinate their mainframes with other types of computer systems. In order to meet user demand manufacturers have begun to supply mainframes which are not only capable of supporting multiple OSs but which can support OSs originally designed for the PC/desktop market. Such advances have meant that corporate users can, when necessary, fully integrate their mainframes with the other diverse parts of their computer configuration.

Mainframe manufacturers have also begun to make significant inroads into the cost of producing and operating mainframes. This has come about by the inclusion of a new breed of processors. Specifically, companies such as Fujitsu and IBM have started to employ CMOS in their mainframe systems. The main advantage of CMOS chips is that they are significantly cheaper to produce and do not require water cooling. Unisys, like IBM, has also broken new ground by launching a mainframe computer which operates Pentium Pro microprocessors alongside CMOS mainframe chips. The concept is fairly revolutionary and is expected be emulated by other major manufacturers.

The arrival of inexpensive mainframes which are not only capable of supporting current Critical Mission Software (CMS) applications but which can also support applications/systems that were originally tailored for the PC/workstation gives corporate users a priceless flexibility.

2.7.1 Barriers to migration

Business users who want to abandon their costly mainframes still face considerable obstructions and experienced staff fully aware of the potential trauma of migrating from sound mainframe systems have well founded doubts. Amongst those barriers supporting these doubts are:

(a) Capital investment

Many organisations have made tremendous investments in current equipment, hardware and software. Mainframe configurations often run into millions of pounds. If they perform adequately, then there may be little short-term advantage in abandoning them.

There is also the straight economic argument that a break-even point exists where a mainframe is actually less expensive to manage than, say, a large network of PCs. The reason for this is that mainframes and minicomputers support an efficient centralised management of data and resources. With computer networks, resources and data stores are spread across a much wider area. Control of widespread networks is not only expensive but can also prove problematical (see Chapter 6).

(b) Customer services

Mainframe manufacturers such as IBM have excellent customer support services. Their staff are usually better educated than those in small organisations and are more likely to be equipped to deal with customer problems over the phone or via a communication link. This type of service is expensive to provide and most small computer system manufacturers/suppliers simply cannot afford to provide this type of backup.

(c) Corporate culture

Corporate personnel who have been raised in a mainframe environment are only now beginning to switch on to the inevitability of change.

Migrating from a mainframe environment not only means a change of equipment configurations but also staff skills. This may involve extensive retraining especially for information systems (IS) management who have progressed up the ladder and are removed from the technological coal face. It could also mean extensive redundancies as modern corporate computers do not need the personnel requirements needed to operate the older mainframes.

IS professionals are also aware of the considerable upheaval involved in transferring data to new systems. Retraining and system transfer could therefore be considered as unacceptably onerous despite possible benefits.

2.7.2 Mainframe software

Mainframe software is often thought of as being turgid and unfriendly. The reason for this is that a lot of the software applications currently used on mainframe computers were often created when screen presentation tools were in short supply. However, mainframe software applications are, despite their reputation for poor presentation, popular with corporate and other large-scale users, mainly because mainframe software is usually of a CMS category. This type of software is generally regarded as an elite class of software which, due to continuous use and development, usually performs with the minimum of error.

Lamentably, most CMS applications running on mainframes are very complex programs and users can usually only make limited modifications. This is a severe restriction on any user wishing to invest in application development and poses major problems for users having to meet new requirements presented by changes in legislation or business activities.

One major hiccup with contemporary mainframe CMS applications which is causing major concern is the manner in which the software deals with the change of century. Unfortunately, a large slice of modern mainframe software was developed in the 1960s and 1970s and is not designed to cope with the next millennium. As from 1 January 2000 this century-insensitive software is redundant. What is even more amazing is that a lot of developers have discovered that they no longer have the original source code of the various applications.

As a result, many corporate and business users will be forced to develop or migrate to new applications/computers. However, CMS applications are extremely expensive to produce. Thousands of millions of dollars have been invested in writing specialist customer software which can only be run using mainframe databases such as IBM's Information Management System (IMS) and Customer Information Control System (CICS).

Nevertheless despite these problems, major developers are pursuing various modification strategies to ensure that many contemporary CMS applications survive in one form or another. For example, because of the trend towards alternative computer systems, popular mainframe software is gradually being converted by specialist companies for use on smaller less-expensive computers. However, this is a very slow and complex process. The impact of this new scaleable CMS software which is beginning to appear has yet to be assessed but an obvious outcome is that users will be able to use these applications on less-expensive hardware.

Interestingly however, not only is mainframe software moving down but PC software is moving up. Contemporary PC software is where the action is and this is reflected by the investment put into PC applications by the software industry, and the increasing sophistication of PC software along with improved performance figures has resulted in many applications being employed on minicomputer/mainframe systems.

2.7.3 An active market

At the time of writing, it is apparent that mainframe technology is still generating huge sales figures as well as attracting huge investment. For example, two large computer manufacturers, Amdahl and Fujitsu, have formed an alliance to launch a new range of mainframe computers for the late 1990s. This venture is backed by an investment budget of several billion US dollars. In addition, IBM, the world's biggest mainframe developer, has demonstrated a clear commitment to continued investment in mainframe technology. The overall picture suggests that significantly smaller and nimbler machines/software applications specifically designed to perform current mainframe tasks will be made available as a matter of course. Mainframe developers are confident that there is unlikely to be a final and dramatic change as was predicted by many industry pundits. Instead, it is expected that mainframe computers/software will simply assume new roles in the emerging corporate computer configurations of the 21st century (see Rightsizing 2.10).

2.8 MODERN MINICOMPUTERS

Commercial minicomputers first appeared in 1960 when the Digital Equipment Corporation (DEC) launched the PDP-1. It was deemed to be a bargain at the time as it was priced at a mere $120,000, considerably less than the millions asked for by IBM to buy one of its mainframe computers. In this respect alone, the PDP-1 was a breakthrough and was to prove the start of an extremely accomplished range of minicomputers, the sales of which were to build DEC into a major computer corporation.

As a rule, the modern minicomputer is a physically smaller machine than the modern mainframe although their respective architectures are, for the greater part, very similar. Modern minicomputers normally run as stand-alone processors supporting clusters of workstations/terminals or they can act as a server computer in various network configurations (see Chapter 5). Smaller models are almost desk-sized whilst larger models are rack mounted. As with modern mainframes new minicomputers are retailed with stringent data security features.

One of the most popular computers in this section of the market in the late 1990s is the IBM AS/400. By 1997 it was estimated that there were over 350,000 AS/400 computers installed world-wide. The AS/400 was originally designed as a proprietary minicomputer dedicated to operating IBM applications.

However, in 1993 IBM broke new ground when they launched three new high-powered AS/400 models. The significance of this particular range is that they were marketed as capable of interoperating with other non-IBM products. As a result, the launch was viewed as a strategic repositioning by IBM so as to enable its minicomputers to fit into the new reality of Open Systems. At the time of writing the latest AS/400 minicomputers are powered by 64-bit technology employing PowerPC RISC-based microprocessors. They can support DOS, Windows, Windows NT, OS/2 (Operating System 2) and Apple Macintosh applications as well as Unix (see 4.10). As a consequence the AS/400 can be employed as a server for networked Unix workstations thus enabling users to access AS/400 business applications from Unix workstations made by Hewlett-Packard and Sun Microsystems, as well as from IBM's own RS/6000 range of Unix computers.

2.9 THE WORKSTATION

The main task of the overwhelming majority of minicomputers is to act as a host or server on a network. Unfortunately one of the problems with early minicomputers was that they could be arbitrary when it came to response times.

The snag was that if you added too many dumb terminals or graphic terminals on to the network, processing would slow down and come to a virtual standstill. The reason for this delay was that most of the terminals

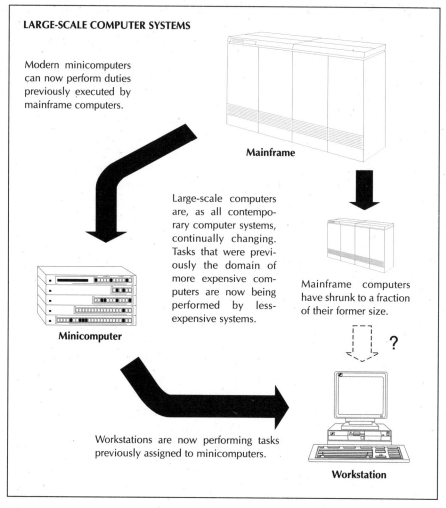

LARGE-SCALE COMPUTER SYSTEMS

Modern minicomputers can now perform duties previously executed by mainframe computers.

Mainframe

Large-scale computers are, as all contemporary computer systems, continually changing. Tasks that were previously the domain of more expensive computers are now being performed by less-expensive systems.

Mainframe computers have shrunk to a fraction of their former size.

Minicomputer

Workstations are now performing tasks previously assigned to minicomputers.

Workstation

Fig 2.2

were principally designed to act simply as an access window on to the central computer's CPU. Users would normally use the terminals to call up various services from the central computer which would then carry out all the necessary processing tasks. This meant that the terminal usually did very little, if any, processing, so the more terminals attached to the central computer the more work it had to do.

So that they might reduce this workload on the central CPU developers came up with the concept of the workstation. The idea of the workstation computer was to provide processing power and graphic facilities locally. What this meant in effect was that some, if not all, of the necessary processing was done by the calling terminal/workstation. A good example would be where an individual terminal/workstation processed the necessary calculations to construct a required screen full of graphics. This of course removed a considerable processing burden from the minicomputer's CPU resulting in an increase in the computer's efficiency as well as a reduction in response time. In order to exploit this gap in the hardware market, an American company called Sun Microsystems was set up in 1982.

2.9.1 Sun Microsystems

The initial game plan of Sun Microsystems was to produce a powerful and cost-effective computer system which would be assembled from readily available components. Sun Microsystems was to become a real good fortune story of the 1980s. It is widely believed that the secret of their success rested on two significant facts. These were the choice of operating system and the choice of market. Sun Microsystems chose Unix as the OS for its new workstations. Unix enabled their systems to support industry standard hardware and empowered potential users to integrate their equipment in the evolving Open System environments. Another major advantage of employing Unix was the fact that neither of the then two industry giants, IBM and DEC, had control of Unix.

The big breakthrough for Sun Microsystem workstations came with their ability to make significant inroads into the Computer Aided Design (CAD) market. Most users of CAD systems employed minicomputer networks and professional CAD users were and are usually individuals or small specialist design teams. The purchase of a mainframe for such a select group was not an economic alternative. Moreover given the problems encountered by minicomputers for this type of work (see above), workstation configurations were welcomed with open arms.

By 1992 Sun Microsystems generated $4.3 billion in hardware and software sales. As a consequence of this success, the Unix OS which was previously the preserve of engineers and scientists was now extended to commercial users. The original Sun workstations employed Motorola 68000 microprocessors. In 1989 however, the company turned to Reduced Instruction Set Cycles (RISC, see 2.9.2) technology with the introduction of the SparcStation 1.

2.9.2 Instruction set technology

The nerve centre or the brain of every computer is the microprocessor. There are, as one might expect, a wide variety of different architectures available and each microprocessor performs various functions and operations according to an in-built list. This list is known as the Instruction Set.

31

As microprocessors became more sophisticated so they were required to perform ever more complicated operations. One major architecture that was developed as a result of this evolution was the Complex Instruction Set Commands (CISC) architecture. The next major development was Reduced Instruction Set Commands (RISC).

Reduced instruction set commands (RISC)

This technology is one of IBM's most important inventions. The idea behind RISC is to achieve the highest possible speed and throughput in a single processor by reducing the number of machine cycles it uses to operate. A *machine cycle* is that length of time taken by a computer to execute a given series of tasks.

IBM's second-generation RISC architecture, given the acronym POWER (Performance Optimisation With Enhanced RISC), raises an individual processor's efficiency additionally by executing several instructions per machine cycle. It is this technology which is behind the new PowerPC (see 3.12).

2.9.3 IBM RS (RISC System)/6000 series

IBM's RS (RISC System)/6000 series is a range of workstation computers which takes full advantage of RISC technology. The significance of these computers is that they were viewed as being in direct competition with Sun Microsystems' workstations. RS/6000 models support AIX, IBM's version of the Unix OS, and have proved to be very popular.

However, IBM RS/600 has proved to be something of a Trojan horse. For example, independent software developers have produced applications that have enabled RS/6000 workstations to emulate a significantly more expensive IBM minicomputer, the AS/400. The situation has now arisen where purchasers can now consider the significantly cheaper workstation, the IBM RS/6000 series as opposed to IBM's more expensive AS/400 mini-computer. A similar event occurred with DEC and the development of the Alpha AXP PC.

2.10 RIGHTSIZING

The early nineties witnessed the birth of downsizing as IS strategists sought to take advantage of the economies promised by the arrival of new nimbler machines. However the zealous pursuit of the downsizing approach by many organisations led to the scrapping of perfectly good mainframe computer systems. One interesting consequence of this activity was a sudden glut of

DOWNSIZING

Mainframe

Downsizing is generally accepted as a strategy whereby corporate mainframe systems are replaced by smaller systems such as PC networks. However there are certain critical barriers to this approach. These barriers include:

1) Organisations which employ corporate computer systems such as mainframes have invested huge sums of money in equipment. Unless the organisation can foresee immediate financial savings it is unlikely to want rapid replacement of such systems.

2) Large corporate computer systems employ CMS (Critical Mission Software). This type of software is extremely reliable and is usually proprietary. In effect, organisations have discovered that in order to use the software it is necessary to keep the supplier's hardware as well.

3) The management and personnel of large organisations have been raised with mainframe corporate systems and are understandably reluctant to transfer to systems that they are not familiar with. In addition, experienced IS personnel know that such new systems have yet to be thoroughly honed and tested by the passage of time and use. Organisations are also only too aware of the trauma of transition and may feel it simply isn't worth it.

PC

RIGHTSIZING

The late 1980s and early 1990s saw many organisations pursue an unrestricted policy of downsizing in order to take advantage of the economies offered by smaller systems. However this policy resulted in perfectly good equipment being assigned to the scrapheap. A more rational approach in the deployment of resources arrived with the concept of rightsizing. Simply put, if the organisation decides to upgrade its equipment then current computers are reassigned to what may be considered a more appropriate role. With rightsizing, computers are not replaced or scrapped unless there is a sound economic or technological imperative.

Fig. 2.3

corporate mainframe equipment appearing in the UK second-hand computer market in the early 1990s. At the time, the computer press was awash with adverts selling mainframe equipment and astute system dealers made immense profits.

Computer-literate accountants suddenly realised that unrestricted downsizing was irrational and uneconomic. They realised that corporate management had to understand that modernisation must be justified beyond an understandable desire to be totally updated with the latest technological developments. This new wave of pragmatism resulted in an approach known as rightsizing. The idea behind the rightsizing concept is the belief that all cost-effective computer hardware resources, irrespective of their technological base, should be harnessed to facilitate the fulfilment of organisational tasks.

Rightsizing is an economic as well as a technological recognition of the advantage in employing all current equipment *in suitable circumstances*. This is especially the case with redundant mainframe and minicomputers which may no longer be suitable for their original duties but could nonetheless prove to be more than adequate for other roles.

A company pursuing a rightsizing policy usually means that if the organisation decides to upgrade its equipment, then current computer systems are reassigned to what may be considered a more appropriate role. Under this strategy, current systems are only scrapped or replaced if there is a sound economic or overriding technological imperative. The concept of rightsizing as opposed to unrestricted downsizing reduces waste and delivers a certain degree of sanity in a continually evolving organisational IS strategy.

2.10.1 A mixed bag

Rightsizing is also a recognition of the necessary mixed computer equipment configuration of many organisations. As has been already stated, many large modern corporate computers possess attributes which are either underdeveloped or simply not available on cheaper computer systems.

However, for many organisations, rightsizing will involve integrating diverse software technologies across different hardware platforms. In order to ensure that a rightsizing policy is made to work, organisations have to make sure that their hardware is fully integrated. Two possible ways of achieving this are by the use of emulation programs and specialist computer systems such as gateways.

(a) Terminal emulation

Most contemporary mainframe terminals and PCs are radically different. To enable their particular PCs to communicate with mainframe/minicomputer systems, some users employ terminal emulation programs. Terminal emulation is a type of application that can, for example, convert the PC's keyboard signals into a format compatible with that of the mainframe the PC is linked to.

(b) Communication gateways

Host services (these usually consist of processing facilities) and software applications can be delivered to LANs (see Chapter 5) by corporate computers by incorporation of specialist communications software on top of that supported by the network. In effect there is a wide range of software applications produced by mainframe and PC developers allowing links between the two classes of machine.

Despite all the commercial theoretical advantages of rightsizing there are practical problems for organisations wishing to pursue a rightsizing strategy. Firstly, any organisation wishing to successfully integrate their systems in this manner must have access to a highly skilled workforce. Secondly, there is a shortage of equipment providing suitable rightsizing support. For example there are practically no mainstream software tools guiding users on data/application conversions so that their systems can run on diverse computers.

2.11 CONCLUSION

Large-scale computer systems such as mainframes and minicomputers are expensive in every way. Even workstations are, generally speaking, beyond the pocket of the average individual user or small business. However what is apparent is that the computers at the higher end of the market will continue to evolve and the underlying technology which made these systems so successful will continue. The evidence for this trend can be gleaned from the manufacturers' continued investment in mainframe technology and the arrival of CMS software on cheaper, smaller machines.

In addition, IT/IS specialists have started to become absorbed in the day-to-day costing of their individual hardware configurations. The current pursuit of complementary rightsizing strategies appears to be an acceptance of commercial as well as technological reality. Nevertheless despite the downsizing and rightsizing trends of major computer configurations in corporate culture, the mainframe retains its position as a colossal, trustworthy data store and data processor. Many organisations have invested heavily in their computer equipment and know that, so long as the equipment performs the required tasks adequately, then change can be superfluous and can in some situations be disastrous.

3

Personal computer technology

3.1 INTRODUCTION

This chapter covers relatively inexpensive computer hardware such as personal computers (microcomputers) as well as peripheral devices such as monitors, scanners, modems and printers. The chapter will place a particular emphasis on the development and architecture of one particular type of personal computer, namely the PC (or IBM PC, see 3.3).

Section 3.2 is a brief overview of Apple's role in the creation of a small office/home owner (SOHO) market for the microcomputer industry along with the subsequent arrival of the PC. The evolution of the PC and its clone competitors are examined in sections 3.4 and 3.5. Sections 3.6 to 3.9 centre on the hardware details pertaining to the PC and other personal computers. Sections 3.10 and 3.11 deal with the relatively recent technological advances such as Integrated Circuit cards (IC) and the arrival of powerful handheld computers.

Sections 3.12 through to 3.14 deal with current issues in the microprocessor market, the concept of the entry level PC and the arrival of the NC. Finally section 3.15 deals with printers and scanners, and the WIMP environment.

3.2 THE APPLE PHENOMENON

For many observers of the computing industry the 1970s and early 1980s, years immediately subsequent to the development of the original microchip, were the years of the Home Computer Wars. Such a label is justified as the period experienced frenetic activity when numerous manufacturers struggled for a share of the ever-expanding SOHO market.

One notable contender was the Apple Corporation. Unfortunately the Apple Corporation fell on hard times during the mid to late 1990s and its future is currently somewhat uncertain. This is in spite of its recent linkup with Microsoft (in the summer of 1997 Microsoft made a huge cash investment in the Apple Corporation; whether this leads to an eventual take-over only time will tell). Nonetheless the Apple Corporation is a company which has had a brilliant track record for producing innovative products and it is often thought of as the organisation responsible for initiating corporate interest in the small business/home computer.

Apple was originally formed in America by a group of young computing enthusiasts who literally came from nowhere and who, it later transpired, had in fact done most of their original development work in the garage. Despite their lack of resources they revolutionised the computing industry and became the first major manufacturer to supply small business computers to the mass market.

Apple's initial achievement appears to have centred on the ability of its founders to make full use of state of the art component production techniques in conjunction with the then relatively new microchip technology. In the late 1970s and early 1980s their computer, the Apple IIe, was the best-selling microcomputer on the market. However, Apple's ability to make good cost-effective computers cannot be viewed in isolation. For example, a major part of Apple's early success was due to the development of complementary software such as the Visicalc spreadsheet. For ordinary non-technical computer users, the arrival of such a program was a considerable boon as it meant that they had access to a small business computer with a ready-made application so enabling them to use their computers without having to program them.

The impact of these various advances meant that by the late 1970s Apple was expanding at breakneck speed and was reputed to have been, from the date of its inception, the fastest ever growing corporation to have entered the Fortune company listing. However, all this success did not go unnoticed and it was undoubtedly the incontrovertible achievement of the Apple Corporation that began to attract other 'blue chip' manufacturers to the microcomputer market. By 1980 elements within IBM, the then undisputed giant of the computing industry, decided to create their own product, namely the IBM PC.

3.3 THE IBM PERSONAL COMPUTER (PC)

When the first IBM PC was launched in 1981 it was viewed by many technical purists to be nothing more than an executive toy. Nevertheless the

IBM PC soon proved to be a serious machine and the computer sold way beyond IBM's own analysts' expectations.

A PC Compatible is a general term used to describe those computers built by other manufacturers but which are capable, for example, of running software designed for computers such as the IBM PC. Another term for a PC Compatible is a PC Clone (see 3.5). It should be pointed out that the terms PC Compatible and PC Clone are basically interchangeable within the context of what might be described as a PC. However, it should also be pointed out that the original PC Compatibles were often built using IBM technology whereas the original PC Clones were designed with a slightly different technology so as not to infringe copyright.

By the end of 1997 it was estimated that there were over 250 million IBM PCs or PC Compatibles in general circulation across the world.

3.3.1 Success factors

The reason for the overwhelming success of the original IBM PC is a somewhat complex issue. Some industry observers have suggested that it was the competitive price of the IBM PC that enabled it to gain such prominence. However in the early days of the IBM PC there were many other cheaper and, some might say, better microcomputers.

Other arguments appear to centre on the machine's logo as opposed to its price. Prior to the arrival of the IBM PC, many microcomputer users were in a quandary as to what machine to buy. They were faced with a vast array of alternative microcomputer systems hosting a whole range of different computing standards, the diversity of which only added to general customer confusion. All this changed with the arrival of the IBM PC. For example, when purchasers saw the IBM label, attached to what was a relatively low-priced computer, it inspired a certain degree of confidence. IBM was, after all, the world's biggest computer company. The obvious suggestion to the investor at the time was that if they purchased a computer with an IBM label, they would be purchasing a machine which would not only give them access to an unrivalled range of software applications but would also give them access to a host of other compatible equipment options/customer services.

What is more significant is that the possibilities posed by the IBM PC not only attracted the attention of individual and organisational end users but also attracted the attention of software/hardware developers many of whom recognised the IBM PC as being an ideal vehicle for their own products. As a result, numerous non-IBM companies began to produce a vast array of equipment/applications specifically for the IBM PC/PC compatible. Such forces meant that IBM PC computing technology was able to facilitate an ever-increasing range of software and hardware development, a situation which has in turn produced a standard locked in by its own positive feedback.

3.4 DEVELOPING THE PC

Computers are an organised system of components drawing on a range of different technologies. However at the core of every computer there are two major constituents to consider. One is the computer's operating system (software) and the other is the computer's microprocessor (hardware).

Because of the success of the IBM PC, the two companies that supplied the critical technological components which made up the computer, namely Intel with an appropriate microprocessor, and the Microsoft Corporation with a suitable operating system, also became global powers in the computing industry.

3.4.1 The operating system

The first IBM PCs launched in 1981 had three different types of operating system. One of these was a Pascal-based program called P-system. Another was Control Program for a Microcomputer (CP/M) developed by Digital Research. This was a simple and relatively friendly program. At the time the CP/M standard was the most widely used operating system for home computers in the world. However for various technical and commercial reasons the OS that was to become the dominant program for the PC market was the Microsoft Disk Operating System (MS-DOS) from the Microsoft Corporation. In fact the deal that Microsoft struck with IBM was in many ways a stroke of marketing genius. What Microsoft did was to sell IBM the rights to use MS-DOS for a moderate one-off payment. By doing this Microsoft was able to entice IBM into purchasing their OS whilst simultaneously retaining the right to licence the program to computer companies wishing to build PC compatibles. The program was to prove a great success, and it was the profits from the PC compatible licence distribution/sales that enabled Microsoft to develop into a major corporation.

In fact, the persistent popularity of the MS-DOS program is such that it is still perceived as being a significant OS. For example, figures compiled as late as 1995 indicated that MS-DOS was still the most widely used OS for PCs employed in the business and commercial sectors in the US. This was in spite of the massive growth in sales of Microsoft's more advanced Windows OSs. It is suggested that the main reason for MS-DOS's persistent popularity is simple economics as it was, and still is, a cheap effective OS that was more than adequate for many of the roles it assumed in the SOHO market (see Chapter 4).

3.4.2 Evolution of the microprocessor

In 1969 Intel produced the i4004 microprocessor. The significance of this product was that for the first time a computer's entire CPU had been placed on a single chip of silicon. In 1972 Intel launched the ground-breaking 8008 chip followed two years later by the 8080, a microchip ten times more powerful than the 8008. The importance of the 8080 was that it was the microchip which powered the Altair 8800, the first ever microcomputer which was, in turn, released in 1975.

By the late 1970s and early 1980s, there were two giants amongst the numerous microcomputer processor manufacturers, Intel and Motorola, currently the world's largest supplier of wireless communications equipment.

In 1979 Motorola brought out the MC6800. At the time it was considered to be an excellent 16-bit microprocessor. However it had already developed the i8086 16-bit processor shortly followed by the i088. This development turned out to be literally a 'gold' chip for Intel which through the success of the i088 was to become the world's largest producer of microprocessors. The reason for this was that IBM opted for the Intel i088 chip as the CPU for its PC range of computers. The main argument cited for this decision is believed to have been one of price. In contrast the Motorola range of chips were taken up by other leading computer manufacturers such as Apple Macintosh and Atari St.

Intel continued to develop its products and the subsequent increasingly powerful microprocessors in the Intel range were the i80186, i80286, i80386 and i80486 which was released in 1989. The last three microprocessors are usually referred to as the 286, 386 and 486. This range of microprocessors was subsequently replaced by the Pentium range. The latest micro-processor to be released at the time of writing, from Intel, is called the Pentium II (see 3.12).

A point that should be made, however, is that Intel is no longer making the 486 or lesser microprocessors. However these previous generations of microprocessors are still being made, in one form or another, by other man-ufacturers. These microprocessors, whilst not being the focal chip of the modern PC, are nonetheless appearing in the handheld computers/periph-eral devices being produced in the mid to late nineties.

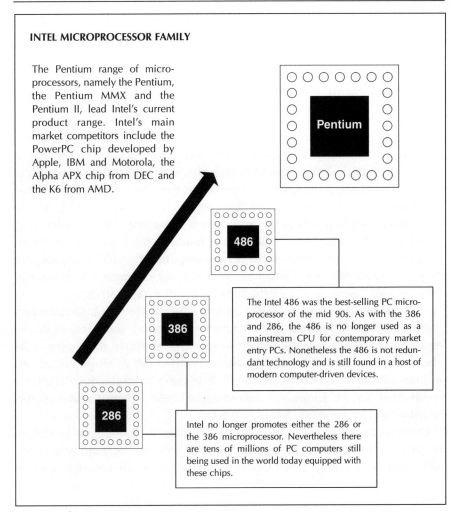

INTEL MICROPROCESSOR FAMILY

The Pentium range of micro-processors, namely the Pentium, the Pentium MMX and the Pentium II, lead Intel's current product range. Intel's main market competitors include the PowerPC chip developed by Apple, IBM and Motorola, the Alpha APX chip from DEC and the K6 from AMD.

Pentium

486

The Intel 486 was the best-selling PC micro-processor of the mid 90s. As with the 386 and 286, the 486 is no longer used as a mainstream CPU for contemporary market entry PCs. Nonetheless the 486 is not redundant technology and is still found in a host of modern computer-driven devices.

386

286

Intel no longer promotes either the 286 or the 386 microprocessor. Nevertheless there are tens of millions of PC computers still being used in the world today equipped with these chips.

Fig 3.1

3.5 PC CLONES

Just as the success of the Apple IIe computer did not escape the notice of IBM so IBM's competitors were only too aware of the IBM PC. Strangely however, IBM appears to have been ambiguous in its initial attitude to the new IBM PC and many industry pundits felt that IBM did not develop the product to its full advantage. Why this was so is subject to much debate.

One suggestion is that IBM were only to aware of the potential power of the PC and did not see fit to exploit the product in case it interfered with its more expensive computers. Another theory suggests that IBM management were simply too rigid in their mind set and were simply unable to make the necessary transition to the new emerging technology. In any event, what is accepted is that IBM took its foot off the pedal and that this lack of leadership along with other factors led to the development of the PC Clone.

3.5.1 Replicating steps

Like Sun workstations the IBM PC was designed and built using readily available components so the basic unit was simple to copy. However there were hurdles for IBM's competitors. A critical complication lay in the original IBM Basic Input Output System (BIOS). The point about the BIOS is that it contained the copyright-protected software that delivered the necessary code for operations such as transmitting data to and from the keyboard or sending data to the printer(s). It was embedded in a microchip called a ROM (see 3.6.2). The BIOS was a major stumbling block for manufacturers wishing to implement IBM compatibility. IBM compatibility meant in effect that manufacturers were offering computers which could support software designed for the IBM PC but at a far lower cost.

The problem concerning the BIOS was transformed when manufacturers such as Phoenix Technology Inc reverse-engineered the IBM ROM so avoiding copyright infringement (the concept of *reverse engineering* is to obtain the same result by an alternative method). A consequence of this technical breakthrough was that the BIOS became another readily available component. The PC Clone had arrived and a consequence of its advent terminated IBM's dominant control of the PC.

The success of the PC Clone enabled companies such as Compaq to take a major slice of the market. In fact Compaq has been so successful with its PC sales that by the mid 1990s Compaq was actually, on occasion, able to outsell IBM's own PCs. For the remainder of this book, any further reference to the term PC will, for simplicity, be a reference to a computer which is either an IBM PC or a PC compatible/clone.

3.6 INSIDE THE MODERN PC

The modern desktop PC is universal in its standard appearance in that for all practical purposes the screen size and keyboard have changed very little since the inception of the PC. Nevertheless technology has moved on since the arrival of the first PC. For example there are fewer electromechanical parts and what parts remain in the standard unit have been considerably compressed. So whilst it is true to say that the outward appearance of the modern PC is not a world away from that of the original, they are nonetheless a universe away in performance and price.

The PC normally consists of a console (monitor), a CPU, keyboard, disk drives and various port interfaces for connections to numerous peripheral devices. Many PCs are now also being supplied with in-built peripheral devices such as modems/faxes and even printers. (See 3.8 Multifunction PCs.)

There are two main types of PC: the portable laptop (or notebook) and the desktop. (See 3.7 for more detail on the laptop.)

3.6.1 Internal architecture

A major feature of the PC computer is that it is not a single homogeneous entity but is in actuality a co-ordinating electronic system which is made up

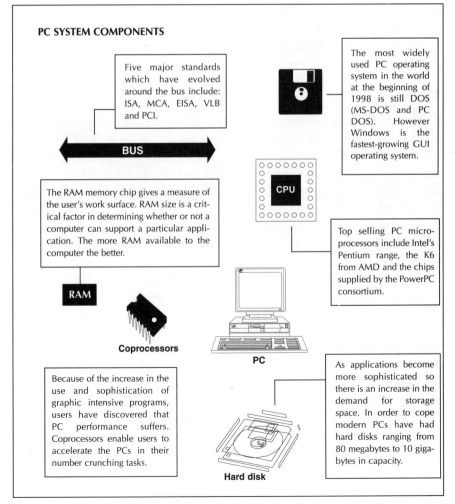

PC SYSTEM COMPONENTS

Five major standards which have evolved around the bus include: ISA, MCA, EISA, VLB and PCI.

The most widely used PC operating system in the world at the beginning of 1998 is still DOS (MS-DOS and PC DOS). However Windows is the fastest-growing GUI operating system.

BUS

CPU

The RAM memory chip gives a measure of the user's work surface. RAM size is a critical factor in determining whether or not a computer can support a particular application. The more RAM available to the computer the better.

Top selling PC microprocessors include Intel's Pentium range, the K6 from AMD and the chips supplied by the PowerPC consortium.

RAM

Coprocessors

PC

Because of the increase in the use and sophistication of graphic intensive programs, users have discovered that PC performance suffers. Coprocessors enable users to accelerate the PCs in their number crunching tasks.

As applications become more sophisticated so there is an increase in the demand for storage space. In order to cope modern PCs have had hard disks ranging from 80 megabytes to 10 gigabytes in capacity.

Hard disk

Fig 3.2

of various critical components. These components are normally made by different manufacturers who in turn supply the PC producer. More often than not a computer's logo is, indirectly, simply a collective badge for a myriad of different products.

The ability of the PC to expand its functions and to integrate products from diverse manufacturers is reflected in a feature which was paramount in generating interest in the original IBM PC. This feature was the ability to add what is known as expansion cards. These *expansion cards* are specialist circuit devices which enable an individual computer to increase the tasks it can perform. A whole range of different cards have evolved over the years and perform various assignments such as the acceleration of processing functions and the provision of network communication facilities. Other cards supply interface channels for peripheral add-ons such as scanners, fax, CD-ROM drives and modems.

However before exploring the major components of a PC we must take a cursory look at the underlying technologies which draw these various components into a working computer system.

The bus

The internal architecture of a computer and the manner in which the major components of a PC such as the microprocessor, memory, and hard disk communicate and co-ordinate rely on a device known as the bus. A bus in a PC computer is an internal electrical connection which enables data to be transmitted to the computer's various components. The physical appearance of a PC computer bus is that of a *parallel* series of thin wires. Five major PC compatible architectures which have evolved around the bus include ISA, MCA, EISA, VLB, and PCI.

The Industry Standard Architecture (ISA) 8-bit bus was introduced with the original IBM PC. Later on a faster 16-bit version appeared inside IBM's 80286 Advanced Technology (AT) computer. This was a ground-breaking design and set the standard for the 386 and 486 motherboard design to this day. The *motherboard* (also known as the mainboard) is that PC component which contains the computer's microprocessor and usually a socket for a coprocessor, a processor cache, main memory, and a range of slots into which expansion cards can be attached. The 16-bit ISA bus is still the most popular standard and is widely supported by third party manufacturers who have created thousands of different expansion cards to fit into it.

In what was regarded by many as the propagation of Proprietary Standards, IBM then introduced Microchannel Architecture (MCA). The MCA connection system or bus was introduced by IBM for its PS/2 range of personal computers. In order to use MCA other computer manufacturers had to pay IBM. Because of this, rival manufacturers of IBM got together and produced the Extended Industry Standard Architecture (EISA) system which became more popular than MCA but nowhere near as popular as ISA.

As computers have developed so we have seen the arrival of the local bus. The *local bus* is an extension of the data connection between the system memory and the processor, and is thus able to achieve rapid data transfers of the same magnitude as the EISA system. One standard that has evolved in this category is the Vesa Local Bus (VLB) .

The Peripheral Component Interconnect (PCI) standard was originally developed by Intel. There are currently two versions of this architecture, one is 32-bit whilst the other is the more advanced 64-bit version. The PCI bus offers a radical way of connecting a PC's internal components and its arrival has conveniently dovetailed with the entrance of the Pentium micro-processor (see 3.12.1). Pentium developers now have what is known as a 64-bit bus to match the power of their 64-bit processor. The next step is to consider the other major components which effectively hang off this device called a bus.

3.6.2 Other major PC components

(a) ROM and RAM

Read Only Memory (ROM) and Random Access Memory (RAM) are the hardware microchip devices containing digital data for use by the CPU. The contents of ROM as its name suggests is not usually meant to be altered and primarily contains permanent information relating to functional routines.

A good example would be the activation of the disk drives. The user does not have to enter the necessary instructions for them to function because the drives are activated by pre-programmed commands resident in the ROM chip. In contrast the RAM is the user's work surface. RAM's contents may be read by the system CPU and overwritten when required. Unlike ROM, the contents of RAM basically evaporates when the machine is switched off.

The size of RAM is a good first indicator of the power and sophistication of the computer. It is usually measured by its byte size. A byte, which is itself composed of up to 8 bits (see below), is commonly regarded as the basic unit of storage for a single keyboard character. The word HELP will therefore occupy four bytes of RAM. The RAM itself is usually denoted in kilobytes (Kb) or megabytes (Mb). A kilobyte is 1024 bytes. The reason for this odd number is that data is organised inside a computer system using the binary number system. Every bit, therefore, represents either a zero or a one. Two to the power of ten is 1024. A megabyte represents 1,048,576 bytes. However, a Kb and an Mb are usually referred to as a thousand and million bytes respectively. A gigabyte (Gb), in turn, is a thousand million bytes.

(b) The PC microprocessor

The microprocessor is usually thought of as the nerve centre of the computer. It executes the program instructions and usually determines the computer's speed of operation. The speed of operation is known as clock speed and is frequently measured in MHz (Megahertz). The microprocessor's clock, usually a quartz crystal, oscillates at so many cycles per second. Therefore a microprocessor working at the rate of 200 MHz indicates that it operates at 200 million cycles per second. However it must be stated at this stage that most IT professionals tend to use benchmark tests such as MIPS (Millions of Instructions Per Second) as a measure of performance for a particular computer. MIPS measures the actual number of machine code instructions executed by the processor each second.

(c) Coprocessors

The primary function of a main microprocessor is to carry out the necessary logic operations. When calculations have to be executed the microprocessor has to employ built-in instructions so as to enable it to perform the tasks.

Unfortunately as programs become more complex so an ever-increasing number of calculations must be performed. Consequently the main processor starts to slow down. In order to alleviate this congestion coprocessors are installed. The coprocessor supplies extra calculating facilities so enabling the main processor to carry on with other routines. Coprocessors are not only beneficial for mathematical tasks but also support the running of sophisticated graphic-intensive applications such as Desktop Publishing (DTP) and Computer Aided Design (CAD). The reason for this is the enormous background calculations that these types of programs have to perform.

(d) Cache

The object of the cache is to predict necessary data and instructions that are required at the next stage of a process and so bypassing constant access to the main RAM for certain blocks of data. A good example of this type of data might be the instructions necessary for the constant refreshment of screen background in a wordprocessing program. This is done is by means of a logic element called a cache controller. When the cache controller supplies the correct data this is known as a 'cache hit' and no doubt it will come as no great surprise to know that incorrect information is known as a 'cache miss'.

A high hit rate can have a considerable impact on a computer's speed but this is heavily dependent on the type of program being used.

(e) Ports

PCs usually come with two different types of port, the serial or RS232 and the parallel or Centronics port. The serial ports are usually used for interfacing devices such as modems whilst the parallel port is usually used for printer connections.

Parallel ports transfer data at much quicker rates than serial ports. In addition printers which support the parallel interface tend to be of higher quality than those which support the serial interface. Parallel printers are also far more available and thus tend to be better supported.

(f) Monitor/VDU (visual display unit)

The computer's monitor, also known as a VDU or CRT (cathode ray tube), is the user's work window. The most common screen sizes are 15, 17 and 20 inches in width. High-quality monitors are very expensive and can make a huge demand on the computer's processing capability.

There are numerous standards but the two most prevalent types of colour monitor in the PC world at the moment are EGA (Enhanced Graphic Array) and EVGA (Enhanced Video Graphics Array).

EVGA which is also known as SVGA (Super VGA) currently supports a graphic display standard of 800 × 600 pixels (some standards currently support 1280 × 1024 pixels). *Pixel* comes from the words picture and element. A pixel is the smallest element of a display that can be controlled by the computer. The size of the pixel determines the quality of computer's screen. The more pixels there are in a given area so the sharper the image that is projected. However, pixels make significant demands on the computer's memory. For example a high-resolution screen containing 1000 × 1000 pixels in full colour requires 24 million bits of memory.

(g) Drives

There are five main types of data drive (storage/retrieval data devices) on PCs:

Hard disk drive
Floppy disk drive
The CD (Compact Disk) ROM drive
PCMCIA card storage devices.
Tape drives

There is also what is known as the RAM disk/drive which, strictly speaking, is not a physical device but is discussed in (f) below.

(a) The hard disk is internal to the PC although removable hard disks are becoming more widespread. It is a fast and efficient means of storing and retrieving data. The capacity of the modern hard disk usually runs from 1 Gb up to 100 Gb(s).

At any rate, whatever the size of the hard disk, users can for the most part employ a disk data compression application so as to increase their disk's data storage capacity. Compression or *data compression* is that technique which compacts data so that it requires less physical space for storage and less time to transmit during any transfer process. What happens is that blocks of recurring information, such as spaces in a text document, are replaced with a single symbol/code. The result is to represent the same data in a more compact form without necessary loss of integrity.

Most contemporary hard disks that occur in non-specialist computer systems are usually of a category known as IDE (Integrated Drive Electronics). However, for professional computer systems required to operate multi-media or Internet/communication applications, both of which can require large disk space as well as fast data speeds, many users prefer the SCSI (Small Computer Systems Interface) standard.

(b) The floppy disk drive usually supports the widely used 3.5 inch disk with 720 K or 1.44 Mb storage capacity.

(c) There are also the CD-ROM drives which access data from compact disk storage media. (More on CD-ROM in Chapter 7 on Multimedia.)

(d) Another type of drive which is growing in popularity is that supported by PCMCIA (see 3.10) credit-card-size devices.

(e) PC tape drives are magnetic tape cartridge type devices that are usually plugged into one of the PC's ports. They are cheap and cost effective and are primarily used for data backup.

(f) A logical drive is also known as a RAM disk. This is a logical partition of the RAM and therefore is only present when the computer is operating. Its advantage is that it enables the user to access temporary work surfaces for various tasks such as copying procedures or platform duties for menu applications enabling PCs to access fileservers on computer networks.

3.7 PORTABLE PCs

Portable computers have evolved at a pace which has been far more dramatic than its desktop counterpart. Power conservation techniques, better screens and improved performance have all made this part of the computer market a massive growth area. The standard A4 notebook portable provides practically all the functions and features of the standard desktop PC but with of course the major advantage of portability.

The attraction posed by powerful portable PCs is compelling. The portable PC user is a mobile worker. No longer restricted to the office, the significance of sophisticated processing operations being carried out in the field has not gone without notice. However modern portable computers still have several major drawbacks that have yet to be dealt with. The keyboards on portables are smaller and the screens are not always as clear or responsive as might be desired. Portables also suffer through their constant movement. Hard disk drives are especially prone to damage.

However as time passes these obstacles appear to be dwindling in stature as the industry makes ever-increasing advances. For example it is expected that the wider employment of PCMCIA cards (see 3.10) will reduce these risks as they do not employ physical moving parts. Portable computers of one type or another are the undoubted future of the computer and predictions indicate that it will be $80 billion by the turn of the century.

3.7.1 Weight

The average weight of the modern notebook/laptop is approximately 3 kilogrammes. Although this is an incredible improvement modern portable PCs are still somewhat bulky and can be reasonably uncomfortable to lug around.

Consequently a slender portable computer has appeared under the Sub-notebook title. It has been suggested that if the computer fits into your attaché case without to much difficulty then it fits into this classification.

The sub-notebooks have a weight of between 1 kg and 3 kg and are mostly PC-compatible. They usually come with an OS such as Windows or DOS. These computers, as one would expect, have certain features stripped away. For example there is usually no internal floppy drive. The absence of floppy drives leads to a big weight reduction and enables better power management as physical disk drives are a big drain on portable battery power. Data transfer is usually through serial port transfer or using PCMCIA cards.

3.7.2 Power

Whilst modern portables support power-saving features, battery life is limited. However some of the latest products support dual alkaline and nicad battery operation. Universal power adapters have also appeared, using what is known as trickle power techniques. This involves the ability to use a computer powered by the mains to restore a chargeable battery at the same time and also the ability to use different voltage supplies, normally between 110-240 volts.

3.7.3 Portable screens

Screens on portable computers are most probably their biggest drawback. Manufacturers have indicated that the liquid crystal display (LCD) screens on laptop computers account for over 50% of the total cost of producing the computer.

Basically LCD devices lack clarity and are horrendously slow in comparison to conventional desktop PCs. Delay and clarity in screen response when using graphic-intensive applications can be severe. These problems have been partly tackled by employing active matrix thin film transistor (TFT) technology. This improves contrast and response time by attaching a transistor switch to each LCD cell or pixel. The majority of the colour portable computers sold use active matrix TFT displays.

Other flat-screen technologies include gas plasma and electroluminescence. Gas plasma screens have the dual advantage of producing their own light and delivering fast response times. In addition they are cheaper than TFT screens. Electroluminescence screens are quick as well and easily support graphic-intensive applications. Their drawback however is that they are a considerable drain on the computer's battery.

The computer manufacturer Dell have manufactured sub-notebooks using a reflective screen instead of a back-lit screen. The power saving has been considerable and is not surprising given that portable monochrome screens reputedly consume 33 per cent of battery power whilst colour screens consume 50 per cent.

3.8 MULTIFUNCTION PCs

PC users in the late 1990s are witnessing a convergence of technologies as new multifunction computers begin to appear. Contemporary new PCs equipped with fax and modem have almost become the norm. However, there is undoubtedly a lot more to come. The current belief by market analysts is that the domestic computer will be eventually transformed into the ultimate home appliance acting as a telephone/communications centre, answering machine, fax, TV and stereo. The cost and technology of these machines varies greatly but the few that have already appeared are beginning to make a significant impact.

One of first of these new hybrid computers for the mass market was Olivetti's Envision which was launched in 1995. The Envision had the appearance and dimensions of an ordinary video recorder. It was equipped with a remote control and cordless keyboard and plugged into a conventional TV. The Envision enabled the user to operate the TV as an ordinary PC as and when required.

Another ambitious multifunction computer is the PC/TV Communication centre developed by Cybertec Ltd. It is, as its advertising literature states, a multimedia PC, TV, radio, hi-fi, Internet and telephony communications centre all rolled into one. Equipped with a Pentium microprocessor, CD-ROM drive, sound card, answerphone, speakerphone, voice mail, fax, TV with remote control and teletext, FM radio and digital hi-fi, it is without a doubt one of the most sophisticated SOHO computers of the late nineties.

In order to accommodate the user with a friendly interface with these increasingly complex computers, manufacturers are beginning to build these multifunction PCs with physical buttons similar to those on conventional TVs or hi-fi systems. The idea behind such buttons is to enable users access to frequently used features such as the fax or even particular software applications such as a wordprocessor, without the need to hunt for specific commands at the keyboard. Other features appearing on these machines include autoload CD drives enabling fast access to frequently used CDs, infra-red facias to enable cordless data interchange and radio-controlled mouse(s).

However, whether these types of computer will become the norm is still subject to much debate. For example, TVs are still viewed as almost a communal activity whereas the PC is still very much for individual exercise. Nonetheless there is an undoubted increase in the public's interest in multifunction PCs. As a result companies have started to develop various strategies to promote the convergence of these technologies within the PC. One notable announcement on this front was the Simply Interactive PC (see 3.9).

3.9 THE SIMPLY INTERACTIVE PC

In 1996 Microsoft, in conjunction with other industry leaders such as Compaq and Intel, announced detailed plans for a new PC called the Simply Interactive PC (SIPC). The computer itself is expected to arrive towards the end of the century. The idea is to provide a blueprint of the technologies that will integrate into a new Windows-driven multifunction computer. The SIPC is designed to fully exploit the recent multimedia/ network technologies by becoming the focal point for education, recreation, communication and work.

The SIPC is to include superior sound/graphics as well as an imaginative range of peripheral devices/activities. The SIPC is also expected to be operated with the same ease as any other domestic appliance and will feature the sealed case concept. In other words, users will not have to interfere with the computer's physical casing to enable them to include various add-ons or upgrades. An interesting feature expected is the OnNow power function. The idea with OnNow is that the computer will be ready for use as soon as the user activates the power button so avoiding a boot-up time delay.

3.10 INTEGRATED CIRCUIT (IC) CARDS

Integrated Circuit (IC) cards are frequently described as being non-disk-based solid-state-memory storage devices. They are usually about the size of a thick credit card and are normally equipped with a tiny lithium battery to enable them to preserve the card's data after the card is removed from the computer. The technology employed in IC cards is not as extensive or 'mechanical' as that employed by other devices such as standard disk drives.

However, because IC cards are so small and because they are practically devoid of any physical moving parts they make ideal storage devices for portable computers. IC cards can also be slotted in and out of the computers whilst they are still functioning and are particularly suited as a means of transferring data between various types of computers. In order to rationalise the various types of IC cards the Personal Computer Memory Card International Association (PCMCIA) was formed in 1989 with the purpose of developing universally accepted standards.

Some of the various types of PCMCIA (IC) cards which support agreed standards and which are currently in use include:

(i) Type 1.0, which is a simple storage device.

(ii) Type 2.0, which enables modem and network connections as well as the creation of extra RAM.

(iii) Type 3.0, which enables hard disk and radio connections as well as 32-bit multi-tasking.

Not surprisingly, IC cards are considered to be one of the biggest growth areas in computing technology and it is rare for a portable PC of the late 1990s not to have a PCMCIA slot. Interestingly the arrival of these IC card devices dovetails neatly with the increased demand for small but powerful portable computers and will no doubt play an increasingly important role in the development of the new handheld or palmtop computers that have started to appear.

3.11 THE HANDHELD COMPUTER

A handheld computer is a general term used to describe those small business computers that can be operated without having to rest them on a surface. For the business sector, useful handheld computers can only enhance the development of a highly equipped flexible workforce. Unfortunately only a few contemporary handheld computers are either DOS or Windows compatible. Nevertheless, as their power increases then so does their popularity and there is a general perception that handheld computers will eventually replace most of their less mobile counterparts.

However mobility and their progressive ease of use are not the only significant factors fuelling the increasing interest in handheld computers. One almost surprising incentive is that of computer crime. Unfortunately, conventional PCs and portables make conspicuous targets for the criminal classes. In addition they can cost as well as contain thousands, if not tens of thousands, of pounds worth of investment. In contrast, handheld computers are easily hidden and, secondly, even when they are stolen, they are not so difficult or expensive to replace.

There are various grades of computer that fall into this category but the main examples are the Electronic Organiser, the Palmtop PC, the Personal Digital Assistant (PDA), the Electronic Book and the TouchMobile. However, although these devices are highly advanced they are still short of the technological ideal of the wallet-sized PC.

3.11.1 Electronic organiser

These are small calculator-size computers with the customary in-built diary applications. They normally support a small alphanumeric keyboard with a small two or three line LCD screen and are usually limited in function.

3.11.2 Palmtop PC

These are significantly more advanced than an electronic organiser and this is reflected in size, function and price. The main difference between a Palmtop PC and an electronic organiser is the software. Electronic organisers usually come with proprietary or dedicated software. In contrast, with a Palmtop PC you have the opportunity of purchasing and running alternative applications.

In addition, unlike most electronic organisers, most Palmtop PCs are purchased with the intention of being used with a PC compatible. Data transfer can be achieved through the use of a serial linkup or, as is starting to appear, through the use of card drives (PCMCIA) or even by means of infra-red signalling.

The Psion range

Although Palmtop PCs have a long way to go they are starting to make a major impact. A range of palmtop computers which proved to be particularly successful was the Psion 3 Series from Psion. Equipped with a neat monochrome screen and running off standard batteries or mains, the Psion 3 range made major inroads into the corporate market and was recognised as a significant business tool.

In 1997 Psion launched its Psion 5 series. The most striking feature of this particular range was an ingenious keyboard enabling the user to almost touch type. As with the Psion 3c the Psion 5 contains an infra-red port for printing as well as a serial port for a hard wire connection to a PC or other peripherals. Besides coming with either 4 Mb or 8 Mb of RAM the computer was designed to run industry-standard software and appeared to be well received by industry.

Windows CE palmtops

In 1997 Hewlett Packard and Casio launched a very sophisticated range of handheld palmtop PCs running Windows CE (the CE was originally believed to have stood for Consumer Electronics). Windows CE is a cut-down version of the Windows 95 OS and although it is early days they are expected to make a huge impact on the mobile computing market.

3.11.3 Personal digital assistants (PDAs)

Personal Digital Assistant (PDA) is the term used to describe those handheld computers which are equipped with handwriting-recognition capabilities. The user writes text using a special pen onto a liquid crystal display screen. Dedicated software then translates the text into data which can be automatically processed.

One of the first mass-produced PDAs was Amstrad's Pen Pad PDA600. It weighed about 1 lb, was PC compatible and came with a PCMCIA slot so enabling access to other ROM-based applications.

A more sophisticated device is Apple's Newton MessagePad. It is approximately the same size as a video cassette and includes a low-power 20 MHz 610 RISC chip (similar to that used in the Acorn Archimedes computer), which gives it a processing capacity equivalent to a 486 PC. Other features of the MessagePad include built-in applications such as diary software as well as a PCMCIA slot.

There have, however, been some setbacks with PDA type computers as the handwriting recognition software has not proved to be the success that was anticipated. As a result of such limitations with the products PDA producers are perceived as having drifted from the domestic consumer market. PDA products are now aimed at providing vertical information solutions for large commercial organisations. For example, PDAs with bespoke applications are supplied to meter readers working for the utility companies such as gas and water.

3.11.4 The electronic book

The Electronic Book concept has been propagated by Sony. Its product, the Datadiscman, is more a reference device although some models do in fact possess the functions of an electronic organiser as well. It is aimed at the growing multimedia market and allows users to page electronic versions of reference books, novels, guides and encyclopaedias, all of which are stored on special 3 inch CD-ROMs each of which can store the equivalent of 120,000 pages of text. The screen on the Datadiscman is a small LCD device with a resolution of 256×200 pixels. Such a device is more than adequate for text display but limited for graphic output.

3.11.5 The TouchMobile

A good example of a robust and practical handheld computer is the IBM TouchMobile computer. This device has a bar code scanner with on-screen signature and data capture. What makes this computer so interesting is that certain models are capable of wireless communication (see Chapter 6) so providing extra mobility to demanding users.

3.11.6 Mobile phone computer

The current computer/communications industry appears to be gearing up to produce a new generation of handheld devices know as mobile phone computers.

One good is example is the device produced by the mobile phone manufacturer Nokia. Known as the Nokia 9000, the unit enables users to employ a mobile phone which also allows faxing, e-mail and Internet access. This particular device integrates the processing power of a PC with mobile telephony. Unfortunately it is considerably more expensive than the conventional mobile phone/handheld computer and is considered to be somewhat ponderous with certain tasks. Nonetheless it is thought to be a ground-breaking device that will have a considerable effect on future market developments.

3.12 THE CHIP MARKET

Intel is currently the world's undisputed leading manufacturer of PC microprocessors, a position which it has held since the early 1980s. It is, however, a widely held view that Intel's market position has been won and maintained because of its incredible investment programmes. For example, in the mid 1990s Intel was building factories costing somewhere between two and three billion US$ almost as a matter of course. Such investment has produced its own dividends and in 1997 Intel was reputed to have control of approximately three-quarters of the world's microprocessor sales.

However in the mid to late 1990s there has been an upward surge in the competition within the microprocessor market. Two companies worth mentioning include Advanced Micro Devices (AMD) and Cyrix. Interestingly both companies have been involved in convoluted legal battles with Intel over licensing agreements concerning the manufacture of various microprocessors. Nevertheless AMD and Cyrix have been reasonably successful in their various business and legal strategies and both have produced microprocessors which have tended to be cheaper than their Intel equivalents.

Another threat to Intel's hegemony in recent times has been the competition posed by the PowerPC microprocessor, produced as a result of an alliance between IBM, Apple and Motorola. Initially viewed as an attempt to wrestle dominance of the PC microprocessor market from Intel it has not had the success that was originally envisaged.

Intel is also believed to be facing increased competition from Sun Microsystem's RISC processors as well as the increasingly popular Alpha AXP chip from DEC. The significance of the Alpha AXP was highlighted when in the middle of 1996 the computer company NCP released the amazing Viper 1000 workstation. The Viper which is based on DEC's 21164 333 MHz Alpha microprocessor caused something of a storm when it was estimated at being able to process 1,200 MIPS. What effect this computer may have on the future of the PC/desktop market has yet to be fully assessed.

Intel is expected to retain its market dominance for the foreseeable future in spite of the PowerPC/Alpha Chip and the ever-increasing threat of companies such as AMD and Cyrix, who are currently producing effective economic Pentium clones. Three reasons for Intel's dominance are:

(a) The pulling power of Intel's brand name is such that users and developers refuse to purchase any other product.

(b) Intel has a good reputation with respect to the performance of its microchip products.

(c) Intel is one of the few manufacturers around with the ability to supply PC manufacturers with practically whatever quantity of microprocessors they require.

3.12.1 The Pentium range

In 1993 Intel launched the new Pentium microprocessor. At the time, contemporary 486 microprocessors operated at speeds approaching 50 MIPS. However, versions of the new Pentium were able to operate in excess of 166 MIPS and the product proved to be a staggering success.

The reason for this leap in performance centred on the fact that the original Pentium had 3.1 million integrated transistors, three times that of the 486 microprocessor. The Pentium also had the added advantage of containing an inbuilt cache and maths processor (see 3.6.2(d)). However, the new Pentium was significantly more expensive than the 486 chip. In order to entice developers and users to take up the new chip, Intel designed the Pentium so that it was totally compatible with hardware designed for the 486 chip. By the beginning of 1996 Intel were shipping large quantities of a new Pentium microprocessor known as the Pentium Pro. Containing over 5.5 million transistors (2.4 million more than that of the original Pentium) and operating at 200 MHz the performance of the Pentium Pro was a dramatic improvement on the original Pentium.

In January 1997 Intel launched the Pentium MMX (Multimedia eXtension). The declared object behind MMX was to enhance the performance of multimedia type applications as well as improve Internet access. MMX Pentium microprocessors included 57 new instructions employing a technique called Single Instruction Multiple Data (SIMD). The significance of this technology is that it provides a processing technique which is particularly suited to those highly parallel operations (those operations where the software applications all make similar demands on the microprocessor) encountered in multimedia/communication type functions. The MMX was in effect designed to cope with those extra processes that are currently performed by add-in boards.

In the summer of 1997 Intel launched the Pentium II. Unlike the Pentium Pro and the Pentium MMX the Pentium II is not so much an upgrade of the Pentium as it is a radically different processor. Pentium II includes the MMX's multimedia technology and is capable of addressing 512 Mb of memory. Initially issued with processor speeds of 233 MHz and 266 MHz top of the range Pentium II PCs are currently operating at 330 MHz and 400 MHz respectively.

3.12.2 Future Intel ventures

Contemporary Intel research and development is working on a new ambitious microprocessor known as Micro 2000. The chip is expected to support up to 100 million transistors and is expected to be in mass production by the turn of the century. In addition Intel has started to collaborate on the development of another new breed of processors with Hewlett-Packard, believed to be the third biggest US computer company after IBM and Microsoft. The declared goal of the alliance is to develop a new class of chips which will include the design of 64-bit microprocessors.

3.12.3 The AMD K6

1997 saw the arrival of AMD's K6 microprocessor. The significance of this particular microprocessor is that it was designed to fit into existing Pentium desktop designs. What is more it was marketed as being a product which could perform as well as its Intel Pentium equivalent but at a significantly lower price. Needless to say the K6 has had a considerable impact on the PC market and seems to be presenting Intel with some serious competition.

3.13 THE ENTRY LEVEL PC

The Entry Level PC is a widely used phrase denoting the minimum hardware configuration a PC must possess to enable it to sell in the contemporary SOHO/corporate computer market. There are no hard and fast rules as to what might be described as an Entry Level PC other than the fact that such a machine should, ideally, be capable of operating the latest software applications as well as interoperating with the latest PC hardware technology at, and this is the critical point, an affordable price.

Obviously, this means that the specification of the Entry Level PC is always on an increasingly upward curve as users and applications make ever-increasing demands. For example PCs which were equipped with 8 Mb of RAM were perfectly adequate to operate Microsoft Office. However, the arrival of applications such as Microsoft 97 has resulted in a dramatic rise in the RAM specification of an Entry Level PC.

3.13.1 Contemporary entry level PC configuration(s)

The contemporary entry level PC would usually consist of a configuration not to dissimilar to the range(s) specified below:

16 Mb–64 Mb RAM
2 Gb–4 Gb Hard Disk
Internal Modem 33.6 Kbps
8–16 Speed Disk Drive
15" – 21" Colour Monitor
On-board Sound Card
300 MHz Pentium MMX/II Processor
1.44 Mb Floppy Disk Drive.

3.14 THE NETWORK COMPUTER

In April 1996 Oracle shook up the business computing world with the launch of the Network Computer (NC). The inaugural NC, which was not too dissimilar from an ordinary computer terminal, consisted of 8 Mb of flash memory, an in-built 28.8 Kbps modem, an infra-red remote control handset and an ARM 75000 microprocessor. However, there were no storage facilities/drives and no end user applications. The reason is that the concept behind the NC was to provide the end user with a cheap cost-effective multimedia client network computer. To enable this, Oracle had to produce a technological framework that was stripped to a functional minimum.

The economic and technical argument for the NC hinges on that which applies to the phone. The point is, just as most phone users employ relatively simple devices which link them up to the phone network so it can be argued that most computer users only need a simple access window in order to take advantage of all the various possibilities which modern computing has to offer. The idea is that the network service provider's central computer system will supply the client computer (that is to say the calling computer, namely the NC) with the necessary applications/services which the user can access as and when they log onto the network.

In this respect it can be seen that an individual NC unit is nowhere near as sophisticated or expensive as a quality contemporary PC. By stripping the potential access window to a bare minimum it is argued that users will not have to spend as much to access the latest multimedia technology. In other words, users will only have to lay out a fraction of the price required to purchase computers which did most of the processing locally. The reason for this, of course, is that all the processing requirements are handled by the service provider's computer in just the same way that the telephone provider's exchange system performs all the necessary tasks in order to connect the user's calls.

Another major advantage of the NC approach is that users will not have to upgrade their hardware as much in order to access subsequent generations of software. With the NC, most major hardware/software upgrades will take place at the point of origin. In other words it is the network service provider that will directly bear the burden of any required technological advances although it must be stated that the cost will eventually be passed down the chain. However, the point is these costs will be more evenly spread over the user base and will not result in the end users having to completely revamp their systems every time there is a major change.

Many contemporary industry observers think that the NC is somewhat of a gamble. Nevertheless it has arrived at a fortuitous time. Data/telecommunication transmission costs are plummeting all over the world and the Internet is really beginning to boom. If the basic cost of purchasing the NC is kept low and if the charges administered by the service providers are reasonable then the NC could be a real success. There is even the possibility that the NC will be provided for free with the idea that the service provider recoups its money in the service contract just the way mobile phone companies do.

In addition, organisations that were not involved in the development of the original NC are starting to develop their own products just in case Oracle has got it right. Sun Microsystems have launched their own NC type computer, the Sun JavaStation. The initial version of this NC is, as with the Oracle model, equipped with 8 Mb of RAM and claims to provide all the major features/utilities of a multimedia PC. By the end of 1996 IBM, Microsoft and Intel also announced plans to make substantial investments in NC technology.

Whether or not the NC will be the success its supporters are implying has yet to be proved. It is suggested, however, that the NC is unlikely to ever totally replace the PC in its present form. The reason is that most users have a strong preference for some form of significant local processing. It is possible, if not likely, however, that the NC will play a major role for those organisations requiring useful on-line services such as round-the-clock Internet access.

3.15 PRINTERS AND SCANNERS

This section details examples of two critical peripheral devices, namely printers and scanners. Other peripheral devices such as modems and faxes are dealt with in the next chapter.

3.15.1 Laser printers

The laser printer is an electro-photographic device that is derived from the same technology used in the office photocopier. As a result, laser printers can produce excellent print copy. Unfortunately laser printers do have a cost penalty. Not only are they expensive to purchase but they are also expensive to operate. For example, laser printers usually employ special toner ink cartridges which cost far more than the conventional print ribbons used in dot matrix printers. Laser printers are also less flexible than dot matrix printers when it comes to paper handling. Most users have discovered that wide paper printing and multi-part forms can be dealt with far better with dot matrix devices. However, despite these drawbacks, a laser printer is a must for most business users and is practically a necessity for those users wishing to exploit their particular systems with DTP type applications. (See also 12.8.2.)

Top of the range laser printers can print at 1,200 dots per inch (dpi) at 24 pages per minute (ppm).

3.15.2 Line printers

Unlike daisy wheel or dot matrix printers which print one character at a time, a line printer, as its name suggests, prints a whole line of characters in a single strike. Line printers are fast action devices that are usually employed within commercial setups for use with a network or mainframe configuration as opposed to the individual PC user.

3.15.3 Dot matrix printers

Dot matrix printers are extremely popular and are the most cost-effective printers to purchase and operate. Companies which have led the dot matrix market include Epson and Hewlett Packard. The crucial focus of a dot matrix printer centres on the print head mechanism. This mechanism is composed of a series of small pins that are activated as the print head moves across the printer's paper.

The calibre of the output of each individual dot matrix printer depends on the number of pins that are to be found on the print head mechanism and the manner in which the print head mechanism adjusts itself every time it moves. The number of pins effectively determines the resolution of the print output. The cheapest standard is the 9-pin dot matrix printer whilst the upper end is dominated by the 24-pin print head mechanism. The 9-pin is usually reserved for low-grade volume output whilst 24-pin printers are used for those print runs requiring near letter quality output. With respect to the adjustment of the print head, this concerns the irregularity of output due to the uneven wear on the printer's print ribbon. In order to counteract this effect, high-quality dot matrix printers are designed to move the print head mechanism very slightly and then reprint an exact copy of each character/line.

3.15.4 Inkjet printers

The inkjet is the most popular type of computer printer currently being sold in the US and the UK. It dominates colour printing technology. The latest examples of inkjet printer technology include printers capable of printing directly from digital cameras.

As their name suggests, inkjet printers operate by spraying the paper with a force of liquid ink. The resolution of an inkjet printer depends on the number of inkjets in the print head. An average quality inkjet printer can accomplish a print resolution of up to 360 dots per inch. Inkjet printers employ special inkjet cartridges and are significantly more expensive than dot matrix printers. However, they can furnish the user with excellent output and are significantly cheaper than laser printers. Leading companies in the Inkjet market include Canon, Epson and Hewlett Packard.

3.15.5 Optical scanners

Optical scanners are light-sensitive data input devices that are used to scan information/patterns, such as printed text or graphs, off paper or other similar medium. This data is then converted into a digital signal which is controlled by a connecting computer operating suitable Optical Character Recognition (OCR)/graphic software.

OCR software specifically enables computers to recognise those varying patterns generated by the varying shades of light that emanate from individual printed/written characters. Computers operating OCR software then match these patterns against a stored group of character templates so that the scanned data can then be translated into a corresponding text file.

The two leading types of scanners are usually referred to as handheld or flatbed. Handheld scanners are so named because the user holds the device over whatever they wish to scan. They are cheap and simple but can prove inconsistent. Users of handheld scanners must make sure that they read the data in a relatively straight line otherwise they can end up with data which is distorted.

Flatbed scanners are a more reliable alternative but can prove expensive. They are usually about the same size as a small office photocopier and users place papers/pictures or whatever, face down on a glass surface. These objects are then scanned by a mechanism from underneath.

3.16 WIMP ENVIRONMENT

Many users have become accustomed to accessing their PC via a mouse in conjunction with the keyboard, in a WIMP environment (WIMP: Windows Icons Menus Pointers).

The mouse is an input device, connected to a computer port by wire, which is manipulated by hand in order to move a pointer or cursor over the menu displayed on the screen. A menu is a range of options, displayed in the form of icons or text. When the pointer has settled on the required menu item, a click on the mouse button activates the task or further menu that is represented by the menu item and its appropriate window appears on the screen.

It is possible for more than one window to be showing on the screen at any one time but only one of them can be active.

For more, see 12.8.1.

3.17 CONCLUSION

Personal computing technology has become part of everyday life. What is more, it is improving all the time. For example, developers are reshaping the PC from that of a standalone wordprocessing/multimedia device to that of central communications Internet tool which combines the best that multimedia/video/telephony technology has to offer.

However, despite the current proliferation of good quality PC products there is evidence of a slow-down in the demand for desktop personal computers. The fact is personal computers have become almost as common as the domestic phone and current figures indicate that Western countries have become saturated with PCs. In addition, there is increasing evidence of users beginning to take greater interest in more cost-effective devices.

Such a trend is mainly due to improvements in PCMICA technology which has in turn led to an increase in the degree and variety of product miniaturisation. As a result, users of every type are taking more note of the new cheaper handheld computers as opposed to their more expensive desktop machines.

Finally there is the perennial problem of the need of all computer users to constantly upgrade their systems in order to access the latest applications/equipment. Whether the new NC will help alleviate this problem has yet to be seen. However, it has shaken the established order and its development will undoubtedly lead to a whole new range of applications.

4

Operating systems

4.1 INTRODUCTION

The subject of computer operating systems (OSs) is a very complex and expansive topic. As a result, an in-depth analysis of computer OSs is way beyond the scope of this book. The main objective of this chapter, therefore, is to give a brief overview of some of the basic concepts underlying contemporary OS software as well as provide some background information to some of the more popular OSs currently in use within the SOHO market.

Section 4.2 provides an overview of what is euphemistically described as computer memory whilst sections 4.3 through to 4.5 centre on the nature and composition of a computer's OS. Section 4.6 concerns the concept of the graphical user interface. Section 4.7 through to 4.12 detail some of the more popular mainstream OSs. Finally, section 4.13 concentrates on emerging object oriented OSs.

4.2 COMPUTER MEMORY

An OS is a program which controls and manages the flow of data, the activities on that data, and its destination. However in order to appreciate the significance of this type of computer program, it is necessary to have an elementary understanding of computer memory.

Computer memory devices usually refers to the various device(s) which hold or accumulate data and programs. User/application access to information stored in computer memory is usually through a sequence of predetermined program instructions the type of which are normally the responsibility of the computer's OS operating in conjunction with the computer's hardware.

Computer memory is generally divided into three main categories: data storage, ROM (see 3.6.2), and primary memory. The first category, data storage, consists of various devices such as magnetic tape, magnetic disks and optical disks such as CD.

The second category, ROM, is a permanent set of built-in instructions inside the computer. The instructions inside the ROM prime the computer for user access and enable the user to load required applications.

The third category, primary memory, consists of the computer's main internal memory. In this part of the computer, devices known as *registers* are used to store and transfer data/programs prior to or during processing. On the PC we would understand this area as being RAM (see 3.6.2(a)).

Another point that must be grasped is that these computer memory devices not only differ in their material composition but also, as a consequence of this difference, in price and performance.

(a) Cost

Data storage devices are usually basic in construction and consequently cheap to mass produce. For example, a standard floppy disk consists of nothing more than an encased disc of metallic-coated plastic containing a series of data-representing magnetised/non-magnetised spots. Even new compact disks, holding hundreds of millions of characters of data, are simply laser-etched plastic mirrors and can be produced for less than the price of a packet of cigarettes.

In contrast, RAM components/chips consist of complex transistor circuits and are therefore far more costly to manufacture.

(b) Performance/speed

Internal memory devices such as RAM process and transfer data at far higher speeds than external memory devices such as floppy disks.

For example, data passing through internal memory devices travels a relatively minuscule physical distance. However, this is not the case with data transferred, for instance, to and from internal memory to the system's external storage devices. Here, data transfer/relay travels via various paths which usually includes read/write mechanisms and internal bus circuitry (see 3.6.1). Although this 'distance' is still minute, it is comparative and is the main reason why data manipulation with external memory is a significantly slower process.

4.3 OPERATING SYSTEM CONCEPTS

Although an OS is a computer program like any other piece of software, it is, nonetheless, a critical application, the importance of which can be gauged by the fact that it is the program which allows the user to operate the computer. For many applications on a PC, particularly software packages, the OS performs its functions in a way which is 'transparent' to the user, i.e. the user can simply assume that the OS will carry out its designed tasks with little or no user intervention (see also 4.5).

At present there are three major classes of operating system: those targeted at:

- Mainframe/minicomputers
- Computer networks
- Standalone PCs/microcomputers.

The OS is in essence the program which enables a computer to control and manage the flow of data/information through its internal architecture

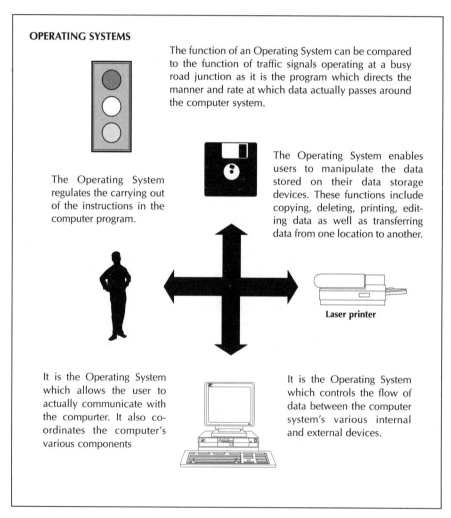

OPERATING SYSTEMS

The function of an Operating System can be compared to the function of traffic signals operating at a busy road junction as it is the program which directs the manner and rate at which data actually passes around the computer system.

The Operating System regulates the carrying out of the instructions in the computer program.

The Operating System enables users to manipulate the data stored on their data storage devices. These functions include copying, deleting, printing, editing data as well as transferring data from one location to another.

Laser printer

It is the Operating System which allows the user to actually communicate with the computer. It also co-ordinates the computer's various components

It is the Operating System which controls the flow of data between the computer system's various internal and external devices.

Fig 4.1

and any connecting peripheral devices. In order to do this, the OS regulates the execution of the various program instructions and it also supervises the allocation of internal and external memory space as well as providing the computer user with a working input/output (I/O) environment/interface.

Because computers cannot function without some form of an OS, the OS has to function as long as the computer is switched on. This means that the computer's OS must be robust and reliable. However, total reliability is not always available on cheaper systems. As a result users have to be fully acquainted with the limits of their particular OS and be prepared to pay extra in order to get what might be described as a relatively infallible system.

The size and sophistication of an OS running on any individual computer is directly dependent on the make-up of the computer system and the type of applications which the user wishes to access. For instance, a cheap and basic single-user desktop computer will often use an OS which could be considered almost primitive when compared to that employed by an individual workstation in an expensive corporate network.

4.3.1 Firmware

Before developing the concept of an OS it is necessary to pause for a moment and consider firmware. Firmware usually refers to those instructions/programs which are encoded within certain hardware components. A good example is the BIOS unit (see 3.5.1) inside a PC. Other examples include the code embedded in specialist microprocessors which control consumer durables such as washing machines or microwaves. Such components are usually instructed by a suite of permanent programs which fall into the firmware category. As a result, the distinction between an OS and firmware is not always so apparent because they both perform control and management tasks.

Nevertheless there are substantial differences. For example, an OS enables a computer/user to operate in a more responsive environment than that which is usually provided by firmware. The reason for this is that firmware applications are usually small programs which are restricted in the tasks they can perform. They are also usually exclusive to the hardware to which they are harnessed. In contrast, the majority of modern OSs are massive programs which can perform a wide variety of tasks as well as operate on an expansive range of computing platforms.

4.4 LOCATION AND FUNCTIONS

4.4.1 Location

The code which forms the OS of a computer is usually stored externally in a series of program files on the computer's hard disk/external memory. However because of their size (most modern computer OSs run into literally millions of lines of code), developers have found it necessary to structure OSs so they do not swamp the computers operating them (see below). OSs are, therefore, usually engineered to operate in sections which page in and out of the computer's own memory/processors as and when needed.

The reason for this is practical economics. For example, it would add greatly to the cost if a computer was designed so that its internal memory could accommodate the whole of the OS all at once, and it would also be a pointless exercise as many OS functions are only required on an occasional basis.

The type of OS routines that fall into this occasional category are sometimes called external OS procedure/file(s). A good example would be a file recovery program (basically a program which returns to 'situation normal' after complications). This type of routine is usually a sophisticated application which can take up a considerable part of the computer's internal memory. To maximise the efficiency of the computer, the file recovery routine is only loaded into the computer's internal memory as and when it is needed.

It should be noted that some parts of the OS must be loaded and running all the time. Those programs falling into this category include instructions facilitating the transfer of keyboard commands or the relaying of information to the computer's peripheral devices. The files enabling these basic functions are usually called internal OS procedure/file(s).

4.4.2 Functions

There is a wide range of OSs available for various computer systems providing a host of different services. However there is a certain group of functions common to most modern OSs. These include those which control:

- User interface
- Peripheral devices
- File management
- Memory management
- Network facilities (see Chapter 5)

- Program scheduling
- Fault monitoring
- Virus checking

4.5 FILES AND DIRECTORIES

OSs function at two different levels, the hardware level and the user level. The interaction of the OS with the computer's hardware level is, for the most part, hidden from the user. For example, signals relayed from the keyboard to the computer's microprocessor is done automatically, under the control of the OS, and without further recourse to instructions from the user.

Even so, the user will, at some stage or another, wish to install programs/applications, copy files, perform search routines or execute any one of a wide and ever-increasing range of tasks. In order to carry out these procedures, the user has to access and operate an appropriate user interface. However, before doing this the user should have an appreciation of the significance of files and directories at the operating system level (see 10.3.1 and 12.4.2 for higher-level interpretations).

4.5.1 File names

A file is a collection of related data, saved on a specific area of the surface of whatever storage medium the system is using. To be accessed, the file must have a name which is recognised by the system. The name is also significant in that it is usually an indication of purpose of the file and the type of data stored in the file. (It should be pointed out that OSs such as Windows 95 and Windows NT place greater emphasis on small icons as a means of identifying the nature and type of a particular file.) For most OSs the file usually has two names. These are known as the prefix and the suffix/extension. The prefix is supplied by the user. The suffix is supplied by either the user or the computer application currently being used.

The prefix is frequently separated from the suffix by a full stop or a slash. For example, in a DOS or Windows environment, the file LETTER.TXT would suggest that it is a letter file containing text data. Below is a listing of some typical DOS/Window file names with appropriate suffixes indicating their contents:

File Name	Data Type
PAY.BAS	Basic program (.BAS – Basic)
COMP.WKS	Spreadsheet data file (.WKS – Worksheet)
ACC.CBL	Cobol program (.CBL – Cobol)
FRED.DAT	Simple data file (.DAT – Data)
SAVE.BAT	Batch file (.BAT – Batch file)
NOTE.TXT	Text file (.TXT – Text)
LETTER.DOC	Document file (.DOC – Document)
MENU.EXE	Executable file (.EXE – Executable)
PROG.COM	Command file (.COM – Command)
REG.DBS	Database file (.DBS – Database)
PIC.IMG	Image file (.IMG – IMAGE)

Reserved names

OSs usually also employ a set of exclusive file names known as reserved file names. These file names are preserved for a list of commands/instructions which perform specialist functions during the operation of the computer. A good example of a reserved file name in a DOS/Windows environment is AUTOEXEC.BAT.

The object of the commands in the AUTOEXEC.BAT file is to automatically configure the PC to the user's requirements. These usually include tasks such as opening menu routines, memory allocation and keyboard recognition.

The AUTOEXEC.BAT file is stored on the computer's external memory. The file is activated as soon as the computer is switched on and initial hardware instructions from the OS begin to take control. The AUTOEXEC.BAT file is also what is known as a batch file, thus the extension BAT. A batch file is a file containing a set of commands which are executed when the file is activated.

4.5.2 Directories

A directory is like a drawer in a filing cabinet. It contains files. In addition, just as a filing cabinet usually consists of multiple drawers so a computer disk usually contains multiple directories. A directory can, if necessary, also contain other directories. The purpose of directories is to enable the user to partition the computer's disk/storage devices in an organised and meaningful manner.

Consider the following:

ACC <DIR>	PAY <DIR>	Here the top directory, on a disk, contains two sub-directories called ACC and PAY

ACC/ COMP.BAT STAR.EXE	PAY/ COMP.BAT	Both sub-directories contain a file COMP.BAT. The directory ACC also contains a file STAR.EXE

A user not positioned in the ACC directory and wishing to access the file, STAR.EXE, must use the file's path name or configure the computer to access the files in the correct directory. The path name for STAR.EXE, from another directory, in a DOS/Windows environment is \ACC\STAR.EXE. This path name is unique. To access the file COMP.BAT in the PAY directory, the path name is \PAY\COMP.BAT, and to access the file COMP.BAT in the ACC directory the path name is \ACC\COMP.BAT. The point is file names are unique in a directory but not on a disk. The reason for this is that different applications use the same file name time and again for its particular mode of operation. Directories therefore help avoid this confusion.

4.6 GRAPHICAL USER INTERFACE (GUI)

The Graphical User Interface (GUI) OS originated at the Xerox Parc (Palo Alto Research Centre) in the USA. The basic idea was to enable users to move away from text line commands, as epitomised by famous OSs such as Unix and MS-DOS, to that of an icon-based environment. In effect users were to activate screen pictures which in turn would execute various actions/commands on the computer. GUI applications reach their peak in WIMP systems (see 3.16).

The first mass-produced competent application of this type of technology was with Apple's Lisa computer. Its success was such that it was to form the basis for Apple's extremely popular Macintosh OS. However, it must be stated that the GUI market didn't really come to life until the launch of Microsoft's Windows (see 4.8).

4.6.1 Advantages of GUI systems

The GUI approach aims to smooth the user's interaction with the computer. Such encouragement has paid dividends and it is now the style pursued by top software developers involved in the production of modern computer applications. Advantages of GUI applications include:

71

(a) Improved user satisfaction

This is usually a direct result of an intuitive and easy-to-use interface so encouraging the user to experiment and to build necessary self-assurance. This is especially important for the novice user.

(b) Reduced learning curve

Usually a direct result of uniform menus, relevant picture/command relationships and a friendly help system. The method also encourages users to use other applications which employ a similar format.

(c) Superior output

Because GUI applications are usually user friendly and encourage use, this can in turn increase user sophistication by enabling the user to access more complex application utilities and so produce work of a higher quality.

4.7 MS/PC-DOS

The origins of Microsoft's Disk Operating System (MS-DOS) lie in the pre-launch era of the IBM PC. As IBM was about to finalise the PC it started to negotiate with other computer companies to secure a suitable OS for the product. Initial contacts between IBM and Digital Research, the company which happened to own the rights to CP/M (Control Program for a Micro-computer) which was, at that time, the market leader in microcomputer OSs, proved unsuccessful.

In 1980 IBM and Microsoft started negotiations for the production of a suitable PC OS. For Microsoft this was the big break. It had just purchased 86 DOS, an OS from Seattle Computer Products. As a result of a joint effort between IBM and Microsoft, 86 DOS was totally modified and upgraded to what was to become a new 16-bit OS called PC-DOS (Personal Computer Disk Operating System). When in 1981 IBM introduced its famed PC, it came equipped with PC-DOS. Because both companies shared in the ownership of the PC-DOS, Microsoft was able to retail an almost identical version of this OS under the title of MS-DOS. MS-DOS was usually that OS supplied with a PC compatible and PC-DOS was usually that OS which was supplied with an actual IBM PC.

4.8 MICROSOFT WINDOWS

The first version of the Microsoft Windows OS was launched in 1983. Like Operating System 2 (OS/2, see 4.9), the original release was not very successful. However, despite this initial setback Microsoft continued to develop the program. Its persistence paid off when in 1990 it launched Windows 3. The program became the world's best selling 16-bit GUI OS. By the end of 1996 it was estimated that Microsoft had sold more than 45 million copies.

Its success is often attributed to its overall design which conveyed an effective and compact user interface, along with the fact that it was a GUI OS specifically designed for the PC. In addition, Microsoft allowed developers to produce software applications to run on their Windows without the need to notify them and so encouraged a whole industry to work with their product.

Besides allowing users/applications to employ increased RAM, Windows 3 enabled true multitasking and allowed users to access programs written for MS/PC-DOS as well as those specifically written for a Windows environment. However, Windows 3 also resulted in a dramatic rise in the processing capabilities of the SOHO PC. To work effectively the PC was required to have a minimum of 4 Mb of RAM along with a 386 processor.

Unfortunately Windows 3 is not recognised as a fail-safe commercial OS as it does, for various reasons, have a tendency to crash. In order to eliminate such drawbacks and expand into the corporate market Microsoft introduced Windows NT (see 4.8.2).

4.8.1 Windows 95

Windows 95, a 32-bit OS (see below), was released in August 1995. It took Microsoft three and a half years to develop. It was a gigantic task as far as computer projects go and was estimated to have taken 75 million hours of testing prior to its release. It was greeted enthusiastically by the computer industry which saw it as a significant launch platform which would enable it to sell even more sophisticated computers.

At the time of the release, Microsoft played to the gallery and Windows 95 was given an advertising budget that was in excess of two hundred million pounds. It was undoubtedly the biggest marketing campaign in computer history. Microsoft even gave away the daily circulation of *The Times* newspaper in Britain for free on the day of the product's release.

However, Windows 95 has been attacked by industry pundits as being based on old technology. Whether this is so is a moot point. For example, in 1987, the Santa Cruz Operation (SCO) launched a 32-bit OS called Xenix 386, eight years before the release of Windows 95.

The significance of a 32-bit OS as opposed to a 16-bit OS can be measured by the amount of internal main memory that can be directly accessed by the user/program. For example, with a 16-bit version of MS-DOS, the maximum amount of directly accessible memory is 1 Mb. However, with a 32-bit OS, the user has direct access to 4 Gb of main memory.

Nevertheless it must be stated that people at Microsoft are not only proficient software producers but they are also rather successful in business strategy. Windows 95 broke all records and Microsoft sold 7 million copies of the OS within the first two months of its launch.

The product

To run Windows 95 users need a computer equipped with a 386DX or higher processor with a minimum of 4 Mb of memory (8 Mb is recommended) along with a hard disk of 50 Mb as well a 3.5 inch disk drive or a CD-ROM.

Windows 95 was designed to have certain critical features over and above what was already supplied by Windows 3.1 or Windows for Workgroups. These included:

(a) A 32-bit architecture which provides for a multitasking environment allowing the user to run multiple programs or execute multiple tasks concurrently. This architecture also enables faster data/file access as well as an improvement in printing delivery.

(b) A friendlier interface fitted with what is described as 'one click' access. One click access refers to the fact that users didn't have to double click on the mouse every time that they wanted to activate an application. Other congenial attributes include the ability to employ long file names, easy navigation routes and 'plug and play technology' enabling users to connect various peripheral devices or add-ons with the minimum of fuss.

(c) Windows 95 is also network ready. In other words the OS is designed for easy access to network resources. The OS also facilitates gateways to e-mail and fax facilities and access to the Internet via the Microsoft Network. In addition Windows 95 is backwardly compatible with most 3.1 Windows/DOS applications so enabling users to migrate from previous systems/applications.

4.8.2 Windows NT

Unlike Windows 3 and Windows 95, Windows New Technology (NT) is what is known as an industry-standard mission-critical OS. The most recent version of Windows NT, version 4, was launched August 1996.

As a 32-bit OS Windows NT represents the preferred platform for Intel's more powerful Pentium range of processors. Although not exactly the same, Windows NT 4.0 is, as might be expected, very similar in appearance to Windows 95. Critical features which allow the program to contest the commercial OS market include:

- A stable multitasking environment

- Enhanced security features
- Increased memory
- Network utilities
- Portability: NT can operate on microprocessors other than those designed for the PC.

Windows NT is, as might be expected, more expensive than the other Window OSs and makes greater processing demands. However, it should be pointed out that Windows NT is making massive inroads into the corporate computing market and is fully recognised as being a competent useful OS.

4.9 OS/2

In 1987 IBM and Microsoft announced a new PC OS called OS/2 (Operating System Two). Unfortunately, as has already been mentioned, the original OS/2 was not very successful. Hindsight suggests that, as with the early versions of Windows, one of the reasons for the slow uptake of OS/2 was the then considerable hardware demands of this particular application.

Another more serious problem with the original OS/2 was that it was unable to support many existing PC applications. SOHO users were not, understandably, impressed by the lack of compatibility between their original applications and OS/2. However, when Microsoft launched their new version of the Windows OS, Windows 3.1, users were presented with an OS which was able to support most existing applications as well as a new wave of exciting applications such as Excel and Word. As a result there was a certain degree of turmoil in the software market as blue chip applications developed for OS/2 were overhauled by Microsoft's products.

Predictably, the initial lack of interest in the original OS/2 resulted in a considerable strain on the IBM–Microsoft alliance. Not long after the launch of OS/2 IBM and Microsoft began to go their separate ways. Microsoft effectively abandoned OS/2 to IBM and chose instead to concentrate on MS-DOS and Windows.

4.9.1 Later versions

Despite the setbacks, IBM continued to invest in OS/2. As result, they produced a respectable GUI OS which enabled them to claw back a considerable share of the market.

At the beginning of 1995 OS/2 Warp version 3 was the world's number one 32-bit OS. Unlike the original version of OS/2, version 3 attracted considerable industry plaudits. Its 32-bit architecture made the OS eminently appropriate for power hungry programs such as those delivering multi-media.

OS/2 Warp version 3 also supported Window/DOS applications as well as a true crash-proof multitasking environment. This meant that multiple programs could run on an individual computer without interfering with each other. Other features included:

- Integrated gateway to Internet or CompuServe
- On-line tutorial
- Intuitive graphical interface
- In-built spreadsheet, wordprocessor and database.

In October 1996 IBM released OS/2 version 4 (Merlin) networking operating system (NOS). It is believed to be positioned as a direct competitor to Windows NT. It includes IBM's VoiceType speech recognition technology and supports Netscape's Navigator. It is also able to run Java applications.

4.10 UNIX

The origins of the Unix OS can be found in the Bell Laboratories of the American Telephone and Telegraph (AT&T) company. Unix first appeared in 1969 essentially for large machines and, as is the case with many successful high quality computing products, it had a slow start but became a highly successful OS for minicomputers.

Industry analysts believe that the initial lack of interest in this OS was due to fact that the original rights to Unix were not the property of any of the contemporary major computer developers. Conversely it was this very attribute which later led so many third parties to take a closer interest in the product.

The success has been such that Unix is now fully recognised as one of the computing industry's foremost OSs. It is particularly strong in the workstation/network sector of the market. However in contrast to other OSs, Unix has been developed by a host of different organisations, a fact which has caused considerable difficulties. The problem with respect to contemporary Unix centres on its limited application mobility. Although most versions of Unix have sprung from the source code originating from the version developed by AT&T or Berkley's BSD variation, there is still a significant level of disparity between the various flavours of Unix. The degrees of difference have meant that many computer applications designed for one flavour of Unix cannot be ported on to a computer supporting a different flavour of Unix, without first undergoing substantial alteration.

As a consequence, software developers have found that this Babel of Unix flavours has generated a precarious application market. The predicament hinges on the fact that professional application development is exorbitantly expensive and requires heavy investment. If Unix software developers pick the wrong version of Unix they can face severe financial penalties. The reason is that they will have produced a product which can only be sold to those users operating a compatible version of Unix.

In order to try and harmonise Unix standards certain regulatory institutions have evolved. One notable organisation, which is bankrolled by the computing industry and which emerged in the mid 1990s as result of a merger between two former organisations known as X/Open and the Open Software Foundation, is the Open Group. It is believed that one of the main reasons for the arrival of such a group is to face the increasing threat of Windows NT. Unix and Windows NT are direct competitors in certain markets such as networking and workstations.

4.10.1 Unix features

Unix is often thought of as a somewhat terse and unfriendly OS. Despite this unhelpful perception it is not as hostile as might first appear and in many ways is not too dissimilar from MS/PC-DOS. Modern versions of Unix can also be operated via GUI applications such as the SCO Desktop from the Santa Cruz Operation.

In addition Unix supports multi-user and multi-processing systems and is considered to be an excellent network OS. Unix has also generated a range of ancillary industry-standard software products. These include program development tools such as the C compiler (including C+ and C++) as well as the usual office applications such as spreadsheets, wordprocessors, electronic mail, etc.

Unfortunately the lack of universal standards as mentioned above means that users do not have access to as wide an application range as that supplied to the PC market. However Unix is an 'Open' OS which means that users do have the advantage of being able to choose from an expansive field of hardware platforms/computers.

4.11 MACINTOSH SYSTEM

The OS used for the Apple Macintosh PC is known as the Macintosh System. This OS was, until very recently, a proprietary OS. In other words the OS supplied with the Apple Macintosh computer was designed by Apple and fashioned so that it could run only on Apple Macintosh computers. However this strategy was perceived as having contributed to Apple's declining fortunes. As a result Apple begun to license its MAC OS to other computer manufacturers.

The latest version of the Macintosh OS is version 8.0. It includes an interactive help system and various facilities enabling file search as well as the ability to exchange software with applications based on MS/PC-DOS/Windows. Macintosh System 8.0 also supports multitasking, networks and a host of other built-in applications.

4.12 VIRTUAL MEMORY SYSTEM (VMS)

Virtual Memory System (VMS) is a 32-bit OS with multitasking capabilities. Originally created in the mid 1970s, it was designed for DEC's very popular VAX range of minicomputers. The chief architect of VMS was an illustrious programmer called Dave Cutler. He later left DEC and joined Microsoft where he helped to create Windows NT.

Unfortunately, DEC experienced a downturn in company profits during the late 1980s and early 1990s as it failed to take advantage of the downsizing trend. The problem was that other manufacturers began to produce relatively inexpensive alternatives, such as workstations, to their minicomputer range. However, VMS has a reasonably solid commercial user base and DEC was able to claw back some of the market with the introduction of its own cost-effective in-house workstation, the Alpha AXP PC. VMS on the Alpha is the same as that on the VAX minicomputer range, a feature which encouraged current users who realised that they could transfer current skills/applications with the minimum of effort.

4.13 OBJECT ORIENTED OPERATING SYSTEMS

To try and reduce the time/cost cycle involved in the development of software applications, a new class of OS is being developed. These are what is known as Object Oriented Operating Systems (OOOS). Although they have yet to become fully accepted, they are expected to spearhead the future OS market. The move towards OOOS technology is a recognition of the difficulty experienced by users in understanding how particular computers/OSs actually work.

The idea behind an OOOS is to create an OS which can easily employ reusable blocks (objects) of computer code or data in order to construct new applications. These blocks usually consist of computer programs, images, graphics, sound or any other digitised source a user might wish to engage.

It is predicted that OOOSs will result in a total change in the manner in which applications are produced as developers effortlessly recycle in-house objects or simply purchase compatible objects from other developers. OOOSs are also expected to smooth out those technical impediments which can and do arise between computer applications and the OS environment in which it has to run. Basically, developers will be presented with a more-structured user-friendly framework on which to hang their data objects.

4.14 CONCLUSION

The SOHO desktop OS market of the late 1990s is dominated by products such as Microsoft Windows, Unix, OS/2 and the Macintosh System. However this is not to say that developers are no longer producing applications for less-demanding OSs such as MS/PC-DOS. Simple economics indicate that many cash strapped users are still unable or unwilling to invest in computer systems employing GUI OSs. In addition developers know that application development for the MS/PC-DOS market is comparatively cheap and will continue to generate healthy sales at least until the turn of the century.

However what is beginning to radically change is the way in which future OSs will be presented to developer and user alike. For example, the arrival of an OOOS environment is a recognition of the need to smooth those technical barriers faced by developers in the creation of future software applications. It is also a recognition of the almost urgent need to try and enable users to increase personal productivity. Many developers realise that even supposedly user friendly GUI OSs can prove to be a formidable obstacle to the novice user. To minimise this problem, leading developers are trying to produce intelligent, user intuitive OS interfaces.

Finally it is necessary to mention the increasing power of programs such as Web browsers (see 9.10.1(l)). Although these programs are currently pitched as applications enabling users to navigate the Internet, they are, by virtue of their design, gradually assuming tasks previously performed by conventional OSs. Whether this trend continues is a moot point. However, it is possible that these applications will continue to develop along these lines and may, as a result, replace contemporary OSs.

5

Computer networks

5.1 INTRODUCTION

This chapter is aimed at providing an overview of the underlying economic, business and technological rationale governing contemporary computer network systems. The chapter will also place a particular stress on what is known as a Local Area Network (LAN). The reason for this emphasis is that a general understanding of the LAN will provide a conceptual platform to the understanding of Wide Area Networks (WANs) and communications, both of which will be covered in the next chapter.

Sections 5.3 to 5.8 cover the major hardware and software components that constitute an individual LAN. Sections 5.9 to 5.11 deal with major areas involving the growing phenomenon of internetworking. Finally sections 5.12 and 5.13 deal with the new networking concepts of Virtual Networking and Clustering.

5.2 THE BASIC CONCEPT

The late 1990s is witnessing a massive growth in computer networks. These computer networks involve computers communicating with other computers or peripheral devices either by means of cabling, of which there are various types such as optic fibre, or through microwave or satellite links.

The initial objective of networking computers was to enable users to share various hardware/software devices/applications and to facilitate, what was for most users, the occasional transfer of data files. However, this has all changed. The fact is that the tasks and roles of contemporary business computer networks have moved far beyond their original orbit of simple computing operations. For example, modern computer networks are used for communication, trading, education, research and a host of other related business activities. Computer networks also enable the pooling of ideas and information across an otherwise dispersed group of users as well as empower remote management to direct organisations far more efficiently.

5.3 LANs AND WANs

A LAN is a configuration of two or more computers, communicating within a particular building or a particular site. A WAN is, as its name suggests, a geographically spread computer network, which enables computers to communicate far beyond their immediate physical proximity.

Unlike a LAN, the limits and nature of a WAN are somewhat indeterminate. The reason for this is that it is now theoretically possible to link all modern computers irrespective of distance. For example, a conventional telephone link will allow a domestic computer to communicate, via the Internet, with countless computers across the globe. However, it should be stated that the term WAN, when used in a commercial context, usually refers to a private or dedicated long-distance computer network system.

For many commercial users, utilising a WAN is an obvious necessity. Consider a clerk working in a high street travel agency. Amongst other duties, the clerk would be expected by the customer to book hotels and most transportation services there and then. Whilst it is possible for the clerk to book services such as accommodation and road and rail journeys by phone or fax, it is more frequent, in a fully equipped modern travel agency, for the clerk to book services such as plane tickets via a dedicated booking computer/terminal. What is more, such a system should be capable of reserving the appropriate seats at that particular moment in time, a facility usually referred to as an online real time processing system (see 5.3.6). In order to perform this service the clerk's computer would have to be linked with a central computer system which contains the appropriate database. This central system could be an airline's mainframe computer which is on the other side of the country or in a different country. The clerk's computer must therefore be connected to a WAN of some description.

However, the necessity and purpose of a LAN is not always so obvious. After all, the communication and exchange of data/information on a LAN is between neighbouring machines. So, as is often asked, what is the point ? The fact is users have discovered that there are major benefits in connecting computers in this manner. As has already been stated, a LAN configuration enables users to share hardware and software resources as well as facilitating various personnel and process operational efficiencies.

The impact of a LAN in an organisation can be examined by considering their effect on the following three areas (it should be noted that most of the points covered in sections 5.3.1 through to 5.3.3 are just as relevant to a WAN configuration as they are to a LAN):

- Equipment economies
- Data processing
- Personnel performance.

5.3.1 Equipment economies

The intrinsic cost savings of a computer network are self-evident. For example, in an office full of computers is it really necessary for every one of them (in network terminology these are also known as *nodes*) to have its own printer?

In most operational situations there are times when the computer equipment employed is, in whole or in part, idle. So whilst it might be ideal for every node to have its own printer, the reality is that such an equipment configuration could prove to be an unnecessary waste of resources. The objective of providing adequate printing facilities can be achieved through sharing printers.

In the likely event of more than one user wishing to access a particular peripheral device such as a printer or fax the Network Operating System (NOS, see 5.8) will simply place the required tasks in an orderly queue and deal with each node's request in turn. In an efficient commercial network system possible delays caused by excessive workloads are minimised by the ability of the NOS to switch tasks to alternative resources. Economy is thus achieved by the sharing of hardware resources by the network's users.

In addition, just as individual nodes on a network do not have to be individually connected to their own printer so nodes do not have to have separate computer applications installed. In a computer network, application software can be distributed to the node computers from a central server as and when required. It is not necessary to purchase multiple copies of the application software. However it is usual to purchase software specifically designed to run on a network.

Another major equipment saving brought about through networking is the ability to link cheaper computers to more expensive and powerful systems. With respect to processing resources it is not necessary for the individual nodes of a network to have the same processing facilities as the server or host computer (see below).

5.3.2 Data processing

A principal advantage of a network is that it enables multiple users to share the same data files as well as the same applications. This has two major effects on the cost and efficiency of data processing operations.

Firstly, the sharing of data files and applications reduces the cost and time of system maintenance. For example, the network manager/administrator is only required to upgrade the server which supplies the required data/applications to the network instead of having to upgrade all the individual nodes which make up the network.

Secondly, multiple access enables users to centralise their data so increasing their processing efficiency operations whilst simultaneously enabling them to maintain the integrity of their data. A good example would be where a network application allows sales clerks operating separate nodes to process orders from the same stock files. A LAN supporting this type of application would usually ensure that stock files are updated after each transaction, a process known as *on-line real time processing*. On-line usually refers to that situation where a node is linked to a central computer, which holds the main data files. Real time processing usually means that the user's node accesses these central computer files there and then. Any consequential changes to the central computer's data files are carried out immediately.

Finally a LAN configuration can, where necessary, enhance data processing operations by enabling users to physically interlock their processing resources in a more efficient manner. Consider, for example, a situation where a particular processing task would take an inordinate amount of time if processed by one node on the network. The reason for delay could be due to the complexity of the task or the limitations of that particular computer. However, with networking, users can harness the power of more than one computer in order to process the task in question and so reduce the time spent on the task.

5.3.3 Personnel performance

Connecting computers in a LAN has also had a direct impact on the working environment/culture of organisations. The sharing of data and applications in this manner empowers what is commonly referred to in the corporate culture as the workgroup.

The term *workgroup* is a business term for a group of workers who are in close association with each other and who share their resources in their drive towards a collective business goal. In a typical commercial organisation a workgroup is thought of as a specialist team sharing a LAN and a common set of data and/or applications, sometimes referred to as groupware. A good example would be a pool of journalists all of whom use the same Desktop Publishing (DTP) program on a LAN to enable them to produce a newspaper. All the journalists will be using the same software but will be working on their own section of the newspaper file produced by the workgroup. The evolution of the workgroup has fitted well with modern management techniques which place great emphasis on the fact that the success of many organisations stems directly from the efficiency of activity in the lower levels.

Computer networks have also resulted in a massive increase in the use of electronic mail (see 6.9) and the application of Electronic Data Interchange

(EDI). Electronic mail enables computer users to exchange documents or messages in electronic form. EDI has been defined by the International Data Exchange Association (IDEA) as the 'transfer of structured data, by agreed message standards, from computer to computer by electronic means'.

Users of these systems can now access text/commercial data effortlessly. It should also be noted that research has shown that the manipulation and communication of data using electronic mail and EDI has led to a sharp rise in job satisfaction and performance.

5.4 NETWORK CONFIGURATIONS

A computer LAN is made up of a specialist combination of hardware and software equipment. The main components governing a LAN configuration are usually centred on the different types of computer which make up the network, the manner in which the computers are linked, the network technology employed and the NOS.

Modern computer networks can be composed of a whole spectrum of computer types and makes. How these computers are linked and their prospective roles or tasks within the network depends on the network configuration. Four possible configurations are

- File Server network
- Client/Server network
- Peer-to-Peer network
- Three-tier Client/Server network.

Unlike a peer-to-peer network, file server and client/server networks are reliant on a central computer known as a file server or a server computer.

5.4.1 Server computers

A computer which takes on the role of a file server or that of a server computer is usually a machine which carries out specialist network tasks. These specialist tasks can include the role of say 'banker', whereby the server computer is dealing application software to the various terminals or nodes as well as supporting the NOS and thereby controlling the flow of data around the network.

Servers can also act as pivotal data stores or provide necessary processing facilities. Whether or not a server computer performs these and other tasks depends on the structure of the network and the type of computer employed as a server.

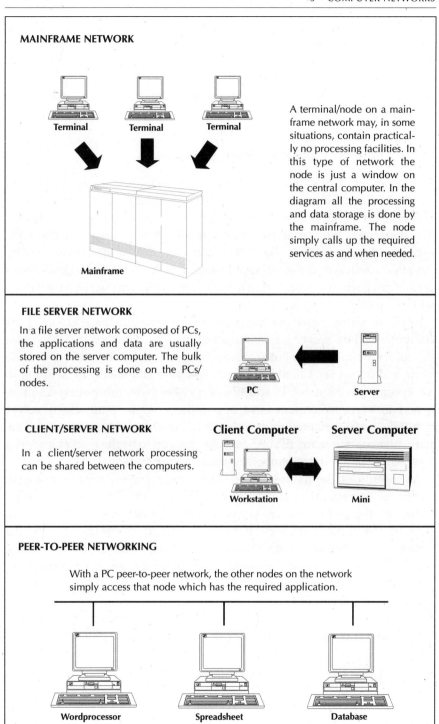

MAINFRAME NETWORK

Terminal   Terminal   Terminal

Mainframe

A terminal/node on a mainframe network may, in some situations, contain practically no processing facilities. In this type of network the node is just a window on the central computer. In the diagram all the processing and data storage is done by the mainframe. The node simply calls up the required services as and when needed.

FILE SERVER NETWORK

In a file server network composed of PCs, the applications and data are usually stored on the server computer. The bulk of the processing is done on the PCs/nodes.

PC   Server

CLIENT/SERVER NETWORK   **Client Computer**   **Server Computer**

In a client/server network processing can be shared between the computers.

Workstation   Mini

PEER-TO-PEER NETWORKING

With a PC peer-to-peer network, the other nodes on the network simply access that node which has the required application.

Wordprocessor   Spreadsheet   Database

Fig 5.1

Besides the file server, client/server and peer-to-peer networks, there are also standard mainframe server networks (see figure 5.3). A standard mainframe-based network can result in all the processing being done on the mainframe computer. The nodes are usually non-processing cheap terminals which access the mainframe for services and are in effect just a 'window' on the mainframe.

5.4.2 File server and client/server networks

File server networks and client/server networks have several common attributes. The main attribute is the use of a main server computer.

File server networks are the most common type of computer network. The nodes and the server are usually made up of industry-standard PC type equipment. With a file server network, the actual server usually supplies a range of different applications which all the individual nodes can access. Each individual node then processes its own data in conjunction with the particular application it is using.

In client/server networks the relationship between the node or client computer and the server is much more subtle. The client computer accesses the server's applications but the processing is usually shared between the client and the server. Client/server networks are more likely to be found in a corporate environment. In addition, the nodes have, more often than not, access to very process-intensive applications. As a result, client/server networks usually employ minicomputers or mainframes as the server. One particular computer, the IBM AS/400, has proved to be the market leader as a server computer in contemporary client/server systems.

As a result of the nature of the hardware and applications employed, client/server networks are usually more costly than file server networks. However, the concept of the client/server approach has proved to be a popular networking strategy. It has two important virtues. Firstly, the strategy coincides well with the concepts of downsizing and rightsizing (see 2.10). In other words the desktop computer (the client computer) can call upon the appropriate server computer such as a mainframe to perform the necessary service or task.

Secondly, the idea of manipulating a mixed-equipment configuration in this manner is central to the strategy of an Open Systems policy.

5.4.3 Three-tier client/server networks

Unfortunately conventional client/server systems have several major disadvantages. Firstly, they can be very complicated and consequently prove very costly to develop and implement. Secondly, because of this complexity, client/server software has proved to be both rigid and vulnerable. In order to reduce these problems, developers came up with the concept of the three-tier client/server configuration. The main difference between this configuration and a conventional client/server system is that the bulk of the management software which details the processing tasks as conducted between client and server is performed by an intermediate server computer. Although this is an expensive option it appears to minimise processing management problems.

5.4.4 Peer-to-peer networks

Because of improved technology and competitive pricing peer-to-peer networking has become increasingly popular within the PC market. With the peer-to-peer network there is no main server computer. Instead the nodes access each other for the required applications or service. This strategy is a common concept with PC LANs, whereby the computers use each other's hard disk for the required application or share common peripheral equipment such as printers.

This type of a network can have some manifest benefits. Firstly, because there is no server all nodes on the network are fully employed. In other types of networks which use server computers, the server computer is usually dedicated in its role. In other words the server is not used for anything else.

Secondly, the network is not totally reliant on a particular computer. With a single server based system, which is what most PC LANs consist of, a server malfunction can result in the network shutting down. In contrast a failure of a node on a peer-to-peer network means that the network can no longer access the applications or data on that node but other than this it should continue to function.

Thirdly, linking computers in a peer-to-peer network is significantly more straightforward. The reason is there is no central server to which all the computers have to connect. The computers can connect to the network cable at any convenient point. With sites and buildings being the shapes that they are this can prove to be a considerable saving.

5.5 CABLE TECHNOLOGY

Most contemporary computer networks link the nodes of the network with a physical cable of some description but there has been a dramatic increase in the use of wireless technology (see 5.6) although this is still the exception. The first point to note is that the technology governing the cable link has a determining effect on the quality and efficiency of the actual transmission.

The most popular types of cable currently in use are twisted pair, coaxial cable and fibre optic.

Twisted pair is physically identical to the cabling used for conventional telephone lines which are simply made up of two parallel copper wires. In turn, coaxial cable is that medium which is used for TV aerials. Data transmitted over coaxial cable does not suffer from as much 'noise' (interference) as twisted pair and is consequently well suited for long-distance transmission as well as local transmission.

Fibre optic cables are considered to be the state of the art cable transmission medium. They work on the principle of using fine glass cables to conduct data by means of light beams. Fibre optic cables have a major advantage over conventional 'copper' based cables in that they support high data transfer rates with high security and without being vulnerable to electromagnetic interference. Optical cables of this type are extremely efficient and flexible but are somewhat expensive.

5.5.1 Network topology

Before the nodes are physically linked by an appropriate cable technology it is usual, for various technical reasons, to give consideration to the topology of the network. There are three main types of physical network topologies for LANs. These are the bus, the star and the ring (see figure 5.2).

The type of topology used depends on factors such as the physical nature of the site, the hardware configuration and the network technology (see 5.7).

The advantage of a bus network is that wiring is simple and additional nodes are not a problem. The disadvantage is with overall size as all the computers have to access a single line. As a consequence increased traffic on the network reduces response time and so network size has to be limited. Star and ring topologies are popular as the technology used on them tends to be higher calibre than that used on bus networks. With the arrival of intelligent and sophisticated 'hubs' or MAUs (Multiple Access Units) cabling is not the physical hurdle it once was.

An MAU is an intelligent central wiring device for a computer network. It can detect whether it has a live node attached to any socket, and will bypass any socket whose node is turned off. Equally, where there is a cable break the network will only lose the one node directly affected.

5.6 WIRELESS LINKS

As has been stated, it is not always necessary to have a physical link between computers so that they might communicate with each other. It is possible to employ various wireless technologies to link the machines. A

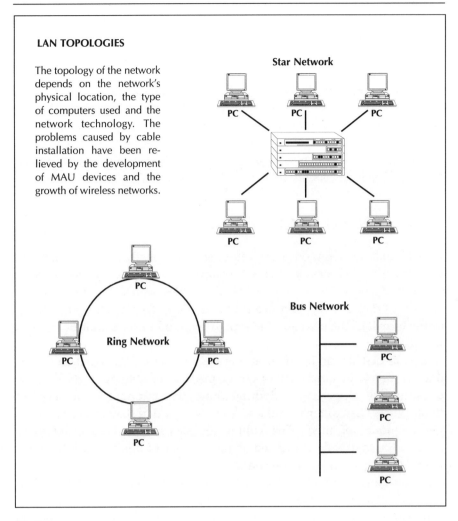

LAN TOPOLOGIES

The topology of the network depends on the network's physical location, the type of computers used and the network technology. The problems caused by cable installation have been relieved by the development of MAU devices and the growth of wireless networks.

Star Network

PC PC PC

PC PC PC

Ring Network

PC PC PC PC

Bus Network

PC PC PC

Fig 5.2

wireless LAN can usually surmount physical problems posed by the site with ease but tend to be relatively expensive.

A wireless LAN is usually linked by one of three systems: spectrum radio, infrared or high-frequency radio transmission.

Unfortunately spectrum radio and infrared have severe distance restrictions. With spectrum radio, signals can currently pass through walls or partitions but the transmitting and receiving nodes cannot be any further than about 250 metres apart. With infrared technology the maximum distance between the server and a node is only a tenth of that for spectrum networks. In addition with infrared networks the server and the node must be in line of sight of each other. The principle employed is the same as that used for a domestic video recorder. Even so, the growing importance of infrared technology for LANs can be gauged from the formation of the IDA (Infrared Data Association).

The third option, high frequency radio, is much more flexible and covers far greater distances. For example a portable laptop computer can be equipped with suitable transmitting/receiving technology to communicate with computers on the other side of the country. As this type of computer communication is usually associated with a WAN system it will be covered in greater detail in Chapter 6.

5.7 NETWORK TECHNOLOGIES

In order that the nodes on a computer network actually communicate with the network it is necessary that the computers use agreed *access protocols*. These protocols are simply a set of fixed rules which describe how the transfer of data between devices is to take place. They specify such things as the format of the data and the signals required to start, control and end the transfer.

A point that should be made at this stage is that a data signal, in theory, doesn't travel any quicker through the medium of fibre optic glass than it does through copper cable. Both mediums transmit data at the speed of light. Where they differ is in the volume of data that they can convey in a given amount of time. This volume of data, normally referred to as bandwidth, is usually calculated as the number of bits that can be transported through a circuit in a second.

It is also important to note the manner in which the various medium and protocols cope with the network data traffic. Cables with a small capacity/bandwidth are usually called narrowband circuits. These cables are employed to transmit basic data signals such as text or sound. Cables with higher bandwidth are usually called midband and broadband. These are used, depending on their individual bandwidth, to convey more sophisticated data such as photographic images, video, audio, etc.

Baseband is where unmodulated signals are used to carry data. Ethernet technology uses baseband. Broadband is the opposite in that it transmits data by means of a modulated signal. It is useful if not necessary for applications such as videoconferencing (see 7.10.3) and is the carrier signal for fibre optic cables.

Modulation uses a carrier signal to transport the message; the message signal modifies the carrier's frequency or amplitude.

There are a number of PC LAN protocol technologies. These include Ethernet, Token Ring, FDDI, CDDI and ATM.

5.7.1 Ethernet

Two of the most common PC LAN technologies are Ethernet and Token Ring. Ethernet was developed by DEC, Intel and Xerox. The aim was to produce an agreed specification for a cable-linked LAN. The protocol agreed uses the concept of CSMA-CD (Carrier Sense Multiple Access with Collision Detection).

The principle behind CMSA-CD means that the node computer which wishes to transmit the data waits until the wire it is connected to is clear before it transmits its data. Once the data is transmitted the computer checks the line to see whether or not the data has clashed or collided with any other packs of data transmitted by other nodes. Thus the term 'collision detection'.

If the data has collided then the computer re-transmits when the line is clear. This type of protocol is common on bus networks.

Fast Ethernet

One major performance advance for Ethernet users was the arrival of Fast Ethernet. Fast Ethernet can transmit up to 100 million bits of data per second (100 Mbps) and is considered to be a sound economic alternative upgrade for users experiencing data delays with their existing Ethernet systems. Users have discovered that their Ethernet networks can be improved by the addition of special connecting switches. The advantage of these switches is that they create dedicated connections between receiving and transmitting computers so avoiding data collision and thus reducing possible delays.

The major advantage of these switches, however, is that they can be attached to the existing hardware configuration. In other words there is no need to purchase new nodes, servers or cables. Because of the familiarity of the technology, Fast Ethernet has proved to be a very popular development.

At the time of writing there has been considerable investment into a new product known as Gigabyte Ethernet. This product, as its name implies, results in a tenfold increase in current Fast Ethernet data transmission speeds.

5.7.2 Token ring

In a Token Ring network, the token is a signal which continuously passes through all the nodes in the network. It basically acts as a carrier of data packets by receiving, transporting and delivering them to their destination. The token must be 'empty' or 'free' before a node can pass data over to it. IBM's Token Ring (LAN) which was first launched in 1985 employs this technique in ring and star network topology.

5.7.3 FDDI

Fibre Distributed Data Interface (FDDI) was fully defined in 1989. Fiddi, as it is sometimes known, is the technology that defines a 100 Mbit/sec network using fibre optic cables. Fiddi data networks are exceptionally fast but very expensive.

Because of this cost factor and the large bandwidth supported by optical fibres, FDDI technology is usually employed in the role of a backbone. The concept of a backbone can be seen on a large site, such as a college campus. Sites of this type usually have a number of LANs all of which wish to interconnect with a central mainframe/minicomputer or other LANs/devices. What happens is that the LANs themselves are wired with a cheaper medium and then feed into an optical fibre cable which runs across the site. This optical fibre is the backbone. Its main role is to act as a trunk or highway for all the machines/users on the site so enabling interdevice/computer communication.

5.7.4 CDDI

As a result of FDDI, vested interests in copper-based cables introduced CDDI (Copper Distributed Data Interface). With CDDI networks it is now possible to transmit data at the rate of 100 Mbit/sec over copper wires.

CDDI technology is cheaper than FDDI. It has a critical physical advantage over FDDI in that copper-based cables do not suffer from condensation problems as have been reported with fibre optic cables. Even so, CDDI technology is not considered a serious contender to FDDI.

5.7.5 ATM

As applications become ever more complicated and as the physical size of networks grow so users are witnessing an ever-increasing demand on their network's transmission capabilities. Certain applications such as videoconferencing can have a dramatically negative effect on the network's response times. The reason for this negative effect is the millions of background calculations which have to be processed by the serving computer processors to generate the graphics.

In order to reduce this problem ATM (Asynchronous Transfer Mode) was developed. Originally designed to integrate data, voice and image technology, contemporary ATM transmits data anywhere between 155 Mbps and 635 Mbps.

The initial developers of ATM were the CCITT (Consultative Committee on International Telephone and Telegraph which in 1994 was renamed the ITU-T), the organisation which sets the standards for the world's public networks. The significance of the technology can be gleaned from the statistic that one ATM connection is capable of transmitting 300 concurrent phone calls and is the equivalent of 240 64-Kb ISDN (see 6.6.1) lines.

(a) The theory

With non-ATM networks, be they WAN or LAN, operational communication across the networks is done synchronously. What this means is that the respective transmitting and receiving computers must be on identical timing cycles. This is not necessary however with ATM. Because intricate real time synchronisation across the networks is no longer needed, data from multiple users can be transmitted almost all at once and without fear of interference.

ATM can differentiate between different types of information, such as data and voice, and transmit them at varying speeds. This results in a much more efficient network as the network separates the various signals. For example, a user of a phone system requires instantaneous transmission whereas e-mail or text files do not require the same degree of speed or urgency in order to be relayed in a useful manner.

(b) The future

ATM has been universally recognised as a major standard in network technology. It can be employed on the desktop using a LAN or across a global WAN.

However, whilst many observers expected ATM to supersede Ethernet and Token Ring, the fact is the overwhelming majority of contemporary LANs still use Ethernet and Token Ring technology. In addition, organisations wishing to change to ATM have discovered that such a change involves considerable extra cost. IBM, a big investor in ATM technology, has taken this problem head on and has developed emulation software enabling ATM to run on conventional computers across current LAN cabling so reducing transition costs.

Even so, the range of applications presently available for which ATM is the only pragmatic bandwidth solution is minimal and the suggestion is that FDDI, Ethernet and Token Ring LANS will continue to dominate the network market until the turn of the century.

5.7.6 Enabling technology

(a) Network interface cards

Most contemporary LANs are what is known as PC networks although it would appear that this is all about to change with the arrival of the NC. In any event, in order for PC node computers to be attached to a network they require what is known as a network interface card.

A Network Interface Card, otherwise known as a LAN Interface Card, is that segment of hardware that enables conventional PC nodes to link with a network cable. The type of interface card which is plugged into the PC node depends on the type of system employed by the network. Of the two most common systems Ethernet and Token-Ring, the Ethernet interface card is the most prevalent. They are relatively cheap and easy to install.

(b) UPS devices

The majority of computer networks are commercial operations many of which are operating around the clock. Unfortunately, there is always the possibility of a power outage due to factors such as adverse weather conditions, accidents, sabotage and so on.

To ensure that their computers receive a continuous power supply, users are turning to what is known as Uninterruptible Power Supply (UPS) devices. The size, price and performance of UPS devices vary greatly. However, the more common units are usually about the size of a small printer and retail for about the same price. In addition, top quality UPS systems have the ability, in the event of a complete power failure, to support the network long enough to enable a smooth shutdown and for the user to perform a complete data backup.

Because of commercial expediency many commercial network users have discovered that a UPS has become a mandatory piece of organisational equipment. This is due to potential huge financial penalties an organisation could face in the event of their computer's power supply failing. Many insurance companies are requiring customers to instal UPS devices as a precautionary measure.

5.8 NETWORK OPERATING SYSTEMS

A Network Operating System (NOS) is a specialist program that enables the nodes of the network to communicate with each other and the server computer(s) or other peripheral devices. Like other operating systems an NOS enables the network's users and administrators to carry out the usual routine operations plus certain critical network management tasks.

A good example of a critical network management task would be those functions executed by the audit feature, a utility common to all NOSs. This feature enables the network manager to keep track of users' access to the system and its various subdirectories and whether it is authorised or unauthorised. Such a feature is useful for security recording as well as billing.

It is also apparent that contemporary NOS developers are paying particular attention to Intranet/Internet (see 14.1 and 14.2). As a result, current as well as impending releases of various NOS applications are making considerable efforts to enhance the delivery of Intranet/Internet technology.

5.8.1 The network administrator

All computer networks have to be supervised to ensure that they function efficiently. If a network is not supervised properly then the network is likely to collapse. For example, activities such as unauthorised or unrestricted use can result in various problems such as data corruption due to breaches in data security as well as an inappropriate and chaotic use of peripheral devices such as printers and fax/modems.

In order, therefore, to maintain a certain degree of supervision most organisations appoint a network administrator. As might be expected the NOS is crucial to the administrator as it is through the operation of this program that the administrator maintains control of the computer network.

A good example of such control is where the NOS allows the administrator to grant certain privileges to users. These privileges include permission to access various applications and, where appropriate, to read, write, modify, create or delete data from the network's computers. The NOS also enables the administrator to redirect data traffic between the peripheral devices across the network and to monitor network use so providing supervision along with useful management statistics.

5.8.2 Netware

The current mainstream version of Netware is a specialised 32-bit NOS which has been designed to work on WANs as well as LANs.

Just as MS/PC-DOS and Windows have enabled Microsoft to dominate the single desktop computer OS market so the Novell Corporation managed, through its Netware NOS, to dominate the PC LAN market. The significance of the Netware NOS range can be gauged by the fact that in 1995 it was estimated that Novell had captured approximately 70% of the market share worldwide for NOSs. However, it should be pointed out that Windows NT, which is also an NOS application, has made severe inroads into Novell's market share and its almost total dominance is currently under threat.

The latest version of Netware is Netware 4.1. Amongst other features, the system offers file compression enabling the user to save hard disk space. The program also appears to have been designed with the specific intention of making network administration easier.

With Netware the central administrator has an option of delegating control to other network supervisors, a very useful facility when dealing with LAN to LAN communications or WAN administration. In addition, the program is very security sensitive and users have to log on to the network using authorised passwords. The password determines a user's access rights and is protected from possible abuse.

The program also has a very flexible interface and can be operated via Windows and OS/2 or if necessary straight from a text-based DOS. It also enables the administrator and other authorised users to access all network utilities regardless of physical location.

Netware 4.1 fits into the Open Systems concept for the seamless integration of a proliferation of desktop systems and servers. This can be demonstrated by Netware's ability to enable users to link a host of different systems and devices irrespective of the operating system they are using be it MS-DOS, Apple Macintosh, Windows, Unix or OS/2.

5.8.3 Lantastic

A good economic alternative to Netware is the PC LAN OS called Lantastic from Artisoft. It is a very popular peer-to-peer OS. In other words there is no necessity for a dedicated file server. The program enables high-speed data transfer, a consequence of which is that peer-to-peer PC networks are put into a similar league to expensive dedicated PC server systems. This is achieved by the inclusion of facility known as LANcache.

Artisoft have also launched Lantastic in a Windows 95 version. Amongst its many utilities is a network administration program which enables supervisors to navigate the network from a central screen as well as add and delete users or groups of users from the network as and when necessary. The Windows 95 version also has a custom control panel enabling supervisors to fashion screen commands and introduce extra levels of security.

5.9 INTERNETWORK DEVICES

Having identified the essential hardware/software components which constitute an individual LAN the next issue to consider is LAN to LAN/WAN communication. Three hardware devices enabling this communication are specialist computers known as Bridges, Routers and Gateways.

Other specialist equipment enabling internetwork communication such as digital telephone links and modems which are employed on some large LAN sites are more appropriate to WANs and will be discussed in Chapter 6.

5.9.1 Bridges

The main task of a bridge computer is to receive and pass data from one LAN to another. In order to transmit this data successfully, the bridge magnifies the data transmission signal. This means that the bridge can act as a repeater as well as a link.

Repeaters are devices that solve the snag of signal degradation which results as data is transmitted along the various cables. What happens is that the repeaters boost or amplify the signal before passing it through to the next section of cable.

5.9.2 Routers

Router computers are similar to bridges but have the added advantage of supplying the user with network management utilities. Routers help administer the data flow by such means as redirecting data traffic to various peripheral devices or other computers. In an internetwork communication, routers not only pass on the data as necessary but also select appropriate routes in the event of possible network malfunctions or excessive use.

5.9.3 Gateways

Gateways are also similar to bridges in that they relay data from network to network. They do not, as a rule, possess the management facilities of routers but like routers they can translate data from one protocol to another.

Gateways are usually used to link LANs of different topologies, e.g. Ethernet and Token Ring, so enabling the exchange of data.

5.10 ISO STANDARDS

Until relatively recently, communication between computers in heterogeneous systems was problematical because of all the different components constituting the network. To facilitate intercomputer communication, the International Standards Organisation (ISO) developed a seven-layer Open Systems Interconnection (OSI) model along with a matching family of inter-network protocols.

The OSI model is used as a reference by innovators and hardware designers in the computing industry to introduce new products/protocols capable of integrating with current as well as future computing equipment and of promoting Open Systems. For example, in order to get over the problems encountered by users exchanging text and graphic files between different computer systems IBM developed two sets of protocols called Document

Content Architecture (DCA) and Document Interchange Architecture (DIA) whilst the CCITT (now the ITU-T) developed X.400 (see 6.9.4). These protocols occupy the higher levels of the OSI model and dictate the means by which a document should be encoded and decoded for transmission between computers.

The model is still under review as are the systems which support it. However, the significance of the model can be measured by the fact that many governments such as that of the US will not purchase equipment unless it satisfies their Government OSI Profile (GOSIP) criteria. Unfortunately there have been problems with this stance as different GOSIPs are produced by other countries.

5.10.1 The seven layers

The seven-layer OSI model is the nucleus of the ISO standards (see figure 5.3). It specifies the relationships between the hardware and software components within a computer network. The more sophisticated a particular device so the higher up the level or stack you will find that device operating.

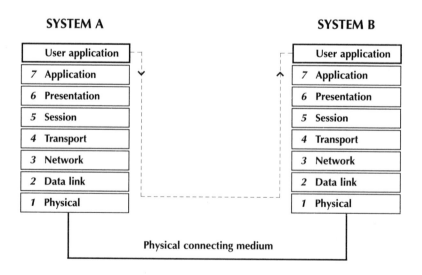

Fig 5.3

The idea behind the layered model is to divide a network system into functionally specialised but interconnected parts, so that each part (layer) uses the services of the one below, performs its own function(s), and passes the completed task to the layer above. When two networks employing the OSI model are connected as shown in figure 5.3, a message from system A's user application is processed down through system A's layers, across the physical connecting medium, then up through the corresponding layers in sysem B until it reaches the user application layer in fully processed form.

The basic function of the layers is as follows:

Layer 7 **Application**

This is that layer which is in direct contact with the user. It governs the services (e.g. e-mail, file transfer, etc.) employed by the users as they interact with other users, applications and peripheral devices. Gateways operate at the application layer.

Layer 6 **Presentation**

This layer makes sure that different devices using data in dissimilar formats such as ASCII and EBCDIC can communicate.

Layer 5 **Session**

The session layer controls the interchange which enables users to request services from the network and manages the connections between cooperating programs.

Layer 4 **Transport**

This layer deals with such details as reliability and error correction as data is physically passed between computers. It ensures that a mainframe in one system does not overload a PC in the other, for example.

Layer 3 **Network**

The network layer carries out various functions such as routing data across the network irrespective of the transmission technologies being used. Routers function at the network layer and because of their sophistication usually perform necessary automatic management routines at this level.

Layer 2 **Data link**

This layer ensures the reliable transfer of data as it passes across the network's physical media. It might, for example, split the data into blocks and arrange for its correct re-assembly at the receiving end. It also controls the necessary protocols enabling the various nodes and peripheral devices to acknowledge the transmission and acceptance of data. Bridges operate at this level.

Layer 1 **Physical**

The physical layer concerns the actual transmission hardware requirements so that the data is transported along whatever media is being employed. A good example at this level is a repeater which extends signals along the network cable.

5.11 INTERNETWORK PROTOCOLS

The vast majority of LANs are PC networks and the greater part of these use the Novell Netware NOS. Nonetheless there is a widespread and increasing use of Unix/Windows NT networks in the commercial sector as well as a large and established user base of various mainframe systems. In addition users will, for various reasons, want to connect these systems to PC networks. One reason for connecting such systems is that users can gain access to the sophistication offered by more elegant PC/Window applications whilst simultaneously harnessing the processing and data facilities of the corporate machines.

To link Unix-based networks to other systems such as mainframes or PC networks either a terminal emulation program can be used whereby the receiving node operates the same system as that of the server computer or full synchronous connection can be established via a protocol such as Transmission Control Protocol/Internet Protocol (TCP/IP). Other major protocols are DECnet from DEC, SNA and APPN from IBM.

5.11.1 Transmission Control Protocol/Internet Protocol (TCP/IP)

TCP/IP is a standard set of data transmission protocols developed during the early 1980s by the US government (see figure 5.4). Its widespread use by the university sector and other institutions meant that it became the de facto networking standard for workstations and other Unix-based systems.

The TCP/IP standard is in fact two protocols. In the context of the seven-layer OSI model as outlined above the TCP (Transmission Control Protocol) protocol is the transport layer and the IP (Internet Protocol) protocol forms the network layer. As TCP/IP is resident between the user's applications and the network's physical links it is in fact indifferent as to the medium used and can be employed on the same hardware connections used by OSs such as Netware and Windows NT. A TCP/IP set-up can run on different network technologies such as Ethernet or FDDI.

As a result of TCP/IP's hardware independence the system can support a uniform front-end interface for a host of different computers ranging from an IBM PC or a Mac to a Unix workstation, a Vax minicomputer, or even an IBM mainframe. TCP/IP is the most prevalent protocol employed to link

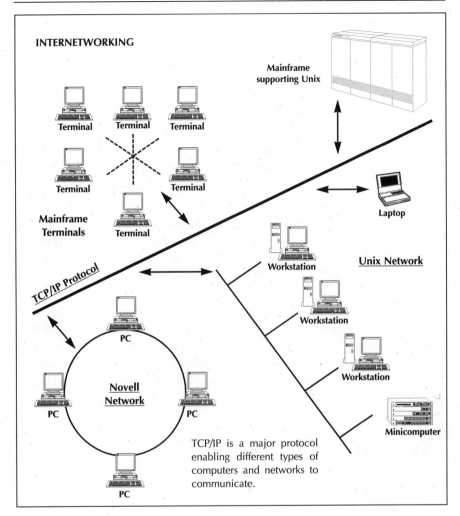

Fig 5.4

PC and Unix systems. In a multi-protocol network, operating systems such as Netware are able to pass TCP/IP signals as a matter of course.

Unfortunately the future of TCP/IP is uncertain. The reason for this is that the US government has (see 5.10) subscribed to the OSI model through GOSIP (Government Open Systems Interconnection Profile). The problem is that TCP/IP is not totally compatible with the OSI model so there is a requirement by users and suppliers to use other approved protocols. However this is meeting a fair degree of resistance as TCP/IP is viewed as a very reliable and competent system.

5.11.2 IBM protocols

Despite its success, TCP/IP has a major fault as far as IBM is concerned. It is not, to put it bluntly, an IBM proprietary system. However it is commonly recognised that a large number of IBM corporate systems are using TCP/IP. It should also be pointed out that the fact that TCP/IP is not an IBM proprietary system is undoubtedly seen as a blessing by many of IBM's competitors.

IBM's two main network proprietary protocol systems which enable large and small IBM computers to communicate across LAN and WAN systems are called Systems Network Architecture (SNA) and Advanced Peer-To-Peer Networking (APPN).

SNA is a reliable network architecture system that has been developed and used for the best part of two decades. In orthodox SNA configurations, server computers such as central mainframes act as a mainstay for all end user applications, administration, security, configuration and communication duties.

APPN technology has originated from SNA and is considered to be in direct competition with TCP/IP. In contrast to SNA networks, APPN systems enable end users to manage intelligent PCs or workstations that can launch intercomputer communication independent of such central control. IBM has committed considerable resources to persuade its customer base to upgrade from SNA to APPN.

5.12 VIRTUAL NETWORKING

The ease and growth of internetworking has resulted in the development of a concept called virtual networking. Virtual networking concerns the means by which users, regardless of location, local or remote, are linked into a transitory or virtual workgroup (see 5.3.3) enabling them to participate in joint undertakings or facilitating data exchange. By employing sophisticated bridges and routers (see 5.9) networks can be partitioned into logical as opposed to physical networks.

The significance of virtual networking is that it allows organisations to establish specialist teams or workgroups irrespective of their individual physical location. Other advantages include increased security options as parts of networks can be sectioned off and improvements made in data traffic through the ability to predict work loads. However, the technology required to enable virtual networking is relatively new and expensive and is unlikely, for the foreseeable future, to move beyond the boundaries of the corporate user.

5.13 CLUSTERING

Clustering is the linking of autonomous server computers, be they mini-computers, workstations or PCs, to establish one large virtual computer system within the same physical area. A computer cluster of this type has several key advantages. Firstly, individual computers in the cluster can, in the event of a systems failure, pass their individual workload to other computers in the cluster. Secondly, the sum power of the clustered computers is greater than that of individual machines. As a result of this total processing power, clustered computers are capable of coping with CMS type applications. With clustering, users/organisations can therefore employ more cost-effective computer configurations in order to operate and access corporate type systems applications.

Clustering was first developed in the 1970s by Digital Equipment to enhance the processing capabilities of its Vax minicomputers. However, the feasibility of enabling PC networks and other similar computer systems to successfully operate CMS has drawn the concept of clustering to the full attention of the corporate market. Computing companies which have decided to invest in clustering technology include Microsoft, Intel, Tandem and Compaq.

Microsoft has included clustering technology in Windows NT whilst major database vendors have started to design systems which operate on clustered NT servers. Intel has developed a quad Pro Pentium processor board for a PC network server and is currently working an eight-processor board. Clustering has significantly increased computer network reliability and is expected to make major inroads into corporate processing.

5.14 CONCLUSION

Computer networks have proved to be a huge growth area in the IT industry. Commercial users have discovered that computer networks enable them to access a wider range of services than that which can be supplied by individual machines as well as enable them to take advantage of the various efficiencies and economies that can be achieved as a result of their computers being connected to a network.

Another point to note is that downsizing trends have fuelled a dramatic increase in the use of systems such as PC LAN networks for corporate processing, whilst rightsizing is encouraging the use of older mainframes and minicomputers as servers in the development of corporate networks.

The increase in computer networks has also resulted in a correlated increase in internetwork communications. As a consequence the computing industry has had to put greater emphasis on the production of systems and devices that are compatible with other products.

6

Wide area networks and communications

6.1 INTRODUCTION

Wide Area Networks (WANs) and data communications are central to the success of the modern commercial organisation. Through the use of the WAN and other communication technologies users are able to access a practically limitless market of clients as well as a vast array of information/ processing services. The objective of this chapter is examine the composition of the equipment and resources which enable users to reach and use these customers/services.

Section 6.2 defines the composition of a WAN. Section 6.3 is about corporate network strategy as embodied by Enterprise Networking whilst sections 6.4 to 6.7 cover the physical systems that currently enable WAN connections. Section 6.8 debates network management technology and sections 6.8 to 6.11 deal with current as well as potential uses of WAN systems and the ever-expanding Internet.

6.2 DEFINING A WAN

A WAN (Wide Area Network) is a term used to describe those computer networks that range far beyond the physical boundaries of a particular site. For example, regional, national and global computer networks are usually encompassed by the term WAN.

However WANs not only differ from LANs in terms of their geographical spread but also because of this geographical spread. A good example is the cost and nature of the communication links used by LAN and WAN networks. With a LAN there is usually no need to consider the expense of specialist external links in order to communicate with other computers on the network. In a WAN, however, there is usually a dramatic cost difference for data transmission as it is frequently dependent on communication services supplied by organisations such as national telephone enterprises, cable companies and satellite broadcasters all of whom will levy various transmission charges.

Even so, whilst there are significant differences between LAN and WAN technologies, what does become obvious is that many of the choices faced by users involved in the design and operation of WANs are similar to those decisions taken when implementing a LAN. What is more, it could be argued that a LAN or indeed any individual computer connected to an external communication system is, in reality, a subset/node of a WAN.

6.3 ENTERPRISE NETWORKING

The phrase Enterprise Networking is another widely used business computing expression with no accepted formal definition. Even so, enterprise networking is generally recognised as a strategy which integrates LAN and WAN technology and places the computer network at the heart of the organisation's operations.

For example, although the day-to-day operational workload of an organisation may be carried out on LAN-based systems or on remote fixed or portable computers, ultimately many of these systems are connected to external networks. It follows that because of the geographical spread and size of many organisations and their need to communicate with external services, the organisation-wide network is by default a WAN or relies upon a WAN configuration.

Commercial applications which are fully dependent on reliable data communication links over a WAN often include the extensive use of Online Analytical Processing Databases (OLAP, see 10.9.4) systems running on various corporate computers. Examples of this type of trade include the use of Teller Machines (TM) or cash machines by high street banks, Electronic Funds Transfer (EFT) systems as used for credit/debit cards, share dealing systems on stock exchanges, on-line booking systems for airlines and so on. In the event of the malfunction of such a network many organisations would simply cease to operate.

The concept of the Enterprise Network therefore is the employment of a strategy which connects large sections of the organisation's computer activities into a unitary and manageable system (see figure 6.1). How this is done depends on a host of factors but the ultimate objective of the systems designers is to develop a network which fully serves the organisation's requirements. This can only be done by involving the whole of the organisation in the provision and processing of the data passing through the enterprise's information architecture.

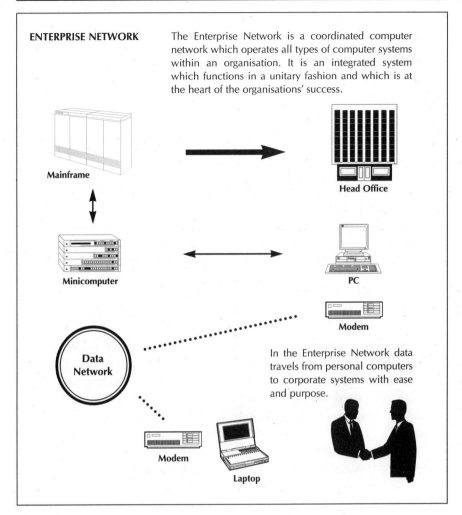

ENTERPRISE NETWORK The Enterprise Network is a coordinated computer network which operates all types of computer systems within an organisation. It is an integrated system which functions in a unitary fashion and which is at the heart of the organisations' success.

Mainframe

Head Office

Minicomputer

PC

Modem

Data Network

In the Enterprise Network data travels from personal computers to corporate systems with ease and purpose.

Modem

Laptop

Fig 6.1

In effect any organisation pursuing an enterprise network is developing a computer network which functions in a synchronised and seamless fashion passing from the local desktop/portable computer through to possible remote corporate systems as and when required.

The remainder of the chapter is an overview of the technology that system designers may employ to bring this about.

6.4 CONNECTION OPTIONS

When users wish to connect their computers/LANs into a wider network they are faced with several choices. These choices as with all other decisions regarding the operation and procurement of computers are dependent on critical factors such as technology and price.

With WAN data communications there are two fundamental transmission technologies to consider, namely analogue and digital. Analogue transmission technology is older, slower but more prevalent. In contrast digital transmission technology is more efficient but more often than not more expensive. However there is no clear dichotomy of performance and price as analogue transmission systems have proved to be cost-effective competition for the digital alternative.

WAN designers are also confronted with a plethora of medium transmission devices. WAN data signals, whether analogue or digital, can pass from cable to ether to cable many times as they traverse the global networks. To ensure efficient data reception/delivery it is extremely important that the equipment and technology employed conforms to approved industry standards, otherwise the data will simply not get through.

6.5 ANALOGUE TELEPHONE TECHNOLOGY

At present the majority of the world's national telephone networks and, indeed, telephones are still based on analogue technology. In order, therefore, to transmit non-analogue data, such as the digital data of a computer, across an analogue-based telephone network, a modem is needed (see 6.5.1). However, despite significant improvements, modems are still relatively sluggish and the fact is ordinary analogue telephone circuits are somewhat restricted in the amount of data they can transmit. As a result of this curb on performance, users have started to employ new silicon-based digital networks (i.e. ISDN, see 6.6.1) as well as other transmission technologies such as satellite broadcasting.

6.5.1 Modems

To enable the analogue Public Switched Telephone Network (PSTN) to send computer (digital) data, a modem (Modulator/Demodulator) is required. The idea behind a modem is that it translates or modulates digital data from the computer into an analogue form so that it can be transmitted over the analogue speech circuits of the PSTN. The process is reversed by the receiving modem so that incoming analogue data is reconstituted in digital form (see figure 6.2).

The modem has proved to be an invaluable partner for computer users enabling them to communicate down standard telephone lines in real time mode. It has meant that the ordinary business/domestic user could perform immediate commercial transactions over long distances. Because of

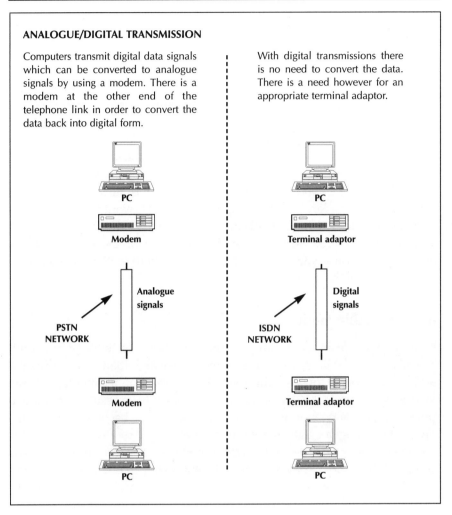

Fig 6.2

improved transmission speeds, some smaller corporate users, who previously employed modems but then switched to the new digital line technology, have started to use modems again. The cost/benefit analysis that companies make hinges on that point where expensive digital lines with high transmission speeds are more costly to use than cheaper modems with slower transmission speeds but consequent higher dial-up charges.

6.5.2 Modem transmission speeds

There are many different types of modems all of which transmit data at different speeds. The speed rates of these modems are usually measured by what is known as the *baud rate* (commonly accepted as thousands of bits per second (Kbps)). The importance of the speed factor cannot be underestimated and is crucial over long distances or with large blocks of data as the slower the modem, so the higher the charge for transmission.

Faster modems are usually significantly more expensive than their slower counterparts, so users are faced with a choice within a choice. Having decided upon analogue transmission as opposed to digital lines users are then faced with the decision of purchasing either a cheap modem with high dial-up charges, or a fast expensive modem with consequent lower dial-up charges.

A modem which has a transmission rate of 9.6 Kbps can transmit up to 600k per minute. A modem operating at 14.4 Kbps, also known as V.32 (transmission standard as approved by the ITU-T), would transmit up to 860k per minute. The majority of contemporary PC modems operate on the V.34 standard at 28.8 Kbps whilst the latest top of the range modems operate at 33.6 Kbps and 56 Kbps. The speed of these modems makes them a serious alternative to expensive digital lines.

6.5.3 Portable modems

Modern portable modems support the very latest technology and until recently have been significantly more expensive than the traditional desktop versions. However, improved miniaturisation techniques and the increasing use of PCMCIA cards/slots (see 3.10) have resulted in a sharp price fall for this type of device. In addition they are becoming multifunctional, delivering fax, data and voice services.

Contemporary pocket-sized portable modems offer transmission speeds of up to 33.3 Kbps. They also have sophisticated data compression and error detection utilities and are designed to fit into standard phone sockets. Top of the range models have universal adapters capable of fitting practically any phone in the world.

Wireless portable modems have also led to a substantial increase in mobility. Wireless portable modems can operate on analogue cellular telephone networks (see 6.7.2) or via two-way radio communications.

6.5.4 Simultaneous voice data modems (DSVD)

Because of their increasing speed users can now employ modems with voice transmission facilities. Simultaneous Voice Data (DSVD) modems allow users whose phones are connected to digital exchanges to employ a solitary phone line to transmit/receive data and voice concurrently. With this type of technology, users of ordinary analogue phone links can talk whilst importing or exporting data.

6.5.5 Cable modems

Cable modems are used for sending data over cable TV networks and are beginning to prove extremely popular. One incentive being given to users by those companies supplying cable services of this type in Britain is that of free local telephone calls.

6.5.6 Fax

The principal use for a fax machine is the inexpensive transmission and reproduction of documentation such as plans, reports, graphics, contracts and so on, i.e. exact copies (facsimiles) are sent and received. It is a device that has been described as a cross between a photocopier and a modem.

Fax transmits text and graphics with equal ease because it treats them as still pictures. They are scanned in at the sending end, sent over the phone network (usually), and re-created at the receiving end by the same technology as used in photocopiers. A fax-modem enables a computer to send and receive computer-generated screens across the phone network.

The principal advantage of these machines is their versatility and ease of use. For example, because of the diversity of e-mail systems (see 6.9) many users find it quicker to simply fax documentation to end users. The recipients can, if they wish, then scan/copy the documentation into their own computer system. Faxes have the added advantage of being generally recognised as evidence in contractual agreements. A disadvantage of fax is that both terminals must be operating simultaneously; if the receiving end is 'engaged', the sender must wait for it to become free.

6.6 DIGITAL LINKS

Although modems are undergoing a resurgence with many business users, the fact is that they are currently inadequate for the extensive data transmissions demands made by many organisations. In order, therefore, to accommodate large-scale high-speed data transmissions special digital lines have been developed. Lines employing digital signals have proved to be more reliable than conventional analogue lines and also enable better voice reproduction over long distances. Digital lines have the further advantage of providing a faster response for users. There is no need to modulate/demodulate the signal. The computer can be plugged straight in with a special terminal adapter.

One way of using digital signal technology is through the installation of dedicated high-speed lines. However these lines are somewhat costly and are limited because they always connect the same two points. A more pervasive and increasingly popular means of connection has evolved through the arrival of the Integrated Services Digital Network (ISDN).

6.6.1 Integrated services digital network (ISDN)

ISDN is a very fast digital network which provides communication transmission services which are significantly superior than those supplied by analogue-based systems. They allow both-way voice and data transmission between terminals such as telephones, fax machines and personal computers.

An ISDN line has two channels known as the data channel and the bearer channel. The data channel oversees the data transmitted along the bearer channels. Each bearer channel can transmit data up to 64 Kbps. A major benefit of ISDN lines is that they can be added together in the event of a need for greater transmission rates. Two bearer lines coupled together can perform as one line capable of transmitting up to 128 Kbps.

The real advantage of the ISDN standard is that it delivers digital network technology straight to the ordinary user as well as the corporate customer. However the ISDN system has not expanded as fast as was originally thought. Two reasons already mentioned are price and modem technology. Another reason is the differing national/proprietary standards currently defined for ISDN networks. Despite this, the increasing demand for greater performance from data transmission systems means that ISDN networks are expected to supplant standard analogue networks in most western countries by the turn of the century.

Broadband ISDN (B-ISDN), the next step up from ISDN, will be possible when the prevailing copper phone cables are all superseded by high bandwidth fibre optics.

6.6.2 X.25 data link

A major non-voice use of ISDN concerns X.25 data links. The X.25 data link is an ITU-T approved standard for packet switching data over networks and is now a common way of distributing data worldwide.

With packet switching technology, data is literally cut up into packets (groups of bits) by a device called a Packet Assembler/Disassembler (PAD). These packets of data are then transported, with their destination address, into what is known as a 'cloud' inside the network where they travel with other user's data packets to be reassembled at the receiving end.

The X.25 data standard forms part of the physical, data link and network layers of the OSI model (see 5.10.1). SNA, OSI, and TCP/IP protocols can be carried over X.25 networks. It is usually used for data networks and can run parallel with the telephone network.

X.25 and packet switching form the basis of most WANs, for example the networks used for cashpoint machines and a bank's central computer.

6.7 WIRELESS COMMUNICATION

As mentioned in the previous chapter, wireless computer data networks are becoming increasingly popular. The use of radio signals, rather than orthodox cabling, to broadcast data from one computing device to another has major attractions. With respect to WAN communications, this type of technology is becoming even more important.

6.7.1 Mobile computing

Mobile computing is concerned with those devices such as portable computers which are used by personnel to communicate even whilst they are on the move. Radio-modem-equipped portable computers allow workers in the field to transmit and receive data from central computer systems. Such workers can access all the usual applications such as e-mail, databases and financial services.

A good example is the system supported by RAM Mobile Data Ltd, a company recognised as a market leader in wireless data networks in Great Britain (see figure 6.3). The RAM network uses radio for real-time two-way communications. It uses packet switched technology (see 6.6.2). Packet switched technology is cost effective as customers pay for data transmission and receipt and not for the length of time that radio channels are allocated. RAM radio modems remain in contact with the RAM network at all times when switched on and in coverage. Not only can RAM deliver data transmissions via radio modem but also via X.25 connections and other public data networks.

6.7.2 Cellular nets

Because of the huge increase in the use of mobile phones there has been a corresponding growth in analogue and digital cellular networks in order to support this surge in traffic. As these cellular networks have become more widespread they have proved to be a great attraction to mobile computing users. Consequently there has been a dramatic increase in the transmission of non-voice data over cellular networks. Portable computers can be used employing specialist protocols and modems designed for cellular working.

Four major companies supplying a cellular net service in Britain include Cellnet, Mercury, Orange and Vodaphone. Orange and Mercury are digital

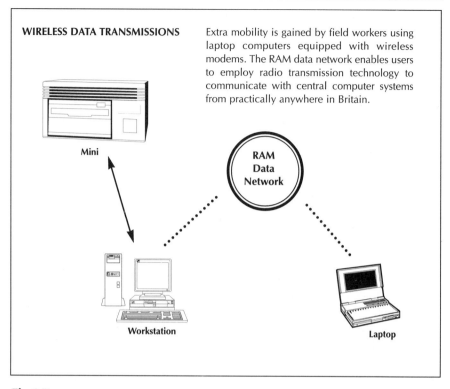

WIRELESS DATA TRANSMISSIONS

Extra mobility is gained by field workers using laptop computers equipped with wireless modems. The RAM data network enables users to employ radio transmission technology to communicate with central computer systems from practically anywhere in Britain.

Mini

RAM Data Network

Workstation

Laptop

Fig 6.3

services and use a protocol system called Personal Communication Network (PCN). Cellnet and Vodaphone use an analogue-based system which is compatible with the new GSM (Global System for Mobile Communications) standard. GSM is a European digital cellular system. It functions in the 900 MHz frequency band and is considered to be a stable and reliable means of transmitting data.

The main advantage of GSM as its name implies is that it is fast becoming the accepted standard on a common set of frequencies in many parts of the world.

6.7.3 Satellite technology

Another growth area in the application of wireless technology is radio satellite transmission. Communication satellites are used mostly in the area of intercontinental transmissions and are usually owned by governments or major multinational communication organisations. They are used principally to receive and retransmit communication signals for telephone, television and data channels. The cost of communication is independent of distance, and the bandwidth of satellite channels means that several thousand simultaneous telephone conversations and a few television programmes can be carried.

With terrestrial transmitter/receivers there is a signal degradation problem due to the curvature of the earth. Consequently earthbound transmitters and receivers have to either rely upon the reflection of radio waves from ionospheric layers outside the atmosphere or use various booster stations to retransmit the signal. With communication satellites this problem is minimised.

Communication satellites are usually placed about 35,800 km above the earth's surface in geostationary orbits, i.e. they are designed to rotate synchronously with the earth so that the signals they transmit always arrive at the required fixed point. It has been calculated that three satellites placed at this height, each appropriately positioned above the equator and equipped with the appropriate technology, can transmit signals to all the planet's surface. A complete satellite communication configuration usually consists of the satellite and terrestrial stations which can, if necessary, communicate with each other via the satellite.

A terrestrial station is simply a disk-shaped antenna and the affiliated electronic equipment for transmitting and receiving telecommunication signals. Until recently some of these satellite receiving dishes were enormous but because of the increased power of satellite transmissions they are now down to about 30 centimetres in diameter.

Microsoft satellites

At the time of writing the Microsoft Corporation has combined forces with Cellular Communications to invest in a new company called Teledisc. The stated goal of Teledisc is to build and operate a satellite network for videoconferencing transmissions, interactive multimedia (see Chapter 7), real time data and speech channels, all of which is expected to commence in 2001.

The satellites will employ ATM (see 5.7.5) technology and transmission speeds are expected to be comparable to fibre optics. A web of ground-based gateway computers will enable Internet Service Providers (ISPs) to offer links to other cable and wireless networks. The projected cost of the venture is 9 billion US dollars.

6.8 NETWORK MANAGEMENT

Most commercial computers/networks are usually part of a far wider network. Consequently as networks increase in size so operational problems start to accrue and command of the network(s) becomes problematical.

WANs are especially complex to comprehend and control because of the multitude of configuration alternatives. More often than not many different types of computer systems and transmission signals have to be co-ordinated so that data passes across the network. In addition, data traffic that actually passes across the network has to be regulated in order that any excess workloads or bottlenecks due to malfunctions on the network do not cause unnecessary delay. IT specialists have discovered that whilst it is very easy to create a computer network it is much more difficult to supervise it.

Because of the size of some networks total control without specialist management tools/techniques (see below) is impossible. Standard corporate LAN networks often have thousands of nodes and peripheral devices whilst WANs can have tens of thousands. Furthermore WAN nodes are usually widespread and can be very remote.

Security is a central matter of network management and at its core is user access; authorised access is usually via user identification and passwords, regularly updated; level of access needs to be defined and managed.

Not surprisingly, a ready pool of network managers and administrators who are familiar with network management protocols/techniques and are capable of performing necessary remote backup and recovery procedures is a priority for any sizeable organisation. In order to control and optimise their networks many large organisations have a specialist team of people operating in what is known as a Network Control Centre (NCC) section. These sections normally employ various generic management tools and concentrate on specific key areas in network management. These areas include:

1 *Fault management*. Fault management centres mainly on maintenance tasks and data traffic routing decisions which result from physical breaches in the network's infrastructure.

2 *Performance management*. Here, network administrators are normally concerned with making sure that processing functions are appropriately distributed and that remote and central systems are configured correctly.

3 *Inventory management*. This area is concerned with the physical recording and positioning of network resources as well as the day-to-day procurement of suitable upgradeable/replacement resources.

4 *Accounting management*. Accounting management means that users of the network, be they internal or external, are charged accordingly.

5 *Configuration management*. Configuration management enables administrators to have central control of resources such as remote server computers.

In order for administrators/managers to have effective control of the networks, various tools have been developed. These tools not only synchronise the network's various resources such as gateways or MAUs but also support the NCC by enabling it to ensure that the network is a successful component of the organisation's operation. The network management tools that have been developed have resulted from industry-standard network management protocols.

6.8.1 Network management protocols

Programs such as these not only provide strategic statistics to the network administrators but also provide useful interpretive reports and suggestions as to appropriate courses of action such as redirecting data traffic through a particular node/resource. It must be stated that products of this type are essentially corporate utensils and are unlikely to be considered by domestic or small business users.

One protocol which has evolved as an economic means of routine but effective network management is the Simple Network Management Protocol (SNMP) standard. It was developed by the Internet Engineering Task Force (IETF). Not only is it cheap but it is the most popular protocol of its type in current use. Advanced versions of SNMP contain various additional features such as increased security.

However, these protocols are being challenged by a new system known as the Common Management Information Protocol (CMIP). CMIP technology is a more expensive system but it is considered to be more rugged than SNMP and is part of the ISO standards. Amongst those manufacturers that furnish generic management systems of this class are Hewlett-Packard with Openview and IBM with Netview.

Two other important standards used for network management include the Remote Monitoring (RMON) standard and the Desktop Management Initiative (DMI).

6.9 E-MAIL (ELECTRONIC MAIL) SYSTEMS

One major benefit of networking computers is the ability to transmit data messages in various forms. These messages can be voice, text, images and so on. One principal application which has evolved is e-mail, an application employed on both WANs and LANs (see figure 6.4).

Interestingly, the primary global carrier of WAN e-mail traffic, namely the Internet, was originally designed to supply governments with communication facilities in the event of nuclear war. However e-mail has since evolved

117

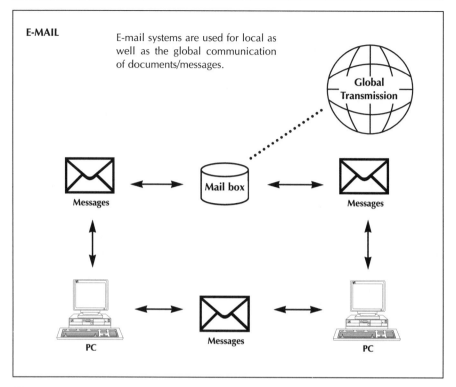

Fig 6.4

to be a more commercially oriented tool and is currently considered to be the killer application of the Internet. In other words, it is the main reason why so many business/domestic users have actually signed on to the Internet. (A killer application not only drives its own market but also the market of products needed to deliver it.)

Business e-mail is usually used for tasks such as Electronic Document Interchange or as a rapid text messaging system. For example, it is possible to relay data from London to San Francisco in just on a minute. E-mail is also considered to be extremely reliable for WAN communications. E-mail is also remarkably cost effective as global transmissions are the same tariff as regional deliveries. Corporate users have discovered that data transmission using e-mail systems are only a fraction of the costs of fax technology.

Moreover data transmission charges are not the only savings. There are also savings in other areas such as the use of printers and consequent consumption of paper. There is no need for users to obtain a hard copy of incoming messages. Messages, documents, etc. can simply be read on arrival and stored for later use.

6.9.1 Junk mail

As more users take advantage of e-mail systems so serious junk mail problems have started to accelerate. Most users of e-mail systems have electronic *mailboxes* which are constantly on-line. The mailbox is usually a storage area on a computer's hard disk. This hard disk may be on an individual node or on a central server as provided by the ISP.

The snag is that users are beginning to transmit messages of an ever-increasing byte size. This is due mainly to an increase in the use of space-hungry graphic applications. Not only this, but unfortunately there is a dramatic increase in the use of unsolicited advertising mail of this type. Consequently users are discovering huge unwanted blocks of data on their systems. The degree of annoyance that this type of activity can energise can be measured by the deluge of litigation in the American courts in the early 1990s.

6.9.2 E-mail components

E-mail systems have two major components. First of all there is what is known as the e-mail 'server' computer, otherwise referred to as the engine. The server's responsibility is to relay the messages/data across the network from one node to the other. The second component refers to the 'client' node. This is the computer which permits the user to access the e-mail application software and thus to supervise the mail.

In order to co-ordinate the server and client computers into an effective e-mail system it is of course necessary that the appropriate software is installed. Unfortunately there are a number of different systems available. Popular e-mail standards include Lotus's cc:Mail Vendor Independent Messaging (VIM), Microsoft's MS-Mail and Messaging Application Program Interface (MAPI), and Novell with Message Handling System (MHS).

6.9.3 Lotus cc:Mail

As a product, Lotus cc:Mail is an accepted global leader in e-mail system applications. Its principal attributes are its ability to interconnect with a host of different systems and its provision of a useful suite of user-friendly utilities.

Like most e-mail servers, Lotus cc:Mail can provide facilities to diverse clients all at the same time. It has been designed to run transparently on MS-DOS, Windows, OS/2, Macintosh and Unix. This means that the client nodes can all be totally different. At the same time the version of Lotus cc:Mail that each individual node accesses is compatible with its own particular OS despite all being connected to the same 'engine'. Lotus cc:Mail can consequently pass messages with other major global e-mail systems across LANs and WANs irrespective of the computer hardware configuration employed be it PC or mainframe.

A major advantage of Lotus cc:Mail is its user-friendly attributes. It is an ideal program for inexperienced computer users. It has an intuitive interface enabling users to transmit documents within minutes of studying the screens. For example, users that receive messages/documents have the following basic operational options. They can:

- Leave message in the mailbox
- Delete message from system
- Send message to printer
- Forward message to other users
- Reply to sender of message
- Copy message to private folder
- Archive message to hard drive
- Post message to a public bulletin board.

As for transmission options, Lotus cc:Mail users can send almost anything that can be viewed on a PC. As well as text messages users can send graphics, files, and faxes. Up to 20 items can be transmitted in a single message.

A major complication of using raw e-mail systems is addressing. With Lotus cc:Mail addressing messages is easy. Everyone accessible by Lotus cc:Mail, including remote and foreign mail system users, are listed on the directory. All the user has to do is remember the recipient's name. Lotus cc:Mail zips through the directory as the user types, zeroing in on the name before typing is finished.

Lotus cc:Mail Mobile is a wireless option and is linked into the RAM Mobile Data network (see 6.7.1). From a user perspective, the RAM network is transparent and allows users to plug a radio modem straight into a portable PC.

Lotus cc:Mail supports all the major networking and data communication standards such as X.25, X.400, X.500 and the Novell MHS (see below).

6.9.4 E-mail standards

Unfortunately, as has already been mentioned, there are a number of different proprietary e-mail systems and as a result there has been a certain degree of incompatibility. Two major standards to consider are the ITU-T standard, X.400, and Novell's MHS.

ITU-T X.400

X.400 is a set of standards ratified by the ITU-T. It is a specification for message formats and electronic mail and is incorporated into the OSI model at layer 7 (application) as the Message Handling System (MHS). The main task of the standards is to harmonise the connectivity and communication of diverse proprietary mail systems.

X.400 separates electronic mail systems into three divisions. These divisions are the User Agent (UA), Message Transfer Agent (MTA) and the Reliable Transfer Server (RTS). The UA is that application, such as Lotus cc:Mail, that enables the user to create, receive and relay messages. The MTA is that part of the system that controls the delivery of messages. It checks the address of the message and keeps handing the message on down the network until it reaches an RTS computer which is local to the recipient and is capable of taking delivery.

There is another important e-mail ITU-T standard, the X.500 specification. X.500 is a specification for message delivery service options across a network of heterogeneous computer systems on a global basis.

MHS (message handling service)

MHS is an e-mail messaging facility which runs on Novell networks and supports WAN and LAN e-mail linkage over an expansive range of environments. It is a rival of X.400 for international e-mail connectivity. MHS is proprietary (it was developed by Action Technologies) but is heavily promoted by Novell.

6.10 VOICE MAIL

A communication application that is beginning to attract more attention from business users is the concept of voice mail. An inability for callers to an organisation to contact a particular individual can be a major cause of frustration or delay. The basic idea of voice mail is to enable callers to post voice messages to particular individuals who they are unable to reach. In addition, called persons are provided with a range of powerful options for dealing with those messages.

6.10.1 VoxMail

A leading system in the voice mail market is VoxMail from Storacall Voice Systems Ltd. The system is supported on a suitably equipped server and can provide addresses for hundreds of mailbox owners. Callers are guided through the system by clear and precise prompts and can leave messages in

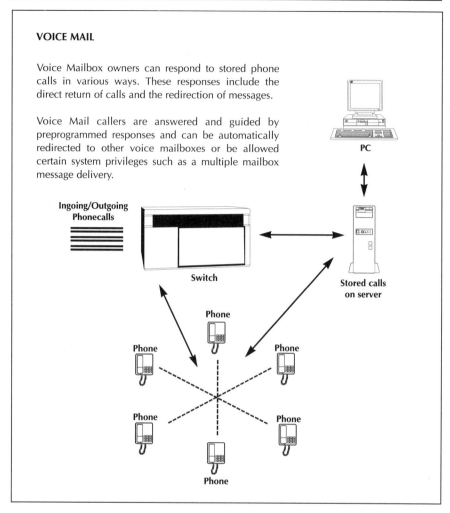

VOICE MAIL

Voice Mailbox owners can respond to stored phone calls in various ways. These responses include the direct return of calls and the redirection of messages.

Voice Mail callers are answered and guided by preprogrammed responses and can be automatically redirected to other voice mailboxes or be allowed certain system privileges such as a multiple mailbox message delivery.

PC

Ingoing/Outgoing Phonecalls

Switch

Stored calls on server

Phone

Phone

Phone

Phone

Phone

Phone

Fig 6.5

one or more of these mailboxes. A box owner once answered by VoxMail dials a unique pin code and is then able to use the full range of box owner usage options for listening, leaving messages, paging and changing options. In addition the box owner then has the option of repeating, deleting or saving any messages. Box owners can, if they wish, respond instantly to the caller or forward the message to another box.

The system also has a group distribution message facility enabling a message to be left in a global box for automatic distribution to all mailbox users or in a distribution box for a specific set of personnel – for example, the sales manager can leave one message for the sales force which is then automatically posted into every salesperson's mailbox.

6.11 THE DIGITAL SUPERHIGHWAY

The concept of an information Superhighway is that of a global interconnected computer network made up of numerous individual networks. It
goes without saying that the Superhighway is expected to be the major
driving force behind any new emerging technology in data communications. However although such a network is undoubtedly beginning to
evolve it has yet to arrive.

This emerging global infrastructure is aimed to encompass any transmission of information which is capable of being processed by a computer. This
network will not only carry standard information such as text, pictures and
sound but also video. Services to be supplied by this Superhighway include
video on demand (VOD), home banking, educational courses, home shopping
as well as other exciting opportunities such as enabling domestic users to
engage in financial transactions on the stock exchange.

The rest of this section concerns an examination of two contributors to the
evolution of the Superhighway, namely the Internet network and the American
ISP CompuServe. The commercial impact of the Internet and the arrival of
the World Wide Web (WWW) will be fully discussed in Chapter 14.

6.11.1 Internet

Principal amongst the popular data networks is the Internet. As its name
suggests Internet is a network of networks. It was set up by ARPA, the
Advanced Research Projects Agency which is an offshoot of the US Government, as a a method for providing secure computer communications in
time of war.

The beauty of Internet is that each network may have its own internal
architecture and networking software, but it can exchange files and data
with other networks via a designated gateway machine that runs a high-
level internetworking protocol (see 5.11). Alternatively all the machines on
the network may run a common suite of software that uses the Internet
protocol which is TCP/IP (see 5.11.1). In the latter case, all machines on the
local network that can access the net directly are said to be 'on the net'.

However the Internet did not have an altogether auspicious commercial
start. The original users were prohibited from advertising on the Internet
and the majority of these users were military, corporate or academic institutions. In addition, navigating the Internet was initially complicated as well
as tedious. There were no e-mail address directories and net navigation was
done via a text-based command line. (This has of course all changed with
the arrival of the WWW and web browsers such as Netscape and Microsoft
Explorer.)

Nevertheless, despite these initial drawbacks the Internet has proved to be extremely popular and is currently expanding at an incredible rate. What is more it is evolving all the time and appears to be moving towards being a full blown trading/service conduit.

6.11.2 CompuServe

Whereas Internet is in actuality a global collection of computer networks/bulletin board systems, CompuServe is a commercial online information service. Headquartered in America, CompuServe is a truly formidable ISP. By 1997 CompuServe had a global membership of over three and a half million users and was reported to be adding one hundred and fifty thousand new users every month. Although the CompuServe system is based in America, it has access points all over the world and is growing rapidly in Europe. In Britain users can log in via regional telephone numbers.

CompuServe's American roots have proved to be a valuable marketing ploy. The reason for this is the substantial dominance of American companies in the computing industry. Consequently a large number of American software and hardware developers use CompuServe as a distributive service platform to provide technical support for their customers. CompuServe is a dynamic service and is constantly updated with extra facilities such as new entertainment guides, news information, directory listings and a host of other suitable utilities. Ultimately, the main advantage of this type of service to small business users is its accessibility. A potential user has only to be equipped with a basic PC/modem configuration and with appropriate software to gain cost-effective access to a global information network.

6.11.3 Offline reader

Most conventional Internet users will dial up their ISP, collect their mail, and, more often than not, surf the Internet, reading notice boards, executing search routines and doing whatever they usually do. However, by the time they have come off the Internet, they could be facing quite a high phone bill as well as a substantial charge from using the pages as furnished by the ISP.

In order to reduce these costs, more and more users are turning to what is known as an OLR (Off Line Reader). What happens with an OLR is that the user logs on to ISP, retrieves any user e-mail and immediately logs off. The user can then peruse their mail, which is stored on their own machine, at will and without incurring unnecessary log-on charges. Then, having compiled e-mail replies the user employs the OLR to log on again, relays the messages and immediately logs off again so keeping service costs at a minimum.

6.11.4 Voice and data transfer

There is a growing realisation by computer users that WANs, of which the Internet is the best example, can be used for the simultaneous transmission of voice and data. Unfortunately this is causing some concern as combined data and voice traffic does in fact cause a considerable slow-down on the computers trying to transmit signals.

The four main contemporary technologies which enable this include Frame Relay, IP (Internet Protocol), ATM and Time Division Multiplexing (TDM).

TDM technology is proving of particular interest to network managers as it enables the network to slice voice and data into segments so enabling the signals to have equal bandwidth. What is more, the technology allows users to prioritise voice signals by simply increasing the bandwidth attached to the various signals.

6.12 CONCLUSION

Computer networks, WANs and LANs, are central to the success of many modern commercial organisation. WANs have, in particular, become increasingly critical as they provide users with practically instant access to an almost limitless supply of services. These services can come in the form of improved long-distance processing power to enable basic commercial transactions or in the form of advanced communication systems such as e-mail and videoconferencing (see 7.10.3).

The impact of effective WAN systems can be judged by their influence on contemporary work routines. For example, employees such as financial analysts/money dealers concentrate on WAN-linked terminals so they can make global decisions whilst journalists with a modem-equipped PC and a healthy credit card have made news scoops an everyday event.

As the networks knit closer together to form the new Superhighway so more exciting services are expected to emerge. Because these services will be more sophisticated they will undoubtedly require substantial improvements in transmission technology. This improvement will not only pertain to the local computer systems but also to the means by which data is physically transmitted across carriers such as the national telephone network.

Such advances in the world's national and global WAN/communication systems will undoubtedly require substantial investment. However there is little doubt that such changes will bring dramatic improvements in their wake and lead to an ever-advancing information/communication rich environment.

7

Multimedia

7.1 INTRODUCTION

Multimedia is an all-embracing term which cuts across a wide variety of technologies. The aim of this chapter is to explore some of the major ingredients of multimedia and to examine certain dominant themes which permeate contemporary multimedia applications. These themes include the high quality of the equipment and personnel used to develop multimedia products and the ever-growing innovative range and nature of the products themselves.

Section 7.2 is an introduction to what is meant by the vexed term multimedia whilst section 7.3 is concerned with the manner in which multimedia is accessed and developed on the PC. Sections 7.4 through to 7.8 deal with the use, role and development of current compact disk (CD) and videodisc technology. Sections 7.9 and 7.10 consider the development of multimedia applications and the various markets in the personal and corporate sectors whilst section 7.11 concentrates on the commercial delivery of mass multimedia.

7.2 THE MULTIMEDIA CONCEPT

Multimedia is an all-encompassing term used to describe a host of computer-delivered services made up of textual and non-textual information. Multimedia computers and multimedia software applications integrate a variety of data sources which can include photographs, animation, moving video, sound and text. The main advantage of multimedia systems is that they enhance communication between users and computers by enabling information to be conveyed in an inventive as well as an attractive and intuitive manner.

With multimedia systems, users can go beyond the semi-static text and graphic screens and actually interact with the computers in a more dynamic manner. Because of this interaction multimedia systems can improve user productivity by projecting applications which are motivating, educating and friendly.

7.2.1 Delivering multimedia

Because of the nature and manner of integrating so many different data types and sources, multimedia systems are far more demanding on resources than the more conventional computer applications. One data type in particular, namely a digitised image, is usually central to any system described as multimedia. However, digitised images, or more particularly the data structures actually manipulated by the computer so as to reproduce still pictures such as photographs or full moving video (FMV), require vast amounts of storage space. The same images also require the manipulating computer system to possess considerable processing power.

The more sophisticated the image, be it colour or monochrome, still or moving, high resolution or low resolution, so the greater the demand placed on the computer system. This demand is reflected in terms of space for the actual data that constitutes the image as well as the processing power of the computer system required to manipulate it. In order therefore that multimedia applications are delivered to the end user in an effective manner, it is necessary that the supporting computer system, whether an individual PC/desktop or a larger corporate computer system such as a minicomputer, not only has sufficient memory and processing power but that the system is designed in such a manner that the various media sources that traverse through the system do so in a co-ordinated environment.

Unfortunately such features as outlined above mean that multimedia computer systems require resources, hardware and software which are more advanced than those necessary for the delivery of most text-based data applications. Multimedia computer systems are therefore almost as a matter of course significantly more expensive.

7.3 PC MULTIMEDIA

Developing and accessing multimedia via the PC is being recognised as a prime development area in business computing. The growing success and importance of PC multimedia can be witnessed by its dramatic impact on PC sales as domestic users seek to take advantage of the new multimedia applications. This increasingly important domestic market is being shadowed by massive investment by the corporate sector. For example, retail businesses have started to develop specialist systems such as CD-ROM mail order catalogues, training applications and so on.

For a desktop PC to handle the inclusion of extra sophisticated data sources such as moving pictures and stereo sound, it must be equipped with sufficient physical attributes. These attributes include high quality screens, adequate RAM, a CD-ROM drive, audio speakers, a sound card, a microphone and a large hard disk.

7.3.1 PC image manipulation

There are several ways images can be conveyed on PCs. For example, users can purchase expansion cards acting as TV tuners enabling the user to watch domestic television on their PC. Alternatively there are also what is known as video capture cards allowing users to grab video/picture clips from cameras or VCRs (see (b) below).

In the late 1980s there was a big leap forward in the development of multimedia products with the arrival of digital video compression. The advantage of this technology was that it enabled digital video to be stored and transmitted efficiently and economically.

The problem is that image data requires a significant amount of storage space when converted to digital form. The compression of images, therefore, is an essential production stage for companies developing titles for various CD formats such as CD-ROM and CD-i (see 7.4.1 and 3). The combination of this new compression technology and fast CD-ROM drive transfer speeds allows motion pictures to be contained on and replayed from a CD-ROM disk.

(a) Compressed images

The two most commonly used standards in image compression for the PC are the Joint Photographic Expert Group (JPEG) and Motion Picture Expert Group (MPEG). These standards were developed over the years by the joint efforts of numerous interest groups.

The original JPEG standard was the standard arrived at for the compression of still pictures. This system compresses each individual image. In contrast MPEG was specifically designed for the compression of moving pictures such as video clips although JPEG does this as well. As MPEG only stores those individual picture frames which are significantly different from the previous frame it is considerably more efficient than the JPEG standard.

MPEG video technology has been recognised as the international standard for mass market digital video in consumer multimedia titles or interactive kiosks. It is now widely employed by the consumer electronics, cable TV and direct satellite broadcast industries.

129

(b) Video capture cards

Video capture cards enable the PC to capture and manipulate video sequences or video still frames. Images can be taken from VCRs (video cassette recorders), camcorders or laserdiscs and saved into a format that can be easily merged into a vast number of applications.

Three crucial classes of video capture cards are frame grabbers, software compressors and hardware compressors. Frame grabbers grab single picture frames from video input. They are declining in popularity as other more sophisticated devices can perform this function as well as other complex operations.

Software capture cards are hardware devices which capture moving video clips. The video input is converted by the software capture card into digital form. This data is then compressed by the PC. Software capture cards of this type are economic but heavily dependent on the power of the computer.

Hardware capture cards are more expensive but enable users to manipulate images with higher resolution. The advantage of these boards is that they are equipped with dedicated circuit devices such as MPEG chips so that image compression is performed on the incoming video before it is stored on the hard disk.

(c) Video Electronics Standards Association (VESA)

In order to help facilitate the seamless integration of video and graphics on the PC, the Video Electronics Standards Association (VESA) agreed on a standard for digital video devices called the VESA Media Channel (VMC). Computer components inside a PC are all connected by a bus (se 3.6.1). However, video processing tasks place an enormous load on the bus. What the VMC does is bypass the bus taking video data streams straight to the screen.

This hardware device which fits inside the PC has been described as a dedicated real time multimedia highway. In essence, the VMC is a new bus, completely independent of the PC's main bus, and is available for ISA, EISA, MCA, VL-BUS and PCI machines (see 3.6.1).

7.4 CD TECHNOLOGY

The majority of users interacting with domestic/PC multimedia systems use CD drives. These CDs have a wide range of standards and formats and are accessed by a variety of devices.

7.4.1 Compact disk read only memory (CD-ROM)

CD-ROM disks are the same disks as used for audio storage. These disks usually contain around 600 million characters of text information or alternatively up to 2000 high resolution pictures or 20 hours of speech. As this data is encoded in permanent bubbles on the surface of the disk by using lasers, CD-ROMs are read-only.

To facilitate greater user interaction CD-ROM disks have been marked with special indexes which integrate with CD-ROM-XA (eXtended Architecture) software so enabling limited image manipulation.

Other different formats besides the CD-ROM format include DVI, CD-i, CD-TV and PhotoCD (see below).

7.4.2 Digital video interactive (DVI)

Digital Video Interactive is another standard for storing images/video data on compact disk. Developed by RCA and currently owned by Intel it enables developers to store about an hour of full motion video (FMV) and audio on a CD. The significance of this technology is that the data is fully under computer control. The user can retrieve and interact with digitised images almost at will.

7.4.3 Compact disk interactive (CD-i)

A competing standard of DVI is compact disk interactive (CD-i). CD-i is a compact disk storage format which was developed by Philips, Sony and Matsushita. CD-i devices are usually player/console kits that are attached to a television. With CD-i, users can achieve vigorous interaction with multimedia products employing sound as well as still and moving pictures. The CD-i system firmly establishes the TV as the focal point for presenting various applications providing services as diverse as entertainment, education and reference. From a consumer point of view, CD-i is an attractive proposition as the player/console kits are significantly cheaper than full blown multimedia PC systems.

However the production of volume CD-i titles has been disappointing. The reason for this, which is dealt with in more detail below, is the exorbitant development costs. The reality of the situation is that many developers have discovered that they can only produce high quality CD-i products at a price which is higher than that which can be supported by the mainstream consumer market. Even so, CD-i appears to have a good future.

7.4.4 PhotoCD

PhotoCD is a CD format developed by Philips and Kodak. The essence of this format is that it enables computer users to capture photo images almost effortlessly. Instead of having to use expensive hardware devices such as scanners in order to digitise high resolution pictures users can now pass their films to ordinary photographic development high street outlets. They in turn digitise the images on the film straight on to a CD-R (write-once CD). The images can be retrieved in one of five different resolution ranges from thumbnail size to a full high resolution photo.

7.5 CD STANDARDS AND DRIVES

As a result of all the different CD formats there are now a widely accepted range of colour codes identifying different standards. This is called the Colour Book Standard, also known as the White Book Standard.

7.5.1 Colour book standards

These were originally introduced by Sony and Philips and are as follows:

(1) *Red Book – CD Audio*. The Red Book standard for CD Audio is now the accepted standard within the music industry.

(2) *Yellow Book – CD-ROM – CD-ROM XA*. The Yellow Book is the standard for CD-ROM (Compact Disc Read Only Memory) and is the standard for all computer-based storage/retrieval systems. Yellow Book is also for CD-ROM XA (eXtended Architecture) which is the bridge between Green Book and MMCD (Multi Media CD).

(3) *Green Book CD-i*. Green Book is the standard for CD-i (Compact Disk – Interactive).

(4) *Orange Book MO CD Recordable*. Orange Book is the standard for MO (Magneto Optical) and CD-R (Recordable) technology. It is now commonplace for clients to have their own CD-R equipment where they can cut themselves a proof disk. This is then given to major manufacturers such as Disctronics who then do a 'binary lift' producing glass masters and finally mass-produced CDs.

(5) *White Book Video CD*. White Book is the standard for Video CD. Philips and Sony have created this standard as the method of using MPEG (Motion Picture Expert Group, see 7.3.1 (a)) for displaying FMV (Full Screen Motion Video) on computer and TV screens. Disctronics are world leaders in this

technology and are able to assist all developers, publishers and film companies in the art of Video CD.

7.5.2 CD drives

Because of all the different CD formats, users must make sure that the CD they are using is capable of accessing the various standards.

In order to ensure compatibility various factors must be taken into account. To use the new PhotoCD systems from Kodak the user must make sure that the drive is capable of supporting such a system. Two crucial factors which have a bearing on compatibility are the multisession feature and speed.

A multisession CD drive is simply a drive which can access CDs which have been written at various stages. In other words, data which is added to the CD in another session can now be accessed. Secondly, features such as dual speed capacity indicate that data can be accessed from the CD at different transfer rates.

7.6 CD PRODUCTION

7.6.1 Small-scale production

CDs can be produced individually through the employment of special CD drives known as Write Once Read Many (WORM) drives. A good example of this type of device is the Kodak 200. It enables users to produce their own CD titles by using special blank disks. It is an ideal system for users wishing to distribute multimedia titles with a limited circulation. However it is not an economical method for mass circulation.

7.6.2 Mass CD production

Manufacturing a professional CD for the mass market is a complex process. Consider the following processes as carried out by Disctronics.

First of all there is the pre-mastering stage. This involves the creation of an image of the CD-ROM data structure onto a computer hard disk. The CD-ROM image is then subjected to a 100% virtual image scan so it might be checked for errors before it is transferred to a magnetic tape for laser mastering. Laser mastering involves the production of a 'glass' master disk using a laser cutter. The glass master is coated with silver and after various tests passed to the electroforming stage. The glass master is then electro-plated with nickel in order to manufacture production stampers. The finished nickel stamper is then checked visually and the back of the stamper is polished and measured to ensure that there are no imperfections.

An initial batch of 50 compact disks are pressed for quality control and process monitoring. Quality control involves a multitude of rigorous tests. All of these tests are completed to the Philips and Sony 'Book' requirements. Once the tests have been passed, the full production run goes ahead. The stamper is fitted into the injection moulding press and a highly automated robotic disk production process is triggered. At the metaliser, the disks are processed in a batch.

The metaliser coats the disks with aluminium. After this, protective ultra violet light dried lacquer is applied and samples are checked for contamination, coverage and integrity on a continuous basis. The finished CD or CD-ROM is then printed using ultra violet cured ink with up to five colours by a flat silk screen process.

Once the disks have been printed they undergo final inspection. All disks that reach this stage are inspected using an automatic laser inspection machine which checks for contamination and physical damage. The disks are packaged in slim line cases ready for distribution.

The overall impact of Disctronics mass production methods is to produce professional CDs at a fraction of the price employed by methods such as WORM drives.

7.6.3 Compact disk erasable (CD-E)

Compact Disk Erasable is a compact disk standard promoted and developed by companies such as IBM, Philips and Ricoh. Whereas ordinary CD-ROMs provide a read-only facility and whereas CD-R disks cannot be erased, CD-E disks can store and erase data as and when required.

7.7 VIDEODISC TECHNOLOGY

Videodisc is a term often used to refer to an early and relatively successful multimedia delivery system called LaserVision, developed by Philips in the late 1970s. Videodisc systems are created by employing laser disk technology on mirror-type 12 inch videodiscs, similar to standard CDs. Videodisc systems deliver high quality image/video displays and give the user effective operational control. The majority of professionally produced disks focus on subjects such as skill development, education and marketing. Despite the high quality and continued significant sales of videodisc systems the overall picture suggests a product in decline. The reason for this appears to centre on the fact that videodisc technology is an analogue format as opposed to digital and that unlike CD technology there was a failure by industry to produce compatible videodiscs or compatible playback devices.

7.8 DIGITAL VIDEO DISK (DVD)

At the time of writing, Sony and other interested parties have launched a new optical CD type disk known as the Digital Video Disk (DVD). This new standard is capable of holding 4.7 Gb of data, six times that of contemporary CD-ROMs. The reason for this increase in storage capacity is due to a dramatic improvement in laser technology as well as a new technique enabling developers to put two layers of data on one side of a disk. For example, DVD technology employs smaller-wavelength signals to govern the laser which is used to encode the data. This in turn allows the corresponding equipment to increase the focus of the laser so enabling data to be written in finer detail. In addition, the top data layer on the disk is semitransparent which permits the laser to read/write through to the bottom layer as well as focus on the top layer as and when necessary.

DVD can store two and a quarter hours of MPEG video and is consequently expected to eventually supersede CD-ROM. A major incentive to other developers in this regard is the fact that DVD players are backwardly compatible with contemporary music/video CDs.

7.9 COMPONENTS OF MULTIMEDIA APPLICATION DEVELOPMENT

As with ordinary software applications, users are faced with the choice of producing their own applications or purchasing ready-made products. For ordinary domestic and small business users, the main advantage of purchasing ready-made CD-based multimedia applications is that they are relatively cheap. However although many ready-made applications are developed for the mainstream market, they are normally restricted to entertainment or reference.

Unfortunately the problem is that producing effective and attractive multimedia applications with a view to selling them to a mass market is an expensive business. For example, one CD-ROM version of the New Grolier Multimedia Encyclopaedia published by Software Toolworks contained 4000 images and 85 video clips. However, it was commonly estimated to have taken around US$ 500,000 to produce. Interactive CD titles have even more excessive development costs. Virgin Interactive says it spent about US$ 1.7 million developing its best-selling CD games title Seventh Guest.

Obviously these costs are usually incurred through employing highly paid experts along with the latest technology. However, smart and attractive multimedia applications can, and do, generate major profits.

7.9.1 Expert personnel

Because multimedia involves the integration of various technologies and disciplines, the personnel that produce multimedia applications usually come from a variety of specialist backgrounds. The types of skill required frequently include animators, graphic artists, photographers, video editors, multimedia authoring software authors (see below), programmers, presenters, consultants, courseware designers, subject specialists. This type of personnel is in high demand everywhere and usually command a high premium for their services.

7.9.2 Specialist software

In addition to personnel with the required skills it is also necessary to have the software to design and compile the systems. In order to actually produce the applications, developers usually employ standard programming languages such as Pascal, C, C++ and Java (see Chapter 9) or an authoring language system.

Authoring language systems of this type have major advantages over standard programming languages in the production of multimedia applications. Firstly, authoring language systems have specialist routines and ready-made menus for constructing multimedia applications. Secondly, although authoring language systems are complex they are usually very user friendly and enable less-experienced users to produce sophisticated applications. Authoring language systems frequently support facilities enabling developers to use hypertext (see below) features in the creation of multimedia applications.

(a) Hypermedia

Hypermedia allow application users to immediately refer to that part of the multimedia scenario which is of interest to them. For example, a user investigating a particular subject can point at various bits of data on a screen, such as a picture or word, which would lead to further screen(s) providing information on further aspects of that subject. These elements on the screen are what is known as 'hot' or 'hyper' or 'node' links; the paths between these nodes is determined by the skill of the designer, and, by manipulating the links, the user can chose between video, sound, text, etc. presentation of the subject matter as appropriate. The development of applications using this type of technology is considered to be especially useful for training applications.

Hypermedia is often called, but is in fact an extension of, Hypertext. A hypertext system stores text in a way which allows users to search through it using a variety of commands and to construct their own links.

(b) Multimedia databases

Most multimedia systems rely upon a complex database so that they can store and 'chain' (a connection to the next data object) all the different types of data which have to be manipulated by the system. A multimedia database could contain a series of photographic stills, video clips, sound recordings or a combination of information structures of this type integrated with conventional text files.

However with hypermedia applications the computer system is required to handle data structures which are far larger than more conventional systems. A video clip, linked to particular word (i.e. hot link) in a multimedia application, can result in data structures which consist of hundreds of megabytes or, indeed, gigabytes of data.

7.9.3 Human machine interface strategies (HMI)

Successful multimedia applications are usually attractive and relatively easy to operate. To ensure that the application possesses both of these qualities, developers regularly deploy those strategies pursued by HMI (Human Machine Interface) specialists. Personnel in this area tend to be a mixture of computer specialists and behavioural scientists. These specialists advise developers on screen layout techniques, user interaction points, screen text interrogation and general user interface.

Interestingly, voice instructing applications provoke cultural discrepancies across national boundaries. Developers have discovered that users in countries such as England and France respond more positively to multimedia applications using a woman's voice whilst users in Germany respond better to a man's voice.

7.9.4 Touch screen

A hardware device that has taken on a significant role in the delivery of user-friendly multimedia systems is the touch screen.

A lot of touch screens operate on what is referred to as surface wave technology, otherwise known as projected capacitive technology. What happens is that a voltage field is projected through a special sensor. A glass screen displaying options is then placed in front of the sensor. Any user wishing to access the system simply touches the screen at an appropriate point, e.g. a menu option. The sensor detects changes in the projected field as a result of the user's touch. These changes are converted into x,y data co-ordinates allowing the software to instruct the computer to implement the user's choice. One application is a touch screen installed between a shop window and an ordinary computer console. The user can consequently control an interactive exhibit by simply touching the window.

Another type of touch screen comprises a rectangular grid of fine electrical wires, which can detect finger position.

The main advantage of a touch screen is that it enables users to communicate and interact with a computer in a positive and direct manner. Multimedia applications developed around this system, such as 24 hour shopping, have proved to be very successful. The reason is that users can access the application's services without any training. In addition these systems are extremely efficient as user error is usually minimised by the implementation of concise menu options. Although the actual screens supporting touch screen technology can be expensive there are hidden economies such as the dispensing of computer keyboards and other input devices.

7.10 MARKETS AND PRODUCTS

Because of the diverse nature of multimedia, it would appear that there is a boundless potential product market to which the concept could be applied. Even so, there are obvious niche sectors to which multimedia appears particularly suited. These include education/reference, videoconferencing, retail and entertainment.

7.10.1 Education/reference

Computer-aided learning has long been regarded as a successful and efficient teaching tool. In fact, it has been so successful that governments and corporations around the world are starting to invest massive slices of their training/education budgets developing systems of this type.

A conventional format usually means the student following a computer screen display, which involves being asked questions and supplying required answers. Most early computer learning packages displayed simple graphics and enabled the user to progress at their own speed.

However, multimedia products have given a special impetus to this type of application. The reason, is simply the attractive and enticing nature of so many multimedia titles, which results in the user not only being informed but also, more often than not, being motivated or indeed even inspired. The deployment, say, of orchestral music combined with full motion video in the study of the movements of the planets in the solar system must produce a positive impression. This type of educational application is a cross-over between education and entertainment and is often referred to as an 'Edutainment' product in retail software listings.

Other achievements of multimedia products of this type are especially critical in the creation of virtual reality (VR) and simulation applications. These new waves of programs have been used to develop problem solving skills, and train staff in environments which are not only hazardous to them but to others as well. This is especially the case with products being developed to aid doctors training for surgery or pilots to fly aircraft. Educational/training multimedia products of this type provide a realistic environment involving touch, sight, hearing and movement. As a result trainees are reasonably competent on the simulation before starting on the job itself.

The economic value of these products depends on their aim. Medical programs or flight simulators cost a fortune to produce but their long-term benefit is undeniable. With respect to less sophisticated aims, such as a program delivering basic proficiency in a foreign language or a particular skill, then development is a cheaper and more straightforward venture. From an organisational/user point of view, educational programs of this type are popular because:

(a) Travelling is minimised, as trainees can learn on site. This means no travelling subsistence or journey time.

(b) Once an application is purchased, it can be used repeatedly by a trainee or other members of staff. Learning is consequently reinforced and spread as necessary.

(c) Training is carried out when it is convenient to do so.

(d) Staff normally used for training can be released to perform other duties.

7.10.2 Publishing

The printed word is undoubtedly under threat from the CD. The power and economics of CD publishing is self-evident if one considers that a single CD-ROM can store literally thousands of texts. However, it is suggested that until the means of accessing the CD-ROM is a much cheaper process than it is at the moment, it is unlikely that books in their conventional form will disappear as rapidly as market makers would imply. The late 1990s also witnessed some big publishing organisations withdrawing from the multimedia/CD-ROM market due to lack of sales.

Nevertheless there are warning signs such as the increasing drift towards investment in handheld CD reading devices. If devices of this type were to become mainstream there is little doubt that it would have a dramatic effect on the future of the publishing industry. Convenience, flexibility, portability would no longer be the special preserve of the book.

7.10.3 Videoconferencing

Videoconferencing involves geographically separated users being in direct visual and audio communication. Standard videoconferencing units consist of a camera, a microphone, a TV monitor equipped with a CODEC (a device that compresses signals for transmission) and a telephone link. Because of the hazards and expense of long-distance travelling and the recognition of the value of visual contact for communication, videoconferencing has experienced a boom. However, until recently videoconferencing was so expensive it was considered to be an application that was the preserve of the corporates.

By the mid 1990s cheaper and more versatile systems started to arrive as manufacturers produced purpose kits enabling videoconferencing via the PC. These kits included specially designed camera equipment to set on top of the computer as well as appropriate application software and a special communications expansion card.

NCR Telemedia Connection

A good example of advanced videoconferencing via the PC is the NCR Telemedia Connection developed by AT&T and NCR. Integrating easily with desktop personal computers such as PCs, TeleMedia Connection computer hardware boards and the associated software enable multiple users to simultaneously exchange full-motion high-quality video images and voice data as well as share and edit files, reports, charts or diagrams from their desktops. The system also enables users to share any Windows application and its associated data.

7.10.4 Retail

Retail multimedia applications are having a major impact on consumer shopping habits. As a result of the introduction of systems such as public-based purpose-built kiosks, shop window touchscreens and interactive TV channel stores, consumers are now being provided with a 24 hour shopping service.

To facilitate these new habits multimedia is altering the manner in which goods are displayed and purchased. For example, mail order users can now access product details via periodical CD-ROMs instead of wasteful and expensive paper catalogues. Similar CD-ROMs are also used by travelling sales representatives enabling them to display their wares via portable PCs.

Domestic users can also link to major ISDN-linked retail networks. Such a link enables users to communicate with the retailer's computers, scan merchandise, place orders and pay by credit card. In order to facilitate this type of home shopping, retailers are investing heavily in systems which are well organised and easy to use. Besides purchasing, these systems also deal with customer credit checks, credit notes advertising, account inquiries and other relevant correspondence.

However as this home shopping data traffic increases so the computing community is beginning to realise that retail multimedia applications such as home shopping are beginning to pose complex challenges to the emerging global information superhighway. This is especially so for networks such as the Internet which has witnessed a dramatic increase in use for just this type of application. The problem is that users/shoppers and retailers employing retail multimedia across national and international WANs require and exchange large volumes of information all of which must be routed at great speed and with corresponding accuracy and security.

Unfortunately high data volume network traffic of this type, for a host of different technical reasons, can have a severe and detrimental effect on the rest of the network. However it should be noted that the computing industry is under enormous pressure to provide cost effective solutions.

Vertical integrated multimedia purchasing systems

Vertical Integrated Multimedia Purchasing Systems (VIMPS) are frontier automated shopping order systems. The idea is to enable consumers to order tailor-made manufactured products via multimedia touchscreen terminals available in high street showrooms. As details of the customer's requirements are fed into the computer, customers are presented with a realistic image of their specifications. The specifications can be altered at will and confirmed orders are relayed straight to the factory. Credit details and payment can be processed through the same system. The overall impact of a VIMPS system is to maximise consumer choice and simultaneously streamline the means of supply.

7.10.5 Entertainment

It is often suggested that a good multimedia product is entertainment in its own right. This has certainly proved to be the case with top quality educational titles. The entertainment market has consequently been recognised as not only being a direct source of income but also as a feed for the sales of other products. Purpose-designed multimedia entertainment products fall into three distinct categories. The first category is the standard game format as supplied on CD-ROM. This is a multi-million pound market which is currently in full swing. The technology is at hand and is being fully exploited by both developer and consumer.

An interesting game called Starship Enterprise became one of the first home computer games employing Apple's three-dimensional (3D) Quick-Time technology. The game enabled users to investigate a realistic 3D image model of the infamous spaceship on practically any PC equipped with a CD-ROM drive. The main attraction of Apple's 3D CD-ROM films is that they project images similar to those employed on virtual reality systems without the user having to purchase or use associated equipment such as special headgear or gloves.

The second category centres on cartridge systems from companies such as Nintendo. However such cartridges which often contain several expensive microprocessors can be very expensive to produce. As a result it is believed that CD-ROM devices will gradually replace cartridge game systems.

The third category is still in its development stages and is in essence that technology which revolves around the generic term Entertainment on Demand (EOD). This category is concerned with services such as inter-active TV whereby viewers can immediately influence program endings, purchase products, rent movies and even vote on various issues without ever leaving the confines of the couch.

7.11 MASS CORPORATE DELIVERY

In order for commercial enterprises to deliver mass domestic multimedia consumer services such as Entertainment on Demand (EOD) or interactive home shopping, they must not only employ sophisticated corporate computers such as parallel mainframes (see 2.5.2) but also suitable database software.

The reality is that corporate multimedia systems such as EOD service providers need specialist database applications capable of manipulating various information objects, moving and still pictures, text articles and so forth, in the same way that other simpler databases deal with more conventional structured data. However these new multimedia formats do not have a simple tabular structure. They are much bigger than orthodox data types and are more awkward to store. A market leader in the development of software enabling the delivery of corporate multimedia systems is the Oracle Corporation.

7.11.1 Oracle

The Oracle Corporation is a world leader in the distribution and development of database software. It has made crucial breakthroughs in the database management of unstructured data types, be it pictures, freeform text, audio, graphics or video. Central to the Oracle range of multimedia delivery applications in the mid and late 1990s are Media Server, Media Net and Media Objects all of which run in conjunction with each other.

Oracle Media Server is a database management system that is designed to run on computers such as parallel mainframes. It works with multimedia data types and will run hundreds of transactions per second as well as manage multiple data types.

Oracle Media Net is a software suite which communicates with interactive televisions to deliver services to the home. Media Net allows applications to transport different data types over a whole range of network systems in real time mode and without noticeable delay. Without such a feature, customers would be deterred as they would be unlikely to accept a system which freezes during the middle of a film as the receivers await the arrival of the rest of the data.

The Oracle Media Objects is a corporate authoring tool used to build new applications such as Video on Demand (VOD). Because the Oracle environment is scaleable, developers can build databases that serve from tens of thousands of users to hundreds of thousands of users.

7.12 CONCLUSION

The ability of multimedia systems to co-ordinate and project applications which employ so many different technologies has resulted in a new wave of exciting user products for both the domestic and business market. As a consequence, consumer/corporate interest means that multimedia has proved to be a tremendous catalyst for the computer industry with respect to development and sales.

However, those new products which might be described as multimedia have required users, developers and manufacturers to make substantial investments. These investments have been in the form of more advanced computers so enabling users and developers to access and produce multimedia products. Users and developers have also invested in the creation of purpose-built software tools to author as well as deliver multimedia applications and invested in highly educated and talented professionals engaged in the actual product creation. Multimedia is not only proving expensive to create and deliver with respect to direct computing technology but a rising level of product sophistication is also having a considerable knock-on effect on the conventional receiving end of the market.

As a result of these high costs, multimedia products are invariably created with a commercial focus. Even so, multimedia development is fostering a hitherto unforeseen convergence of different technologies and skills. The fact is multimedia applications are creating a mesh of technical knowledge so enabling the computing industry to offer the public an ever-increasing wealth of applications.

What is more, these applications are being used now. Users, in various parts of the world, are already shopping from the comfort of their own homes via conventional TVs/computers, driving cars with dashboards supplied with small terminals displaying ordinance maps and built-in voice navigators as well as employing Web browsers to interact with various training programs available on the WWW.

Future multimedia development and applications can only be guessed at but as they evolve in the eye of the imagination no doubt they will then appear.

8

Computer security

8.1 INTRODUCTION

This chapter has two main objectives. The first objective is to drive home to the reader the necessity of adequate computer security. In order to highlight this necessity the chapter will cover legal as well as operational obligations. The second objective is to examine the various areas of potential breaches in computer security whilst simultaneously highlighting possible countermeasures.

Section 8.2 deals with some of the arguments for users to consider and improve their individual computer security procedures. So as to underline this, sections 8.3 through to 8.6 consider security issues relating to hardware, software and personnel.

Section 8.7 is concerned with some of the major legal aspects of the Data Protection Act whilst sections 8.8 and 8.9 centre on the various forms of damage inflicted on computer data and the possible means that users can employ in terms of data damage limitation/recovery.

Sections 8.10 through to 8.12 concentrate directly on those security breaches which are an immediate result of unlawful or unauthorised interference in the user's computer systems. Section 8.13 deals with those measures which corporate users might take in order to recover from serious disaster. Section 8.14 is concerned with the increased threat to computer systems as a result of the recent global surge in Internet traffic.

8.2 SECURITY MATTERS

According to numerous surveys it appears that the majority of computer users still have scant regard for computer security. Unfortunately such indifference can, and very often does, prove to be an excessively expensive oversight. In many such situations businesses have been bankrupted and unique user data has been corrupted or indeed lost forever.

Notwithstanding the current apathy there does appear to be, albeit slowly, a gradual change in user attitudes to computer security. There is, for

145

example, a growing realisation that criminal elements are beginning to make greater use of computers to commit various illegal acts. There is also a growing awareness with respect to the need to enforce user responsibility towards personal privacy, an awareness which has in turn resulted in binding legislative imperatives such as those emanating from the Data Protection Act. On a micro level, individual users are also becoming more conscious of other issues such as computer viruses as well as the ad hoc havoc caused by computer glitches, be they deliberate or accidental.

Computer security is, as a result of these and other pressures, a commercial imperative. As a consequence computer security has become a growth area within the computing industry as more and more companies develop security-conscious products.

8.3 HARDWARE SECURITY

The most obvious form of computer security concerns those measures necessary to provide a secure environment for the user's physical hardware. Threats to these hardware assets are usually the result of unforeseen natural disasters such as fire and flood or human behaviour such as criminal activity.

8.3.1 Unforeseen natural disasters

Natural disasters are, by their very nature, usually difficult to predict and consequently difficult to prevent. Nevertheless it is possible to limit damage through basic strategic planning. For example, corporations in countries which are prone to earthquake activity would usually ensure that important computer configurations were well distributed and, when located within the earthquake zone, housed in buildings designed to withstand potential shocks.

Other potential natural disasters such as flooding can also be minimised with a little foresight. For example, placing equipment in buildings or on the floors of buildings well above sea level in countries such as Holland is only common sense. Even the risk of fire, for whatever reason, can be minimised by the installation of effective sprinkler systems. The point is, if users, domestic or commercial, give due consideration to the computer system's housing, positioning and surrounding environment they can, with a little thought, usually side-step the effects of hazards such as fire or flooding or at least reduce their effect.

8.3.2 Criminal activity

Human endeavour is speckled with criminal activity and the reality is that modern computer systems present a rich hunting ground. The simplest way of reducing the criminal threat is by restricting access to the equipment. This is usually achieved through rigorous site security. Measures which fall under this category include the use of secure locks, guards, alarms and other basic barriers. However, even when measures such as these are in force, users have often discovered that they are not enough.

(a) Theft

Computer hardware is invariably expensive and thieves have discovered that there is a ready and willing market.

Organisations/individuals have therefore discovered that the best way of deterring equipment theft is to render it worthless to unauthorised users. This is usually done by immobilising the equipment through the employment of password controls (see below) or through the inclusion of special electronic token/key devices. Such devices deny access to unauthorised users and consequently make the equipment, if not totally ineffective, then at least expensive to fix. The keys themselves are usually smart cards (credit-card shaped devices with built-in microprocessors) or plastic keys/dongles. The keys can be copied but this is usually a difficult and prohibitively expensive process. Some systems go one step further and employ radio transmission keys. Security marking is also proving to be an effective countermeasure against hardware theft. In Britain most police forces have access to massive databases with details full of serial numbers pertaining to stolen computer systems.

(b) Chip crime

Another growth area in computer crime concerns the theft of microprocessors. In 1997 global 'chip crime', as it is frequently called, was estimated to be a two billion dollar activity. As well as involving considerable amounts of money it is perceived as being a soft racket. For example the criminals specialising in chip crime just have to undo the computer's casing in order to gain access to these small valuable components.

What is more computer chips have the added advantage of being highly resaleable, practically unidentifiable and very compact. It has been estimated that the average-sized attaché case can carry a million dollars worth of top quality contemporary computer chips. Chip theft also brings the added problem of being almost respectable in its criminality in that even if the criminals are caught the sentences handed down by the courts are usually much lighter than those for more unsavoury activities despite the fact that microchips can in fact be worth more than hard drugs or even precious metals.

(c) Criminal damage

Criminal damage to computer systems is usually committed by people such as vandals, disgruntled employees and terrorists. As with theft, such actions are usually best minimised by restricted access. The truth is that it is proximity which enables people to inflict such damage.

With respect to disgruntled employees, extra steps have to be taken. For example, many computer consultants are now advising employers to ensure that newly redundant employees are instantly escorted from the organisation's premises so as to minimise the possibility of a backlash. Other steps the user could take include closed circuit TV or video, which is employed by many organisations wishing to monitor employee operational activity, especially when they are using expensive corporate computer systems.

8.4 SOFTWARE SECURITY

Software security is centred on issues such as software reliability, software piracy and breach of copyright.

8.4.1 Software reliability

Software reliability is a major headache for users and developers alike. For example, users employing faulty software have alienated customers due to misallocated accounts whilst developers have experienced falls in sales due to loss of reputation or possible litigation as a result of their software's disastrous effects. It must be said, however, that blaming the software can be an excuse for user error, and it is not always easy to distinguish between them.

Sadly there is no magic bullet or instant solution which would enable developers to produce fail-safe programs every time. The problem is that as software applications become ever more complex (sophisticated software applications usually contains hundreds of thousands if not millions of lines of computer code) so they are becoming increasingly difficult to control.

Complex software usually delivers more sophisticated features but also invariably results in the application containing more potential avenues of error. Countermeasures to this problem include the rigorous application of strict programming methodologies as well as thorough program testing. However even these approaches are not foolproof and do in fact invariably fail. For example during the Falklands conflict, which was believed to be the first true example of electronic warfare, software controlling Royal Navy computer-controlled anti-missile guns locked onto an incoming French-built Exocet missile and identified it as a NATO weapon. Because of this identification, the anti-missile gun treated the Exocet as friendly and consequently failed to attack it despite the fact that it was fired by the enemy. As a result of this oversight the defending ship was sunk. This, with hindsight, was an obvious error, but unfortunately typical of that sort of error which is practically impossible to plan for.

In addition to these logical/functional errors users/developers are also faced with the increasing problem of computer viruses and the inclusion of mischievous code by third parties attempting some form of fraud. As with logical errors, checking and correcting software tainted in this manner can prove extremely difficult and sometimes practically impossible.

8.4.2 Software piracy

Software piracy or bootlegging is that situation where users have made multiple copies of a particular piece of software without any payment or reference to the legal owner. Unfortunately software piracy is notoriously difficult to detect and suppress.

One reason for this is, yet again, due to social attitudes. For example a friend supplying a copy of a particular program or a retailer installing a pirated version of an application on a computer to enable them to clinch a sale is not seen as the most heinous of crimes. Even so developers have lost countless millions of pounds in revenues from such activities. As a consequence organisations such as the Berkshire-based Federation Against Software Theft (FAST) have appeared. In the early to mid 1990s this organisation was heavily involved in numerous successful court cases involving piracy and breach of copyright.

FAST also provides a service for enabling companies to keep track of their software and ensure that they are not breaching software licensing. Services such as this are becoming increasingly popular for organisations with vast computer configurations. The problem is that management, more often than not, is simply unaware of all the software currently installed and is therefore open to litigation by rightly aggrieved parties.

8.4.3 Breach of copyright

Pure breach of copyright usually concerns those cases where software developers have been perceived to have used computer code/ideas belonging to others. This is a very grey area which encounters varying degrees of enforcement throughout the world.

For example, developing computer code is practically identical to the effort invested by an author in a book. It is obviously unique and has to be protected as such. However if a developer uses a program and then writes a program which performs matching tasks and looks remarkably similar on screen but the code is entirely different, is this breach of copyright?

This is a notoriously moot point and has been debated across the planet. The difficulty is that various countries have dissimilar laws (some have no such laws) governing software copyright. In the US where such laws are very strict, most of the major blue chip computer companies appeared to have fallen foul of the courts at one stage or another. However despite the possibility of severe sanctions there are an increasing number of instances where software developers have quite deliberately and blatantly copied other people's work. The reason why they are prepared to take such risks is that they expect projected profits from their own product to comfortably meet any future legal costs. To a certain extent it would appear therefore that some developers are treating such penalties as a cheap alternative to research and development.

8.5 PERSONNEL ISSUES

Two critical areas regarding computer security are the skills gap and the generation gap. Other related personnel issues such as computer fraud are dealt with later on in the chapter.

8.5.1 The skills gap

In order to operate most contemporary computer equipment in a successful and efficient manner users have to be trained with certain basic critical skills. Fortunately most IT users do not need an excessive amount of training to perform their tasks as most of their duties, as with the systems that they employ, are reasonably routine.

However when organisations need to complete more complex tasks such as a software development project, then the organisation usually has to employ personnel with, or the potential to have, very high levels of understanding and experience. Unfortunately many organisations have discovered that personnel of this type are expensive to recruit or expensive to train. Given the fact that commerce across the globe is requiring more and more such high calibre workers and given the fact that there has been a substantial under-investment in such workers, so economies everywhere are beginning to discover that they are falling into what is known as the skills gap.

What is more this skills gap not only exacerbates future development but also causes organisations particular problems with their computer security. For example, because so many IT/IS projects are relatively short term so most IT professionals are hired on temporary contracts. As a result employers often discover that such workers have very little organisational loyalty. Even with personnel such as permanent programmers, where employers might expect a modicum of organisational loyalty, certain questions must be asked. For example, what happens if key IT/IS personnel are demotivated or involved in industrial action? What happens when they are poached by competitors and they are the only ones who understand how the systems work? What happens when former employees take their ideas to their rival's R & D departments ? (See 8.5.3.)

8.5.2 The generation gap

Yet another quandary affecting organisations everywhere is the realisation that current mainstream computer skills tend to be the preserve of younger members of the workforce. Although time is beginning to erode this quandary, a high percentage of the management of many organisations in the late 1990s appears to be computer illiterate.

As a result of this generational skills gap, management are often in the insidious position of simply not having the necessary underlying knowledge that would allow them to supervise the workforce in an appropriate and effective manner. This in turn has serious security implications as ill-informed management can be hostage to the whims of unscrupulous staff without being fully aware of the consequences of various actions until it is too late.

8.5.3 Countermeasures

To reduce some of the traps outlined above organisations are gradually being persuaded by management gurus, consultants, etc. to pursue various personnel strategies. These strategies include:

(a) All IT/IS staff to be thoroughly vetted irrespective of the tenure of their contract.

(b) Key personnel to be monitored constantly and, where necessary, nurtured, so as to try and reduce disaffection.

(c) Management to undergo regular training in order to ensure that they are fully informed as to the operations of the organisation's systems.

(d) Organisational IS/IT systems to be, where possible, of a mainstream technology so enabling the employer to replace specialist staff as and when necessary.

(e) Employers to make more use of restrictive covenants so reducing the possibility of staff switching to the organisation's competitors.

8.6 DATA SECURITY

Unlike hardware and software security, data security is not such an obvious concept and is often overlooked. However such an omission can prove to be extremely damaging to the user. The reason for this is the unique nature of a user's data. For example, whilst it is easy to replace a user's hardware or software it is practically impossible to replace the data because data is usually peculiar to the user's needs. In order to reduce the magnitude of harm due to data loss successful users operate strict backup procedures.

8.6.1 Backup procedures

Experienced computer users know that data backup (making a copy) is a top operational priority. For data backups to be effective they must be regular and precise. Users usually make backups of backups and ensure that the backups represent sequential generations of data.

Another important point that should be noted is the fact that many users having made the actual backups forget that they must also ensure that these copies are secure in their own right. To clarify this, the question that must be posed is: what good are backup data disks if the user then leaves them next to the computer in an office where a fire/theft occurs?

To ensure that their backup procedures are effective, users frequently arrange for backup media to be stored in fire safes and/or arrange for data to be backed up on alternate sites usually through standard data communication links.

8.6.2 Document security

A relevant subset of data security is document security. It is all very well installing a detailed and sophisticated data-encrypted password-protected computer system only to recklessly discard documentation outlining the procedures. Printout documents can contain strategically important information such as account details or company marketing ideas. In any event, steps must be taken to secure printouts, magnetic storage media, etc. Techniques usually include conventional security measures such as combination safes, or, when the data is no longer required, paper shredding, incineration and so forth.

8.7 DATA PROTECTION ACT (DPA) 1984

The original impetus for the British Data Protection Act (DPA) which came into force in 1984 was a legal directive from the European Commission. The Act is a recognition of the need to control and regulate the use of personal information which is accumulated and manipulated in computers or which is stored on computer data storage devices.

The current version of the Act is aimed at those situations where people who, through no fault of their own, can be refused credit, jobs, club membership and so forth all as a result of computer abuse/error. In order therefore to combat such anomalies the DPA requires computer users who keep information about living individuals, subject to certain exemptions (see 8.7.2), to register their information with a civil servant known as the Data Protection Registrar. The DPA created the office of Data Protection Registrar and it is the Data Protection Registrar who enforces the Act.

The DPA also requires data users to take reasonable precautions in protecting the data and preventing it from being accessed by unauthorised users. Failure by a user in this respect can result in substantial compensation to individuals suffering injury from such disclosure. The DPA enables individuals a right of redress in such circumstances and empowers the government to regulate personal data users.

There is however one noticeable and glaring loophole in the current Act. The legislation only deals with that personal data which is used by a computer system. It does not cover that information which is stored in manual files. The obvious ramification of this loophole is that personal data users can secretly keep sensitive information on living individuals without necessarily infringing the law. This has been the cause of great political angst and is expected to be reversed in the not too distant future.

8.7.1 Data protection principles

The DPA requires all organisations/users to abide by the eight data protection principles. Data users must:

(1) Obtain and process the information fairly and lawfully.

(2) Register the purpose for which they hold the data.

(3) Not use or disclose the information in a way contrary to those purposes.

(4) Hold information which is adequate, relevant and not excessive for the purposes.

(5) Hold only accurate information and where necessary keep it up to date.

(6) Not hold the information any longer than necessary.

(7) When requested, give individual copies of information about themselves and, where appropriate, correct or erase the information.

(8) Take appropriate steps to keep the information safe.

8.7.2 Registration exemptions

There are certain restricted exemptions where computer users are not required to register their use of personal information. These exemptions include information which is:

(1) Held in connection only with personal, family or household affairs or for recreational use.

(2) Used only for preparing the text of documents.

(3) Used for calculating wages and pensions, keeping accounts, or keeping records of purchases and sales for accounting purposes only.

(4) Used for distributing articles or information to data subjects.

(5) Held by a sports or recreational club which is not a limited company.

Personal data users must be very careful. If they hold data which is not exempt then they are committing a criminal offence. Professional advice suggests that users who are unsure should apply for registration.

8.7.3 Access rights

The DPA gives certain rights to data subjects (individuals who have their personal details recorded on a computer). These rights include a right of access so that the individual can see the information, a right of correction if the data is incorrect and a right of deletion if the data user is no longer permitted to hold the data. The data subject is also permitted compensation in the event of inaccurate information or unlawful disclosure to a third party, a result of which causes them financial loss. The data user is permitted to charge the data subject a modest access fee.

There are however a limited number of exemptions preventing data subjects right of access to information stored on them.

These include information which is held for the purpose of:

(1) Preventing or detecting crime.

(2) Catching or prosecuting offenders.

(3) Assessing or collecting tax or duty.

(4) Certain sensitive issues relating to health or social work.

8.8 COMPUTER VIRUSES

Computer viruses are simply computer programs which take control of computers and manipulate them and their ancillary equipment in a manner which is usually contrary to users' wishes. Most computer viruses have certain common characteristics such as the ability to replicate onto connecting computers or other peripheral devices. Computer viruses are, unfortunately, mobile, and can travel along telephone lines or via computer networks.

Computer viruses come in several different categories. Some have little effect in their original form whilst others are malevolent and cause a tremendous amount of damage. Lamentably all computer viruses have a destructive potential. Even where computer viruses have been deliberately designed to be little more than an innocent diversion they can evolve into a more vicious form. This can come about because of a lack of understanding by the original author as to the effects of the virus they have created or where the virus has been intercepted by another programmer who then transforms the program into a more malignant device. For example, instead of just displaying amusing messages the program may contain extra code which encrypts the user's files.

Other types of damage caused by viruses include data and file erasure, the absorption of storage space (as a result of the virus program continually replicating itself), flashing terminal screens and continuous fax and printer outputs. Distinct, more subtle viruses interfere with application performance by the introduction of typing errors or the destruction of competitor's products, e.g. 'Delete all files containing the words IBM!'

8.8.1 Types of virus

Computer viruses are usually classified according to their behaviour and the manner in which they are stored and triggered. Three common types of computer virus are the Trojan, the Time Bomb and the Resident.

(a) Trojan

A Trojan is a program that appears to perform a useful task but is in fact rather destructive. A famous Trojan program that appeared in the late 1980s was the 'Aids' information disk which originated from Panama. The disk purported to give users important health data. Unfortunately when users loaded the program it encrypted their hard disk and gave a message instructing the users to send money to an address in Panama. The idea was to force the users to buy the decryption program so that they might reinstate their data. Sadly the decryption program, when it arrived, proved to be defective and a lot of valuable early local aids statistics on the computers in doctors surgeries across the world was lost forever.

(b) Time bomb

The Time Bomb is a virus which will trigger on a particular date or when some other condition has been satisfied. Famous Time Bomb viruses include the virus celebrating Leonardo da Vinci's birthday. As with other viruses this type may just slow the computer down or display witty messages/ graphics or then again it may destroy valuable destroy data.

(c) Resident viruses

Resident viruses are those viruses which hide in the computer's run time memory (i.e. RAM). They can usually only be eliminated by a complete shut-down of the computer system.

8.8.2 Countermeasures

It is an accepted fact that computers can never be guaranteed total protection from invasion by a computer virus. However the risk can be minimised by the employment of anti-virus software and strict operational procedures.

(i) Anti-virus software

The late 1990s has witnessed a massive growth in the development and use of antivirus software. These applications usually contain a large database storing the details of virus patterns or signatures. These patterns are simply an arrangement of bytes which are usually unique to a particular virus. The anti-virus application searches the computer's memory or storage device(s) for a matching signature or pattern and, if a match is found, then depending on the type of virus an appropriate course of action is suggested (see below).

Because different computer viruses are appearing all the time, it is necessary that the application's pattern database is constantly updated to meet the latest threat. One popular anti-virus application in Britain is Dr Solomon's Anti-Virus Toolkit. It is continually updated and purchasers are able to obtain the latest update every quarter.

So that they might maximise their anti-virus security some users employ the concept of the sheep dip. The sheep dip is simply the engagement of multiple anti-virus applications to any new programs about to be installed. This way the user gets as wide an anti-virus sweep as is possible.

However the late 1990s is witnessing a new more virulent type of computer virus aimed specifically at defeating this type of detection. A good illustration is an infamous program called the Satan Bug. The Satan Bug is what is known as a polymorphic virus. It changes its byte pattern as it replicates and passes from computer to computer. As a result of this ability to evolve it can of course out-race conventional scanning applications which haven't been updated with the latest virus signature/pattern.

In order to counter the problem of the unrecorded virus pattern, be it a new pattern from a new virus or a polymorphic virus, anti-virus applications are now being supplied with intelligent or heuristic search/monitoring features. What happens is that the application not only scans for known patterns but also triggers on what appears to be suspicious code. For example, an intelligent scan could highlight blocks of code which are not uniform in structure and do not appear to fit in with the program's overall structure. Other examples include a resident monitoring feature which activates an alarm as soon as it realises that the program contains a virus which is attempting to inflict damage by means such as data/file deletion or data encryption. These intelligent anti-virus applications often generate false alarms, nonetheless they are proving very popular.

To prevent computer viruses actually causing damage, anti-virus application users are usually presented with three possible alternatives. These include immunisation, renovation and deletion.

(a) *Immunisation*
Many computer viruses tend to only infect or corrupt uninfected files. Consequently virus attacks can be deflected by kidding the virus that the target file has already been corrupted. However this immunisation procedure has a limited effect. The reason is that whilst specific viruses can be avoided through such a technique, it is not possible to immunise against multiple viruses.

(b) *Renovation*
Renovation is that technique by which infected files are restored to their original state. Unfortunately it has only got a limited success rate and the best bet for the user is to replace their infected data/files from backup systems.

(c) *Deletion*
Invariably the best way to deal with infected files and viruses is deletion. How this is done depends on the application employed and the nature of the virus.

(ii) Operational procedures

Users who follow certain operational procedures can make it practically impossible for a computer virus to gain entry to the system. Even if the virus does gain entry it must be remembered that a computer virus is just a program and unless the program is actually executed on the computer it cannot cause any harm. Below is a list of some of the operational procedures that users are advised to follow in order to minimise a computer virus infection/damage:

(a) Users, where possible, should always employ the latest update of their current anti-virus program.

(b) All software should, where possible, be bought from bona fide sources.

(c) All new software should be scanned prior to installation. Users have discovered that even software from so-called bona fide sources have proved to be infected with viruses.

(d) Users should always operate a good backup system.

(e) Users should immediately investigate any differentiating behaviour by the computer. This type of behaviour usually includes unfamiliar error messages, slower response times, vanishing files and encrypted disks.

In the case of the computer system becoming infected, users usually find that they can deal with the situation if they employ their current anti-virus software or simply switch the system off. However, in the event of serious damage, users are advised to hire specialist anti-virus consultants. Unfortunately such services are usually somewhat expensive.

8.9 PC RECOVERY

Considering the huge number of PC computers in use, it is not surprising to learn that data loss is more prevalent amongst this type of machine than any other. The PC is particularly susceptible to :

(a) Computer viruses

The overwhelming majority of computer viruses are written for the PC. In addition these viruses are consistently passed on by PC users casually exchanging files without any proper checks.

(b) Non-critical software

A lot of the software running on PC systems is not as secure as users would wish. Consequently they contain various errors/bugs which can cause the computers to crash without the user having time to save their data. Other problems include those situations where the software has not stored the data correctly or where the data has overwritten important code.

(c) Inexperienced users

Most inexperienced computer users start on a PC. As a result they may inadvertently cause damage by deleting files or reformatting disks.

(d) Hardware failure

As with the software, PCs themselves can and do fail. For example the computer's hard disk may be corrupted due to faulty installation by the manufacturer or because a speck of dust has entered the computer and landed on the disk drive's writing heads.

In the event of the PC user suffering from one of the disasters above, it would be reasonable to assume that, in fact, all is not lost and that, provided certain steps were taken, then some, if not all, of the data can usually be recovered. For the majority of PC users the best way to recover/ prevent data loss is through the application of various utility applications.

8.9.1 Utility applications

In most situations PC data corruption is limited to a small area of the disk. Those applications specifically designed to assist users in recovery tasks are known as utility programs. Some of these applications have been so successful that the main OS suppliers such as Microsoft and IBM have been forced to include similar features as extra utilities in their respective OSs. Even so, specialist applications such as anti-virus software or disk recovery programs are usually more popular and sophisticated than those supplied by mainstream OSs.

Popular and effective anti-virus software include Dr Solomon's Anti-Virus Toolkit from S&S International, PC Defender from American Megatrends Inc. (AMI), Microsoft's Anti-Virus program (MSAV) and McAfee's Scan.

Two top of the range utility applications are Norton's Utilities' from the Symantec Corporation and PCTools for Windows from Central Point Software. Norton's Utilities' initial popularity was as a result of its ability to enable users to painlessly recover deleted files/data. The application suite also includes features such as unformat and file search routines as well as anti-virus facilities and the Norton Disk Doctor (NDD). The NDD enables the user to automatically detect and repair physical and logical errors on a floppy or hard disk.

PC Tools for Windows is similar to Norton Utilities. It also includes two programs Crashguard and INI-Consultant. Crashguard warns users when resources, such as their hard disk, reach critical levels and a crash is likely. INI-Consultant allows the user to read cryptic files in plain English text.

8.10 COMPUTER FRAUD

Computer fraud involves the theft of money and is usually achieved through such means as the falsifying of records held on computer systems. Unfortunately computer fraud is proving to be a major headache for both the private and public sector. It is a growing problem and is one that is difficult to detect and difficult to prevent. Repeated surveys also indicate that most computer crime is committed by internal personnel.

Computer fraud as with chip crime and software piracy (see 8.3.2 and 8.4.2) also has an image problem. It is seen by vast sections of the public as an almost glamorous occupation and the courts have often found juries overtly sympathetic to the offenders. This is especially so if the victim is a an organisation such as a high street bank or, as in Britain, a recently privatised public utility. Public antipathy to visibly rich institutions such as these combined with the often onerous task of understanding the means by which the crime was committed frequently complicates the situation and makes it very difficult for the authorities to clinch a conviction.

8.10.1 Detection

Computer fraud by its very nature usually demands a certain intelligence. As a result most criminals involved in computer fraud are usually highly educated individuals. Consequently not only are such people good at committing the crime but they are usually good at covering their tracks as well. In fact, many are so successful that some organisations are unaware of the fraud until long after the event has occurred.

The actual detection of computer fraud is usually the result of a noticeable deficit in cash assets in the organisation's bank accounts or as a consequence of diligent work by computer auditors. Good examples of auditors uncovering fraud of this type include fictitious employees on payrolls, payment for delivery of non-existent goods from non-existent companies, and the employment of the organisation's funds in the purchase of illusory stocks and shares.

8.10.2 Prevention

Computer fraud is best avoided by employing suitable personnel and constructing systems preventing hostile access. Access can be restricted by making certain computers/locations off limits to all but necessary personnel. However, given the arrival of data communications and the interfacing of computer systems with external as well as internal data traffic, users have discovered that the most effective means of access control is through the employment of effective password systems.

According to the Computer Emergency Response Team (CERT), an organisation funded by the US government, the majority of computer break-ins are a result of users adopting vulnerable passwords. North America is particularly vulnerable as many US phone companies make no charge for local calls. Consequently hackers with limited resources are able to make significant raids. These intruders, with computers equipped with modems and simple character-generating devices, are able to make multiple password attempts and as a result simple passwords prove no barrier. Some hackers have even designed what is known as sniffer programs. These are special programs designed to seek out the user's password(s).

To try and minimise password violation users are often given the following advice:

(a) Use passwords that are at least six characters long.

(b) Passwords should contain non-alphanumeric as well as numeric characters.

(c) Passwords should be changed on a regular basis.

Users are also encouraged to attempt to hack into their own system or employ others (although this could be dangerous) and so expose any unforeseen weaknesses. The idea then would be for the user to plug the gap.

8.10.3 Prosecution

Unfortunately many fraudsters working in busy computing departments have often escaped prosecution by simple denial. For example, how do prosecutors prove that a particular individual sat at a particular keyboard and typed in a particular set of instructions which then resulted in the crime? The only sure way, with this type of activity, is through the use of video equipment. However, this is not always practical and is, for the greater part, an expensive option.

The fact is, unless the aggrieved party has well documented evidence and strong eyewitness testimony, conviction without a confession is, in many cases, practically impossible. In addition, computing concepts can be very subtle and sophisticated. Such complications can confuse a jury and studies have shown that juries are reluctant to convict in situations where they are unable to comprehend the manner of the crime.

Finally, there is the aggrieved organisation's reputation. For many organisations such as banks, insurance companies and other city institutions, the public's belief in the integrity of the institution is paramount. What is more, they know that any suggestion that their systems are vulnerable can have a significant impact on their market value. As a result, organisations of this type which have been caught out by various acts of computer fraud have often failed to prosecute the offenders for fear of undermining customer confidence.

8.10.4 Computer auditors

Central to the fight against computer fraud are a new breed of information specialists commonly referred to as computer auditors. The main duty of a computer auditor is to assess the reliability and accuracy of the financial information which is stored and manipulated by the user organisation's computer systems.

Unlike the personnel employing manual systems, computer users have to be trained to a certain level to enable them to gain access to the information stored in the system. Computer auditors are therefore usually equipped with multiple skills including accounting as well as computing expertise. Computer auditors are also employed as front-line expert witnesses in any legal proceedings pursued by potential victims of computer fraud. Consequently, professionals of this type are also expected to have good report writing/presentation skills.

In order to execute a successful computer audit an audit trail must be established. The idea behind an audit trail is to analyse the system's various transactions and totals and to pinpoint the source of any inconsistencies. Painless and efficient audits are facilitated by computer information systems which produce reports tracing data from an initial input stage through to final output. Computer information systems of this type are produced by pursuing a rigorous audit methodology.

Modern computer audit methodologies usually result in users and auditors making more use of specialist auditing software. These programs can be sub-routines in applications such as accounting programs or they can be applications in their own right. They usually allow users to interrogate ad hoc data files and support sophisticated file report facilities.

8.10.5 The Computer Misuse Act 1990

In 1990 Britain introduced the Computer Misuse Act. It was a ground-breaking piece of legislation in that it classifies unauthorised access to somebody else's computer system as a crime. Under the legislation there are three offences:

(a) *Unauthorised access to computer programs or data* (maximum penalty is six months imprisonment or/and £2000 fine). This offence is directed at the computer hacker. In order that the hacker is convicted of this offence the prosecution must prove that the hacker intended to access the system whilst knowing that they were unauthorised to do so.

What is interesting about this offence is that it not only applies to outside parties who are unlikely to have access authorisation but also to people such as wayward employees who suddenly decide to roam the organisation's computers. However in order to secure a conviction of someone such as an employee the organisation must prove that the employee had knowingly exceeded their access authority and that the transgression was duly recorded.

(b) *Unauthorised access with intent to commit or facilitate the commission of a serious offence.* This offence is more serious and is really directed at those hackers whose intentions are more serious than joy-riding hackers. To get a conviction for this offence the prosecution must prove that the hacker was intending to commit an offence, e.g. theft by deleting a recorded debt, or by aiding someone else in the commission of an offence, e.g. securing information for a third party which the third party can then use as a weapon of illegal intimidation. If convicted of this offence the hacker can face an unlimited fine and a prison term of up to five years.

(c) *Unauthorised modification of computer data or programs.* This offence makes it a crime to cause the unauthorised modification of computer data and is directed at virus authors or those who would deliberately disseminate viruses. On conviction, an offender may receive an unlimited fine or a jail term of up to five years.

8.11 COMMUNICATION AND NETWORK SECURITY

The recent phenomenal growth in the use of data communications and networks has resulted in an exponential increase in security breaches. These breaches are either non-aggressive, that is to say intercepted data is simply read, or the breach is proactive, in other words the interceptor alters the data or the transmission.

163

Whilst passive interception leaves the data or data transmission intact, such a security breach can, nevertheless, result in untold damage, e.g. informing the opposition of financial or military secrets. Proactive breaches usually result in data/data transmissions being altered, delayed, misdirected or even erased. One way of combating this kind of third party interference is through the use of data encryption.

8.11.1 Data encryption

The most successful way of protecting data transmissions is through the use of computer cryptography. Computer cryptography is the process of encrypting data by the application of intricate numerical operations which makes the data transmission incomprehensible to any third parties. All data including text is converted into numbers. These numerical operations are in the form of an algorithm which is employed in conjunction with a data item known as a cryptographic key. In order to decipher encrypted text the receiver must have details of the algorithm and the necessary cryptographic key.

8.11.2 Encryption algorithms

Users and organisations have access to a number of useful data encryption algorithms. The most successful contemporary encryption system is the Data Encryption Standard (DES) which was developed by the US government and made publicly available. This is what is known as a symmetrical system. The reason for the name is that the sender and receiver use an identical cryptographic key to encrypt and decrypt the data. However the problem with this system is that the cryptographic key forms part of the data transmission and therefore poses a possible security risk.

Another important encryption algorithm method which goes some way to reduce this risk is what is known as the Public Key Encryption System. With this system the data is encrypted by the sender using a public cryptographic key. The receiver then decrypts the data using a second and secret cryptographic key. This is also known as an asymmetric system and is thought to be almost impossible to breach. However, even when the contents of data transmissions cannot be breached, third parties could gain a useful insight into the user/organisation's activities by simply analysing the volume, destination and rate of data transmissions. A good illustration could be a sudden increase in military activity prior to mobilisation or possibly the movement of company assets prior to a restructuring announcement.

The best-known public key algorithm was developed by three mathematicians and is known as the RSA algorithm.

8.11.3 Commercial use

Modern financial institutions which rely on huge paperless money transactions employing technologies such as Electronic Funds Transfer (EFT) and Electronic Data Interchange (EDI) (see 14.8(e)) are particularly susceptible to data transgressions. As a result users know that it is critical that communication messages of this type are genuine and cannot be changed without the user's knowledge.

One way for the user to protect such transmissions is to arrange for the data streams/messages to be shielded by the inclusion of a special block of data called a Message Authentication Code (MAC). The MAC is produced as a consequence of the data stream being encrypted by a DES machine. The process is reversed by a similarly equipped party at the receiving end. Matched MAC codes indicate a successful and unadulterated data transmission.

Another popular security technique for financial transactions is the use of dial-back systems. What happens is that when external users wish to gain access to the system they are required to supply a contact number/code. The connection is then broken and contact re-established by the system, so confirming the external user's identity.

8.12 SURVEILLANCE AND ESPIONAGE

As products and services become increasingly more expensive to develop so industrialists have realised that shortcuts can be achieved by poaching ideas from competitors. What is more, such information is not restricted to technical 'ideas'. Vital intelligence concerning marketing strategies, pricing policies, take-over considerations, indeed any information giving external parties a competitive edge, is currently traded by certain groups in the business sector.

Such activities have been accentuated by the end of the cold war, an event which has resulted in a huge pool of appropriate espionage personnel/equipment suddenly appearing on the open market. Industrial espionage has consequently come into fashion and is now considered to be big business. Obvious examples of this type of espionage include human operatives, phone tapping, hidden cameras and electronic bugs. Conventional countermeasures to this type of activity include the constant monitoring of staff and the regular sweeping by users of their sites for any bugging devices.

Another information source which external forces can tap into is provided by the energy which is released from all electrically powered equipment. This energy takes the form of electromagnetic signals transmitted as radio waves or along wire or metal objects as electric currents.

This phenomenon is referred to as Transient Electromagnetic Pulse Emanation STandardizing (TEMPEST). Emanations of this type, directly from computers or indirectly from other sources such as network copper cables, are capable of being intercepted and interpreted by third party interests.

In order to prevent any potential abuse of such emanations, users must take steps to minimise the intensity of such signals. Fortunately these signals have a limited range and fade significantly after 100 metres. In addition, reasonable countermeasures can limit their potential. These countermeasures include the isolation of equipment configurations from the possibility of prying from suitably equipped vehicles or the possibility of eavesdropping from curious neighbours. Other precautions include the removal of unnecessary metal items from the equipment area as these only amplify signals and the constant refreshing of terminal screens.

8.13 DISASTER RECOVERY

In the event of a severe disaster such as an earthquake, bomb blast or even a computer virus attack, the user/organisation will want to re-establish their computer system as quickly as possible. Business acumen dictates that failure to recommence commercial operations to a near normal state can mean financial disaster.

To facilitate a swift recovery users need to be aware in advance of any potential catastrophe, what has to be protected, the manner of the protection and the cost. To this end corporate users are beginning to invest in contingency plans. These plans are usually formulated with the help of specialist consultants. To be effective the plans must be regularly tested and updated. In addition plans of this nature must have a holistic business approach. In other words, plans of this type are not just concerned with repairing technical damage but are also concerned with maintaining the user's business operations.

Companies which provide a sophisticated recovery support usually supply services such as mobile computing facilities or other temporary replacement systems. For example, in the City of London, it is possible to transfer to fully equipped dealing rooms. IBM consultancy services offer what is known as warm site and cold site options. A warm site option is where users can immediately start using fully equipped IBM computers at a choice of locations. The cold site option is where users can have a computer system reconstructed at their choice of site.

Recovery plans are usually made the responsibility of operational management, the very people who should know and understand how the organisation works. They will consider issues such as backup procedures, anti-virus measures, insurance (organisations have often found that adequate and effective insurance is very difficult to obtain) and other alternatives. Once the scheme is formulated, it is crucial that key staff are fully trained. This training has two main purposes. The first is to make staff fully aware of the need for security and the second is so that staff can implement the plan as and when necessary. The plan is usually distributed on a need to know basis so minimising unnecessary security leaks.

8.14 INTERNET SECURITY

The massive rise in data traffic and the ever-increasing use of the Internet (see Chapter 14) for trading/communication purposes has resulted in a host of new problems. However the problem which is causing the most concern is the sudden increase in the possibility of contamination by a computer virus. In order to try and eliminate the possibility of virus infection WWW browser applications (see 9.10.1(l)) now include anti-virus software. In addition most ISPs are currently virus checking user downloads from the Internet as a matter of course. Nevertheless for larger organisations with sophisticated internal networks more stringent measures are required. One means of preventing unwanted intrusion is the firewall.

8.14.1 The firewall

The firewall is the term given to the security buffer which separates an in-house computer network and the Internet. As such, there are two categories of firewall. The first category is considered to be the economic approach and works on network routers. The routers act as a filter deciding whether or not a particular piece of code should enter the network. The second category of firewall, which is not too dissimilar from the sheep dip (see 8.8.2(a)), are usually operated from a dedicated desktop computer equipped with appropriate anti-virus software. Incoming data traffic is analysed prior to network entry. Both categories of firewall are usually configured so that the internal network can pass data to the outside world without any interference. Only incoming data is usually analysed.

8.14.2 Secure trading technologies

Another growing concern of Internet security is the crucial issue of secure trading. VISA is currently collaborating with Microsoft to develop new technologies in order to provide adequate security for communication across the Internet. These include Secure Transaction Technology (STT), which is purported to be a protocol for handling credit card sales over private and public networks, and Private Communication Technology (PCT) which is a system enabling a secure means of transmitting everyday communications over the Internet.

Internet developers are also moving towards producing applications which comply with Secure Electronic Standards (SET), a protocol which is centred on RSA encryption (see 8.11.2). The concept behind SET which was initiated by VISA and Mastercard is to prevent hackers or any other unauthorised user from being able to change transaction information or obtain credit card particulars. In addition, the idea behind SET also enables users to confirm the identity of the other party.

8.14.1 Cyber terrorism

Unfortunately, the success of the Internet and other similar network systems has resulted in a new fear, namely cyber terrorism. Cyber terrorism is a term used to describe that criminal activity which takes place on the Internet or other similar networks and which is designed to disrupt those strategic computers that govern everyday life. Cyber terrorism can result in criminals not only appropriating property, but can, when directed, endanger people if not actually cause loss of life. The prospect of terrorists or other criminals causing nuclear power stations to over-react, subway trains to collide, national communication failures and the collapse of financial institutions cannot, sadly, be exaggerated.

The arrival of the Internet means that individuals with the minimum of resources can gain access to the most sensitive systems from practically any point on the planet. In 1997, it was estimated that there were two hundred and fifty thousand attempts to access the computers in the Pentagon. These are official figures and obviously reflect those attempts which were detected. The obvious question is what about the ones nobody other than the perpetrator knows about?

The problem is that whilst users can take certain preventative measures, some of which are discussed above, there is no such thing as a totally secure system. Unfortunately, the threat of cyber terrorism is a phenomenon which would appear to be on the increase and which will undoubtedly be a constant threat for all computer users for years to come.

8.15 CONCLUSION

As computers become ever more pervasive, so it is becoming more and more apparent, to users and organisations alike, that computer security is a serious issue. However it is also clear that a significant number of users have a tendency to ignore the issue. Unfortunately attention to security is costly and requires extra resources. Such investment, for example a special password-protected lock on a door, does not always produce an immediate and obvious return. Nevertheless users have discovered that failure to invest in appropriate security procedures can be catastrophic and is an issue which can no longer be ignored or skimped.

9

Software: development and applications

9.1 INTRODUCTION

This chapter is concerned with examining the nature of computer software and the manner in which various software applications are used and created. Because of their strategic importance, database applications are covered in detail in the next chapter.

Sections 9.2 and 9.3 discuss the concept of computer programming and the basic structure of a programming language. Sections 9.4 and 9.5 examine the various levels and generations of computer languages. Sections 9.6 and 9.7 outline some of the methods as well as trends in application development. Section 9.8 looks at the increasing use of Object Oriented Languages whilst sections 9.9 and 9.10 cover the substance and variety of modern computer business applications.

9.2 COMPUTER PROGRAMS

A program can be defined as a predetermined sequence of events or instructions, whilst programming is basically thought of as being the means by which the programs are actually created. The concept of a program is of particular relevance to computers. The reason for this is that computers are still, to all intents and purposes, unintelligent electronic machines which are driven and directed by human dictat.

If a computer is to perform in a functional and purposeful manner it must be provided with an appropriate set of commands. Consequently a computer program is simply a sequence of instructions. However the manner in which a computer can be programmed differs according to the technology employed. For example, setting the timer on a video recorder or adjusting the settings on a modern washing machine effectively corresponds to programming the microprocessor which controls the operation of that particular appliance. However this is an entirely different format to that of a computer programmer keyboarding a formalised set of instructions. In order to create and execute all the sophisticated operations and functions that go to make up a computer program, developers use what is commonly referred to as a computer programming language.

The programs developed as a result of the employment of a computer programming language are commonly referred to as computer applications. From a user's point of view, applications should be easy to use, work reliably and at a reasonable speed, and be resilient in the face of mishaps.

9.3 LANGUAGE CONCEPTS

Computer programming languages are composed of a defined list of commands and symbols which can be combined, according to rules of grammar (or syntax), into a sequence of logical statements to form a computer program. This written program is known as source code (see 9.4.1) and, before the computer can execute it and before the user can use it, it must be fed into the computer's memory (and stored as machine code).

Although there is a wide variety of computer programming languages (see below), with different vocabularies and syntax, there are underlying concepts which are common to all of them. These concepts refer to the manner in which a language frames the basic logical structure of a computer program. The concepts include the procedures which enable sequence, repetition and decision.

(a) Sequence

All programs follow an ordered sequence. The sequence is usually a top-down event. In other words, the program starts at the first line of the program's code and works its way through to the last line. In addition the computer executes each line of code according to the logical direction of the program.

(b) Repetition

From time to time program users or the programmer will want to re-use a particular program or part of a program or repeat a particular task. In order to do this the program language must be able to support a repetition construct. The type of computer coded statement which might execute this type of action could appear as follows:

REPEAT PAY_CALC UNTIL STAFF_RECORDS = 0

PAY_CALC is a block of code, otherwise known as a subroutine, which calculates the individual worker's pay packet. A subroutine might be a part of a program or a program in its own right. In this instance the REPEAT/UNTIL command is simply a way of instructing the computer to repeat the PAY_CALC routine until there are no more STAFF_RECORDS left.

(c) Decision

The decision facility within a particular program allows options for the user to control the direction and manner of a computer program's execution. For example, an accounting program may have a subroutine enabling the user to issue warning letters to customers who have exceeded their individual credit limit. The type of computer coded statement which might implement this type of decision could appear as follows:

IF SPENT CREDIT_LIMIT THEN PRINT WARNING

where SPENT is a memory location which contains the amount spent by the customer and where CREDIT_LIMIT equals the customer's actual credit limit. WARNING would be that document printed by the appropriate section of code if the statement was found to be true.

9.4 LOW-LEVEL COMPUTER LANGUAGES

Computer programming languages are split into two main categories, known as low-level and high-level languages. Within these two categories there are what is commonly known as language generations. As the language generations evolve so we get *versions* of particular languages.

The lower the level of the language the closer the language is to the computer's requirements; the higher the level, the closer it is to human requirements and the nature of the problem for which the program is designed.

9.4.1 Machine code

Low-level languages usually refer to machine code and assembly language. Machine code is basically a binary coded language consisting of 1s and 0s. It was the original and indeed only programming language of the first computers and a program written in machine code mirrors the hardware configuration of the system. It is often described as a first-generation language. Unfortunately it is a very difficult and cumbersome language to manipulate. However whilst it is no longer used as a mainstream programming language it is the language of the computer itself. As a result all instructions received by the computer must, one way or another, be translated into machine code in order that the computer can operate. Programs written in a language other than machine code are frequently referred to as source code. Source code is usually translated into machine code by special translation software.

9.4.2 Assembly languages

In order to alleviate the arduous task of programming in machine code developers began to produce more intuitive languages. The first of these was assembly language. It was an immediate spin-off from machine code and is consequently classified as a second-generation language.

Assembly language differed from machine code in that it employed symbolic names or mnemonics to represent computer operations. For instance, instead of writing 01011 (say) for multiply in machine code, assembly language allowed MULT in program statements. Computer programmers were able to raise their productivity levels. However, despite certain advantages, assembly languages do have some severe limitations. For example, they are usually developed for a particular processor and are consequently tied to a specific computer range. As a result, assembly language programs are not, as a rule, transferable.

Assembly language programmers tend to be more concerned with optimising the internal processing tasks of the computer or the operation of a microprocessor-based system used, say, for control purposes; it is a language favoured by engineers therefore. In this respect, the machine-specific functions of an assembly language are ideal. However this is a radically different task to that being performed by a creative application programmer. In order to devise useful task-led applications, programmers have to employ high-level languages.

9.5 HIGH-LEVEL COMPUTER LANGUAGES

The majority of contemporary high-level programming languages are portable (transferable between different computers), task-oriented and English-like in construct. They are also known as problem-oriented languages because they allow programs to be tailored to suit the problem not the computer configuration and to be structured clearly into subroutines, etc. to keep the logic flow uncluttered.

Most computer programs written with a high-level language are translated into machine code via specialist software known as compilers or interpreters. The difference between a *compiler* and an *interpreter* is that a compiler creates a machine code file from the original source code which the computer then executes, whilst an interpreter takes an original source file and interprets/executes each line at a time.

The majority of blue chip PC application software developers prefer to use compilers to distribute their particular program (this might however be about to change – see 9.8.1 Java). The reason is that the compiled machine code file can usually be distributed as an independent executable file. In other words, there is no need to supply potential purchasers with the original source code. In addition, because the object code file is extremely difficult to decipher, it prevents outside parties from being able to tamper with or pirate the original software.

9.5.1 Third-generation languages

The first group of high-level computer programming languages, known as third-generation languages (3GLS), are the most widely used of all programming languages. There are dozens of different types of 3GLS, many of which have been developed for particular applications or disciplines. Some of them are designed for scientific use whilst others are aimed at the business community. Among the most common of these languages are COBOL, BASIC, Pascal, C and C++.

(a) COBOL

COBOL (Common Business Oriented Language) was first developed in conjunction with the US Navy in the early 1960s. Originally designed as an all-round business data processing language, COBOL is viewed by computer professionals as a verbose and cumbersome language.

However despite its age and the advance of more sophisticated programming languages, COBOL is still widely used in the commercial world. It is a relatively straightforward language which is particularly suitable for processing mass data files such as payroll, sales orders, invoicing and so forth. In addition, a substantial volume of the source code of corporate software systems were written with COBOL. As a result the language has made something of a comeback as organisations seek to maintain and upgrade their software systems and to deal with the millennium date change.

(b) BASIC

BASIC (Beginners All Purpose Instruction Code) was originally developed in the early 1960s in order to teach computer programming. It has however been transformed from its initial version and is widely used by education and commerce. The Microsoft Visual Basic Professional for Windows, a best-selling PC application in 1997, is considered to be just about one of the most powerful computer programming languages ever devised.

(c) Pascal

Where BASIC was designed to convey the concepts of programming, Pascal was designed to teach structured programming. Structured programming is aimed at encouraging good programming techniques. These techniques include the performance of tasks and functions by clearly defined blocks of computer code as well as the close control of data passing through the program. Pascal's emphasis on subroutine structures known as procedures, and its rigorous data definitions, make it an ideal vehicle for structured programming (see below). Modula and Ada are languages of the same type.

(d) C, C+, C++

Formulated at the Bell Laboratories in the USA in the early 1970s, C was initially developed to enable systems/application programming for Unix. It is considered by many users to be a hybrid language. For example, C's structure is such that it is relatively friendly and easy to use, but it also contains certain utility features that are common to assembly languages. C is also a very mobile language which enables users to produce programs that are compatible (with minimum adjustment) with a host of different computers and OSs. C+ and C++ differ from C only in their range of features/utilities. C++ is particularly suited for graphic-intensive computer programming and has proved to be remarkably successful in the corporate sector.

9.5.2 Fourth-generation languages

Despite their versatility, 3GL languages do pose some considerable problems. Firstly modern 3GLs have a vast array of functions and commands and can, as a consequence, involve potential programmers in a steep learning curve. As a result there tends to be a constant shortage of the right people with the right skills. Secondly there is more often than not a considerable time period required by developers employing 3GLs for medium or large-scale application development. Software projects tend to be almost open ended and their delivery is often very difficult to predict. This delay is very frustrating and significant bottlenecks can occur when developers fail to satisfy demand. In order to counter these and other problems a new and disparate range of computer languages known as fourth-generation languages (4GLs) were developed. Some of them were designed for team-working on larger systems.

What actually constitutes a 4GL has caused considerable angst amongst the computing fraternity. For example, many IT specialists view 4GLs as user-oriented programming languages designed to enable the development of database applications. A good example might be SQL (Standard Query Language). This is an industry-standard 4GL which uses simple English commands to interrogate databases.

Another example of a 4GL type application includes those programming languages known as natural languages. Natural languages are designed to enable the user to communicate with the computer in what could be considered as almost a two-way human dialogue, prompting and questioning the user as well as providing relevant answers. Other commonly held relevant 4GL language characteristics include a restricted vocabulary, helpful screens and useful error messages. 4GLs also usually only require a minimum amount of technical knowledge on behalf of the user and are basically designed to enable inexperienced users to manipulate and use the computer without undue delay.

In addition, 4GLs unlike 3GLs are also what is known as non-procedural languages. The difference between a procedural and a non-procedural language is that with a procedural language (most 3GLs) the programmer has to be very precise and has to specify a detailed sequence of instructions. With a non-procedural language the programmer/user simply outlines their requirements and the application generates the appropriate code. For example a 4GL user could create an appropriate input screen by simply moving data items across a computer screen. When the screen was finished, the 4GL would construct the required computer code in order to make the screen appear.

4GLs have had a considerable amount of success in improving programmer productivity; however, they can lack depth and detail and professional applications usually have to be augmented by subroutines written in 3GL format. In addition 4GLs can be expensive to operate as they usually require computers with considerably more processing power than required by a 3GL. Also, compiler programs for 4GLs can be massive undertakings.

A revealing portrayal of the increasing sophistication of computer languages is shown in figure 9.1 – each generation simplifies the instructions and aspires to normal English.

9.5.3 Prolog

Prolog was first launched in the early 1970s but is recognised as coming to particular prominence with the arrival of Borland's Turbo Prolog language application. It is often thought of as being a fifth-generation language.

Technically speaking Prolog is not too dissimilar from 3GL/4GL languages. Prolog enables the production of programs which are more in tune with the manner in which human beings reason in that, essentially, Prolog programs manipulate large numbers of facts and rules in order to

Fourth Generation 4GLs	Third Generation (High-level languages)	Second Generation (Assembly language)	First Generation (Machine code)
JOIN RECORDS	A=B+C+D	MOVE B,R1	0001 001100 000010
		ADD C,R1	0110 010100 000001
		ADD D,R1	0101 001110 000010
		MOVE R1,A	0111 000001 001111
			1010 010110 010101
			1100 110110 100110

Fig 9.1
(Courtesy: Yeates, Shields, Helmy, *Systems Analysis and Design*, Financial Times Pitman Publishing)

reach decisions or conclusions. As with some 4GLs, Prolog is a declarative (non-procedural) language which promotes an instinctive level of abstraction and is recognised as a move away from conventional number/data processing. It is closely associated with Artificial Intelligence (AI) projects and is used extensively in the development of professional expert systems.

9.5.4 Hypertext markup language

Hypertext Markup Language (HTML) is that language used by programmers to create Web pages for the Internet. It is also used for creating Intranet systems. HTML not only allows users to compose the various text data required for the actual screen but also enables users to insert various instructions (Uniform Resource Locators URLs) linking a particular Web page to other pages on the WWW.

9.6 APPLICATION DEVELOPMENT

The specialists that actually write computer programs are usually known as application programmers. Computer programmers that adapt or maintain current programs are usually referred to as maintenance programmers. A significant number of computer programmers work on short-term contracts. For example, a team of application programmers could be employed to create a particular application such as a payroll system. When the task is completed and the payroll system is up and running so their contract comes to an end. Because of this and other factors, employing application programmers to build a particular application can be an extremely expensive option. As a result the overwhelming majority of computer users tend to employ ready-made software applications made by corporate software houses.

Ready-made or, as they are sometimes known, off-the-shelf software applications are two of the terms used to describe those computer programs that can be purchased and which are ready to use as soon as they are installed. Ready-made applications are usually created by teams of computer programmers working in specialist companies known as software houses. The number of programmers employed to produce a particular software application varies. A small unsophisticated application may be developed by a handful of programmers whereas a complex professional application can involve hundreds if not thousands of programmers. Notwithstanding the difference in scale it should be noted that the majority of competent business computing applications follow the same development format (see 9.6.2).

9.6.1 Development bottlenecks

It is true to say that high-level programming languages have enabled software developers to raise their productivity levels. However as computers have become ever more powerful so users are beginning to demand applications which are even more sophisticated. Such needs are not always satisfied by off-the-shelf ready-made applications. As a result users often have no choice but to invest in their own expensive software development projects.

In addition, because application development is a very time-consuming project, western programmers/developers have discovered that increased global commercial competition has meant a considerable intensification in pressure from users/organisations to develop applications with the minimum of delay. Unfortunately, throwing extra resources into software projects employing dozens, if not hundreds, of programmers/IT experts may not be the solution and can prove counterproductive. In order to try and relieve some of the development pressures whilst simultaneously producing suitable applications, software developers employ what are known as structured programming methodologies (see 9.6.3).

9.6.2 Phases and techniques in application development

Computer programs usually contain a series of various operations and can be incredibly complex to write and understand. In order to minimise confusion, and to streamline application development, software houses and professional programmers employ various techniques or methodologies. The following is simply an overview of some of the phases and techniques found in a typical program development life cycle.

(a) Program specification

A program specification is the term usually applied to that documentation spelling out the tasks to be fulfilled by a particular piece of software. The level of detail is dependent on the programmer's work practice. It could simply contain basic input/output criteria or it could be a specific blueprint outlining the program's exact structure. In either case, the main aim of the program specification is to give the programmer a clear and unambiguous mission in order to produce a program that meets the user's requirements.

(b) Diagrams

In order to gain an overview of all the tasks to be performed by a computer program, programmers usually employ various diagrammatic techniques. This usually involves depicting all the various functions and data transformations in a visual format. A *program flowchart* using standard symbols is a diagrammatic representation of the sequence of operations required in the program. A *system diagram* or *data flow diagram* shows the relationships required between the data and the processes that work on the data. Other diagrams show the connections between the various types of data required by the application problem. In addition they act as useful reference points for the programmer and the potential user in the event of any crucial misunderstanding.

(c) Decision tables

Decision tables enable the programmer to decompose the various processes into simple steps which can be transformed into computer code with the minimum of effort. For example, the outcome of many processes is determined by a series of simple decision steps (e.g. yes/no steps); depending on the outcome, certain actions then follow; decision tables clearly display all the options.

(d) Pseudo-code

Pseudo-code, sometimes referred to as structured English, is simply a way of describing the processes of a computer program in a methodical and elementary format. The idea is to transform the tasks and functions as highlighted in various documents and/or diagrams into a comprehensive

English-like description prior to actually writing the computer source code. The main advantage of using pseudo-code is that it allows the programmer to collate, check and cross-reference all the necessary processes and tasks. This detailed description is then used by the programmer as the template for writing the actual program, usually in a 3GL.

(e) Coding conventions

Many IT specialists consider the actual writing of the computer code to be a mechanical process. This can be a fairly accurate perception provided all the necessary functions and tasks required of the program have been fully analysed and specified. However, despite the apparent routine task of coding there are some useful conventions used by programmers. These conventions include the use of relevant file/memory location names, appropriate indentation highlighting program control, and comments within the program annotating what particular parts of the program are actually doing. The main advantage of such conventions lies in enabling programmers to fully understand what the code is actually instructing the computer to do.

(f) Testing

Before a computer application is released for general use it must be fully tested. In order to adequately test a program, the programmer must pass specious as well as valid data through the program. However program testing is a controversial issue within the software industry as many programs are so complex that it is practically impossible to test them for every possible data input combination and for every possible outcome.

However, a carefully designed test plan should detect syntax errors, simple logical errors, run-time errors, etc. and generally debug the program.

(g) Documentation

Documentation is the final stage of a program's development life cycle. The actual documentation usually falls into two distinct categories. The first category concerns the composition and parameters of the application's code and any other relevant technical development data; it is essentially intended for program maintenance and directed at the computer professional. This documentation is usually created by the application's programmers. The second category of documentation can be loosely described as user documentation. This usually includes details concerning the application's setup and implementation procedures as well as the user manual(s). Because this type of documentation is distributed with the applications it is usually the responsibility of specialist documentation experts known as technical authors.

(h) Feedback

Constructive feedback on the performance of a software application is critical to programmers and developers. For example, user feedback enables the programmers to make any necessary corrections or adjustments to any errors which were not discovered during testing. Feedback also enables the application's developers to consider possible advances or additional features and utilities which would enhance the application.

Unfortunately, because modern mainstream computer applications are so complex, many application shortcomings are not discovered until the application goes on general release. The ensuing publicity can cause the companies concerned heavy financial penalties such as lost sales revenues. In order to combat this, most of the big companies dispense thousands of beta versions of their products prior to final release. *Beta versions* of an application are programs that represent the finished product or as near to the finished product as possible at the time of issue.

The main idea behind the beta version launch is to enable professional users and other approved corporate/business customers to evaluate the program and to pass confidential comments on possible alterations. By following this procedure, most of the major problems can be resolved prior to the application's final release.

(i) Update

Because of the ever-changing demands of the customer and ever-advancing new technology, there will come a stage in an application's life cycle where it has to be either substantially upgraded or totally replaced.

The degree of modification or change depends on prevailing circumstances. However when a mainstream commercial application is modified, it is normally augmented with a version number. For example, an application when first released might be called Module 1.0. A follow-up version, which is practically identical to the original release but which contains (say) extra printing facilities would, as a rule, be called Module 1.1. If, however, the next release was radically different from its predecessor it would be called Module 2.0.

This type of numbering system alerts potential users as to the nature of their knowledge/hardware requirements. If the version number change is fractional then it is more than likely that the user's current knowledge and hardware are more than adequate. If, however, the version change consists of a whole number, then this usually suggests a very different program. So different, it is possible that the updated application may not be able to support or interface with the data files or hardware as used by the previous version without certain technical adjustments/upgrade. For example, file structures may have to be changed, RAM size increased or even a change in the OS.

9.6.3 Structured programming

Early computer programs were usually created by independent individuals for use on isolated computers. The programs themselves were relatively simple and consequently easy to maintain, nevertheless they were usually designed in an undisciplined format. This lack of discipline meant that software disasters were common, but because of the limited nature of the damage, e.g. failure in payroll program, they were almost accepted as being part of the scene.

However as the same computer software became increasingly complex whilst simultaneously entering a wider market so commerce began to require a more disciplined approach to programming. This demand for a new and more rigorous style was not only fuelled by numerous software catastrophes but also by the recognition of the need to produce logically sound applications which could be understood, developed and maintained by programmers other than the original authors. As a result of this pressure, various programming systems known collectively as structured programming methodologies began to appear. The main significance of structured programming methodologies is that they place particular emphasis on program design.

Two of the techniques which are central to the concept of structured programming are the design of independent program modules, and iterative walkthroughs.

(a) Independent program modules

The most striking and useful concept of structured programming is that of the independent program module. Sophisticated applications can require tens of thousands if not millions of lines of code. Because of the sequential nature of most computer languages and computer programming, modern software systems can consist of long, almost immeasurable columns of computer code. However, if the programmers have failed to structure the code in an appropriate manner, the program(s) will, almost certainly, be prone to error and the programmers will lose control of the program simply because it has become so complex.

In order to combat this spaghetti-type programming, structured programmers decompose the full program into independent program modules. The idea is that these modules perform a single or a specific range of functions. Prior to all the various modules being connected into a full blown application each of the modules are tested in their own right. For example, the programmer might write a specific module to deal with the application's printing routines. The point is that, if the print routine failed, then the programmer would not have to wade through the whole program but simply deal with that particular module in order to correct the error.

Another major advantage of modularising computer code in this manner is that it enables the programmer to re-use the same block of code throughout the program. For example a module which is responsible for constructing the screen can be used by the programmer time and time again.

Modular construction favours programming teams.

(b) Iterative walkthroughs

In order to minimise potential shortcomings, such as a lack of functions or inaccurate processing procedures, structured computer programmers place a significant stress on feedback from potential users as well as from colleagues or other co-workers. This is usually accomplished by exposure of the user to the various stages of an application's development by encouraging them to walk through the various routines with the programmers so they might be able to give the programmers an objective evaluation of the work to date. Walkthroughs of this nature are often described as iterative walkthroughs, which is simply a recognition of the fact that such a technique usually has to be practised over and over again until the programmers produce a satisfactory application. They are also called dry runs. The obvious strategy behind such a technique is to enable the programmers to produce a program which will meet the users' requirements.

9.6.4 Software prototyping

An application development technique which is becoming increasingly popular with developers/programmers is known as software prototyping. Software prototyping is the term given to that technique whereby programmers produce functionally limited versions of a particular software application. As a result, prototype programs are typically shell-like in form. In other words they are usually relatively unsophisticated applications frequently featuring just the screen formats and menus expected to appear at the user interface in the final product. Not surprisingly programmers can produce prototype software much faster than normal application software as the detailed programming is left to a later stage.

Prototyping has several major benefits. Firstly programmers can produce inexpensive demonstration applications in a remarkably short space of time and consequently enable the user to consider the particular merits of a software project before any major commitment is decided upon. Secondly prototyping enhances the user's understanding of the program under development and enables them to settle on the tasks that the finished program is expected to perform. Thirdly the work invested in a prototype application is rarely wasted as it becomes, more often than not, the foundation structure for the final application.

9.7 END USER DEVELOPERS

In view of current technological changes, non-specialist end users are beginning to play a far more active role in the development of the applications that they use. The arrival of user-friendly 4GLs and other similar software development tools has resulted in end users being able to create sophisticated applications without having to constantly refer to programmers or other expensive IT professionals. This approach has several major advantages. End user developers are able to program their own computers so they are more likely to produce applications which satisfy their particular processing requirements. What is more, end user developers can alleviate possible organisational IT bottlenecks by taking on some organisational application development.

Various studies have also shown that many end user developers can produce applications far quicker than conventional programmers. One reason for this is that most end user development is done through the use of 4GLs and other high productivity tools. However there is a sting in the tail as it is believed that another common and more damning reason for this rapid application development is the slipshod manner in which the applications are actually produced. For example professional programmers spend considerable time carefully designing the programs prior to coding. In contrast end user developers tend to dive straight in and start coding straight away. As a result, end user applications tend to be unstructured and riddled with errors. In addition they can lack certain critical basics such as user documentation or programming features such as data validation routines or user security procedures such as password control.

End user development can also play havoc with an organisation's overall information/computer strategy as various departments and users within the organisation create applications which are invariably totally incompatible with each other. However in spite of these limitations, end user development is becoming increasingly popular. The fact is that professional programmers are costly and simply beyond the resources of many users. Simple decision support type applications such as spreadsheet models or database interrogators, developed in house by non-specialist staff, may not be ideal but they can, and often do, prove to be a viable working alternative to more costly software projects.

9.8 OBJECT ORIENTED SOFTWARE

Object Oriented Languages (OOLs) enable programmers to develop programs made up of a collection of objects. An object consists of a related set of data *and also* the operations that are permissible on that data; the objects making up a program pass messages between each other or receive messages input by the system user. Thus, an object oriented system is a network of interconnected self-contained objects. They are often stored in the form of tables.

To illustrate the nature of objects, take the manufacture of a range of retail products. Each product can be recorded as an object which specifies its design specification, raw materials required, manufacturing resources required, and projected production demand. If a situation suddenly arose where the demand for one of the products outstripped its projected demand, then additional raw materials would be needed. Passing suitable messages to other relevant product objects could elicit information which would help to establish which of the other products could release suitable raw materials.

OOLs were first developed in the 1960s but because of their processing requirements they were considered somewhat expensive. However the current advent of relatively cheap modern powerful computers and the increased use of Windows style OSs have resulted in an upsurge in the use of this type of programming language.

OOLs are considered to have certain critical advantages over rival conventional computer languages. For example, the use of objects enables programmers to represent processes and actions in a more realistic and intelligible manner. Applications produced using OOLs can more accurately portray factual situations. In addition, applications built on OOLs structures are more robust and less likely to fail. OOLs also enable programmers to reduce the time spent on coding since an object, once coded, can, where appropriate, be reused time and time again. As a result, OOLs enhance rapid application development as OOL programmers take advantage of the growing object code archives which enable them to use ready-made tried-and-tested programs.

OOLs are particularly well suited for producing sophisticated commercial applications such as Object Oriented Databases (OODs – see Chapter 10) and current trends suggest that OOL application development is gradually beginning to move to centre stage. The growing popularity of OOLs is such that they are expected to eventually replace other conventional computer languages in the development of mainstream commercial applications. However this replacement is expected to be a long-term process because of the heavy investment commerce has in terms of current conventionally developed applications and the lack of OOL programmers.

9.8.1 Java

One of the fastest, if not the fastest, growing OOL programming language of the late 1990s is Java. Devised by Sun Microsystems it is, in effect, a derivation of C++ and is believed to have been originally developed to program the microprocessors inside domestic appliances. The reason for its sudden success centres on two critical features.

Firstly Java is a multiplatform language that can run on virtually any computer. The reason for this is that programs authored using the Java programming language are not released like ordinary software applications but are, instead, distributed in a special byte code. Users who wish to access a particular Java program do so by running what is in effect an interpreter which converts the Java byte code into a fully functioning application. Sun Microsystem's Java interpreter application is known as the Java Machine. Its main attribute is that it occupies only a small part of the computer's memory and can be incorporated into practically any computer. Various versions of the Java Machine are currently being released for most major OSs. Versions of the Java Machine are also being incorporated into top of the range Web browsers. In other words, even the very programs that users employ to navigate the WWW are capable of translating Java programs into meaningful instructions.

Secondly Java enables programmers to place multimedia objects such as video, sound, animation and applets (mini Java applications) onto otherwise static web pages. Users of a home banking system could, for example, go to the foreign currency screen and click on an icon representing the dollar. A small Java application embedded in the screen could then check the current exchange rate so giving the user immediate and up to date information.

The significance of the versatility of the Java programming language means that Java application developers can promote their products in what is a practically unrestricted market as they are no longer tied to the OS or architecture of any particular range of computers. This versatility in conjunction with its multimedia tools makes it highly suitable for developing applications on the Internet/network market.

At the time of writing the full magnitude of Java has yet to be fully assessed but its arrival is viewed by some industry commentators as being a seismic event in the computing industry. Whether this is an exaggeration or not, only time will tell. However, the arrival of a programming language which can run on almost any computer linked to the Internet, independent of that particular computer's OS, is certain to cause shock waves as well as enable Sun Microsystems to wield an inordinate amount of power within the computer industry.

9.9 APPLICATION TRENDS

As the price of computer processing power has decreased so the cost of developing sophisticated software which takes advantage of this cheaper capacity has started to rise. Professional mass market software applications can be particularly expensive to produce. For example developing a new OS could easily involve hundreds and hundreds of expensive programmers. In order to try and recoup some of these costs, software developers are beginning to follow certain critical trends:

(a) Mobility

Most commercial developers are concentrating on software projects which centre on mobile computer applications. An application which is considered mobile usually possesses certain critical characteristics. For example the application should be able to run on multiple OSs. In addition the application should enable a user to employ the application regardless of the class of computer they are currently using.

(b) Graphical user interface

The software market of the late 1990s indicates that the overwhelming influence of OSs such as Windows has resulted in applications of every description employing GUI technology. Surveys indicate that users have a strong preference to using programs employing GUI techniques. Icons, pop-up menus and a mouse-driven interface are considered far more intuitive and friendly than a terse text-based environment.

One emerging specific graphical feature of contemporary software products is that of spatial navigation. The concept of spatial navigation concerns those applications which enable users to access necessary information by allowing them to interact with a realistic screen-based model/map of the current system. For example users can access library programs by pointing at books on shelves or they can access details on car engines by pointing at particular parts.

(c) Data interchange

Because of the proliferation of business applications, the arrival of multi-tasking OSs and the need to integrate information in a host of different

187

environments, users require programs which support sophisticated data interchange facilities. As a result developers are producing applications which can not only transfer data within its own boundary of programs, but can also, when required, transfer data between itself and other applications. Two common features which enable this activity are data conversion and data linking.

Data conversion is that process whereby applications are able to convert the data files of other programs into a compatible arrangement. For example a user may receive a data file which is a wordprocessed document created by an application other than the one the user is currently using. In order to use the file it is necessary that the user's application has a menu option which allows the file to be read straight into their program or that the application has a utility feature which allows them to physically convert the file into a useable format. The latter technique usually results in the user accessing an import option. Conversely, when users wish to send their data file to a program other than the one they are currently using, they will often employ an export option, so making the file compatible with the receiving program.

Data linking is concerned with the transfer of active data between particular applications. For example a user employing a Windows-based spreadsheet application may be editing various cells, the result of which simultaneously transforms a graph which is currently visible in another window. This type of action, sometimes referred to as a hot link, can be found on applications running on a Windows multitasking configuration. Applications which enable this facility support an attribute known as Dynamic Data Exchange (DDE). Less sophisticated software applications which update connecting applications as soon as the user leaves their current program are usually operating in what is known as a single-task OS.

(d) Help systems

Software purchasers, private and corporate, are realising that essential user requirements such as software training and software technical support can prove to be very expensive. In order to entice purchasers to their products, developers are adding in-built tutorials to their application menus. Most in-built tutorials act as ice breakers enabling a novice user to get a basic appreciation of a particular application. In addition, many developers are including intelligent Help systems. For example, when users enter erroneous commands in some applications, they are provided with practical error messages informing them of a more appropriate course of action. Other features which are beginning to become the norm include comprehensive indexes and drip-fed tips, the likes of which appear briefly in order that they may gradually increase the user's application expertise without overwhelming them with information.

9.9.1 The games market

One computer software market which appears to be expanding at an almost exponential rate is the games market. Contemporary estimates suggest that the games market is currently worth about thirty billion US$. The games market also appears to be shifting towards the PC as CD-ROM applications take over from cartridge type systems. The main reason for this is simply cost. CD-ROMS are cheap to produce and can store significant amounts of data. The technology to drive the CD-ROM is basically built into the PC and the CD-ROM drive. In contrast, games cartridges can be rather complex devices containing several megabytes of memory chips along with graphic processors. As a result, cartridge-driven games tend to be far more expensive than their CD-ROM competitors and many purchasers appear to be favouring PC game systems as opposed to those applications which can only be accessed via purpose-built devices.

9.10 COMMON BUSINESS APPLICATIONS

Most users have discovered that the price and quality of computer business applications vary according to the technology employed and the profile of the customer market. For example CMS type software running on mainframe computers is usually far more expensive and far more robust than the software found on a SOHO type PC. However such price and quality differences are not as acute as they once were. Two reasons for this are the sharp rise in the standard and quantity of corporate PC software development and the arrival of industry-standard applications which are capable of being supported on a variety of computer configurations, large and small.

With respect to the actual choice of developers most PC users are aware of the overwhelming domination of companies such as Microsoft and Lotus both of which control a disproportionate share of the PC software market. Microsoft as the world's leading PC software developer has developed a unique reputation in combating potential competition by reverse engineering their rival's more successful products and, where necessary, flooding the market with their particular version. As a result users often end up with a Microsoft equivalent product which is usually cheaper and more effective than that provided by the original developer. What is more, even when Microsoft has not been able to emulate a particular product it has often reacted by simply buying their rival out.

However despite certain technological and economic advances, users know that choosing a particular application can be fraught with difficulties. For example, most software purchasers are only too aware that there is usually a multitude of alternatives to their specific requirement. Selecting the optimum alternative can prove a forbidding exercise. In order therefore to pick a suitable application users must consider factors other than the individual nature of the product. These other factors can include the application's compatibility with current equipment and applications, network capabilities, licensing restrictions, overall security consequences, and help and service provision.

9.10.1 Shopping list

Users poring through computer magazines know that there are currently many thousands of business-oriented computer applications available on the open market. Some applications, such as wordprocessors, are non-specific tools, whilst others, such as share pricing systems, are specialist applications which concentrate on particular industries.

Throughout these lists of computer applications two features have emerged. Firstly, as with other products, there are best-selling applications which, according to contemporary demand, move up and down various sales league tables. Secondly there are companies, such as Microsoft, Computer Associates and IBM, who market a wide range of high quality computing applications and who do, in effect, dominate much of the software market. The reason for such dominance has, for the most part, been because of their ability to produce software products which are effective, presentable, and relatively reliable. In addition, because of their ability to produce successful applications, a lot of the original products have been constantly revamped and updated. As a result, many software products are beginning to move down the computing generations.

Microsoft in particular has also proved adept at a marketing technique known as the cross-collateralisation of products. What this means in effect is that Microsoft produces software applications that enhance its other software applications. When these software applications are taken *en masse* they provide users with an invaluable software platform.

What follows is a brief listing of some common contemporary business applications, along with the trademark/logo of a few of the more popular of these software products.

(a) Wordprocessors

The most commonly used computer application is undoubtedly the word-processor. It is the one major application that has proved to be an invaluable tool to all sections of the community. The purpose of this type of application is to enable the user to compose text files in a suitable and useful manner. Wordprocessors usually offer certain facilities such as spell check, thesaurus, font types, page layouts and various print options.

Because of improved technology the wordprocessors of the late 1990s bear little resemblance to the text editing applications that were available on earlier computers. Some wordprocessors are so advanced they can predict words about to be typed, check the grammar of a particular piece of text and provide graphic facilities the likes of which used to appear only in desktop publishing programs (DTP) and some even enable users to create pages for the WWW. In addition many blue chip wordprocessors, as with other top class applications, also enable the user to change the program's menus so that they appear in a foreign dialogue thus expanding the potential customer market. For example, French-speaking users of the program can tailor the program so that the various menus appear in their own language.

Interestingly, wordprocessing programs provide the classic example of the changing fortunes of applications in the software market. During the early 1980s applications such as Wordstar led the PC wordprocessing market. However the original Wordstar was built on DOS-based technology. When the Windows OS was launched the wordprocessing market changed course and DOS-based applications were soon being supplanted by Windows-oriented wordprocessors. The wordprocessing market in the late 1990s is currently dominated by applications such as Wordperfect, Microsoft's Word and Lotus Word.

(b) Spreadsheets

Contemporary spreadsheets are basically arithmetic grids which are capable of containing and manipulating millions of pieces of data. Spread-sheet applications enable users to build sophisticated data models the composition of which allow users to assess particular outcomes. For example, the user could build a spreadsheet which takes account of varying levels of interest payments and inflation and which could consequently predict an organisation's varying profitability. It is for this reason that spreadsheets are frequently classified as being a business decision tool. Interestingly the first mainstream computerised spreadsheet, Visicalc, was developed from concepts devised by the Harvard Business School.

During the mid 1980s Lotus 123 was generally considered to be the leading DOS-based PC spreadsheet. Its success was mainly due to the fact that it was seen to be a very friendly and useful application which not only allowed users to produce powerful spreadsheets but also enabled users to create simple but effective graphs. However Lotus lost their domination of the spreadsheet market when they decided to concentrate their future development efforts on OS/2 as opposed to Windows. As a result Microsoft were able to make major inroads in Lotus 123's market with the launch of their Windows-compatible spreadsheet Excel.

The spreadsheet market of the late 1990s is basically dominated by Excel and Lotus 123. Two other respectable contenders include Supercalc from Computer Associates and Quattro.

(c) Databases

See Chapter 10

(d) Desktop publishing

Desktop Publishing (DTP) applications are sophisticated text manipulation programs. They differ from wordprocessors in that they place particular emphasis on page layout and design as well as the ability to incorporate photo images and graphics within the page make-up. They are used in conjunction with high-quality output devices.

DTPs usually place considerable processing demands on the user's computer. For example DTP users employing inadequate or underpowered PCs soon discover their computer performing in a sluggish manner and, on occasion, the computer simply grinding to a halt. Even when employing a relatively powerful computer, DTP users can experience a certain reduction in response time.

Three of the most highly regarded DTPs are Aldus Pagemaker, Microsoft Publisher and Corel Ventura.

(e) Accounting

Computerised accounting systems have proved to be one of the most popular business applications. Modern accounting applications usually enable users to produce routine financial statements such as balance sheets, profit and loss accounts and VAT/TAX returns without the need to refer to accounting experts. Other regular features of modern accounting systems include invoicing, stock control, payroll and statements.

The number of features available in a particular accounting system depends on the particular application. For example some accounting users require a whole range of sophisticated routines whilst other users need only a simple book-keeping program. As a result, many business/accounting software developers offer users a range of products, otherwise known as an application suite.

One of the most popular PC accounting application suites in the late 1990s is that offered by the Sage series. The Sage suite offers users the opportunity to purchase basic, less expensive accounting programs as well as the more up-market full-blown applications such as Sage's best-selling Sage Financial Controller.

A leading accounting application for Unix-based systems is the Chameleon range from Tetra. Tetra Chameleon was particularly successful as it deliberately planned to present users with a congenial interface which enabled them to make full use of the application as well as enabling the user to integrate the application with other complex business applications.

(f) Drawing/Art

DTPs are excellent for page layout but are usually deficient when it comes to creating drawings, artwork, etc. However there are numerous applications that fill this gap and which enable the user to create the graphics which are then exported to the DTP.

One highly successful application is Corel Draw. It enables users to produce sophisticated drawings/artwork and to access large ready-made clip art libraries. Another best-selling popular drawing application is Visio. This application is particularly useful for flowchart type diagrams.

(g) Presentation software

Presentation software enables users to employ sophisticated graphics to create standalone PC-based side shows. Users of presentation software are usually able to project these side shows on output devices other than the PC. Such devices include TV monitors and video projectors as well as liquid crystal display panels on overhead projectors. Other features common to this type of application include the ability to prepare and print audience handouts like slide reprints and notes.

Two leading packages in this field are Corel Presents and Lotus Freelance.

(h) Project software

Project software is that term used to describe project management applications.

Project management software usually supports control techniques such as Gannt charts, Pert Charts and Critical Path Analysis required in large and complex undertakings particularly in civil engineering.

Each technique requires the undertaking to be subdivided into identifiable tasks. The Gannt chart concentrates on the time allowed and the time taken for the tasks; Pert charts concentrate on the interdependency of the tasks; and CPA identifies the critical path and the tasks on it, and any delay in these tasks delays the whole project. Such techniques are 'naturals' for computerisation.

Two of the more successful user-friendly project applications are Microsoft Project and CA-SuperProject from Computer Associates.

(i) Groupware

Groupware refers to those software applications which allow clusters of workers (workgroups) to concentrate on the same task irrespective of their physical location. Lotus Notes is a leading industry-standard application particularly suited to this type of activity. With Lotus Notes the user is provided with an application that includes an electronic mail system, a database and a bulletin board. An application such as Lotus Notes can be described as a distributed document database. Workgroups employed on groupware activity function on the basis that organisations centre their activities on documents not data. Workflow is the term used to describe information/data moving within the workgroup.

(j) Integrated office software suites

Integrated Office Software Suites usually refers to those software packages which are composed of a combination of individual applications. These packages include a range of programs such as a spreadsheet, word-processor, database, DTP/presentation program, electronic mail, personal organiser/diary as well as a front menu system enabling the user to switch between the various applications. Applications such as these are considered central to the concept of what is commonly referred to as Office Automation Software (OAS).

Software suites of this type have proved to be extremely popular. Firstly users find that because the applications are from the same developer there is normally a uniformity in the manner in which menus/commands are accessed. Secondly these suites are usually designed so that they enable the user to integrate data between the various applications so allowing them to perform ever more sophisticated tasks. Thirdly they are usually competi-tively priced. For example many developers selling this type of package know that whilst a potential purchaser may be interested in buying their spreadsheet they may not be so interested in buying their wordprocessor or database application. In order to entice purchasers, developers usually retail Integrated Office Software Suites at a price which is considerably less than that which would be charged if all the applications were purchased on an individual basis.

Two of the most successful competing examples of this type of package are Microsoft Office for Windows 97 and Lotus Smartsuite 97 for Windows 95.

The Microsoft Office 97 suite includes Word which is a wordprocessor, Excel which is a spreadsheet, PowerPoint which is a presentation applica-tion, Access which is a relational database and Outlook which is a desktop information manager.

The Lotus Smartsuite 97 for Windows 95 includes the famous Lotus 123 spreadsheet, the Word Pro wordprocessor, Lotus Approach relational database, Freelance Graphics, a presentation program, and Lotus Organiser, which is described as a personal information manager (PIM).

(k) Development software

This is a term that can apply to a whole range of software applications. For example, computer languages such as C++ and Java can be described as development software as they are the means by which programmers produce the various programs. Equally, applications which require little technical expertise and which enable inexperienced users to create suitable applications, e.g. database interrogation programs, can also be described as development software.

(l) Internet browsers

Internet browsers is the term currently used to describe the user-friendly computer navigation applications which enable end users to access and traverse the WWW.

One company which is currently leading the way in this particular market is Netscape Communications. In many ways Netscape was to the mid 90s what Apple was in the 70s and early 80s and what Microsoft was in the 80s and early 90s. It was established in 1994 and did in fact experience spectacular success having grossed eighty million dollars in sales in its first year of trading. By the beginning of 1997 it was estimated to have a global base of forty million users.

One reason for its initial achievement was a clever marketing ploy. Netscape gave away its first viable version of its popular browser Netscape Navigator. As a result, Netscape was able to establish a major foothold in the browser market. At the same time Netscape was able to recover revenues by selling companies compatible software applications enabling them to set up WWW sites and services.

Netscape Navigator is currently believed to be the most popular browser in the world. It contains an array of sophisticated facilities including e-mail, HTML (Hypertext Markup Language), chat line functions, Java compatibility as well as useful text formatting and graphic functions and file import/export utilities.

Netscape however does not appear to be a company that is resting on its laurels. As well as bundling anti-virus software with their applications, version 3.0 caused a bit of a stir with the introduction of a software utility called Cooltalk. The idea behind Cooltalk allows users to avoid conventional telephone services by transporting telephone calls via the Internet.

The result of such an innovation is that users can talk to other suitably equipped users for the cost of a local phone call. The consequences of such a service have yet to surface but they are obviously very significant. However, Netscape's current market dominance has lessened greatly now that the giant of the PC software industry, Microsoft, has entered the browser market.

The latest version of Microsoft's browser at the time of writing is Internet Explorer 4.0. It places a particular emphasis on its use of multimedia and is designed to present the user with a single desktop interface. The latest version of Netscape's browser is known as Netscape Communicator. Observers believe the product is pitched at the corporate sector.

9.11 TIME BOMB YEAR 2000

As has been previously mentioned, many if not most contemporary mainframe/minicomputer CMS applications have been developed through the decades. The major advantage of this extended albeit sometimes inadvertent development life cycle has been the almost total elimination of software failure from most CMS type products. In fact it was this feature of CMS, that is the comprehensive reliability of the applications, which has deterred so many corporate users from downsizing to the smaller, cheaper systems. However, this could all be about to change with the arrival of the year 2000.

The problem is that the original creators of the initial source code of many of these CMS applications, many of which were started in the 1960s, did not foresee their software applications being used beyond the year 2000. The significance of this date is considerable and does in truth impact on the operation of the various program(s) within most CMS systems as well as other conventional software applications. The heart of the matter is the manner in which so many contemporary CMS applications store the date data. This date data is, for the most part, stored in a six-digit field. The consequence of such a simple action is that, as time passes, the numerical size of the date gets bigger and bigger. Using such a technique, the final date of the century is, in American format, 991231 (i.e. 31 December 1999). The first day of the 21st century is 000101. The latter date is numerically less than the former date, which means that a program geared to having subsequent dates at progressively higher values will, after the last day of the 20th century, be completely out of sync.

Unfortunately, this date problem is not one that can be easily remedied. One reason for this centres on the actual age of the programs. Because many of these programs are so old, governments, companies, developers and just about everybody else have lost the original source code. In other words, it is extremely difficult, if not impossible, to modify the programs. What is more it would appear that current users are not taking the problem as seriously as they should or even when they do take notice the evidence seems to suggest that they are simply ignoring it.

Having said this, governments and commerce are beginning to wake up to the situation and are beginning to take appropriate measures. These measures include the replacement of current CMS systems with new applications as well as the attempted modification of existing software. Companies and users are being advised to check all their current software and to ensure that new application purchases or developments can accommodate, or have already accommodated, the change in century. However such necessary actions are time consuming and exorbitantly expensive. It is has been estimated that the problem could cost the global economy hundreds of billions of dollars. The quandary faced by software users with the arrival of the year 2000 is literally a ticking time bomb.

9.12 CONCLUSION

Users know that computers are only as useful as the software they support. There appears to be an insatiable demand for increasingly sophisticated applications. Unfortunately such application development involves complex and expensive time-consuming activities. In order to streamline the development process, developers are employing improved programming methodologies. As well as this, users are beginning to indulge in end user development. However both of these activities have proved somewhat counterproductive. For example professional developers have discovered that improved software productivity has simply led to ever more user demands. In addition end user development has also resulted in a certain degree of chaos within organisations as the various departments produce applications which deal with their own particular information requirements.

Software developers have also realised that high quality applications are the key to any potential sales success. However, because quality software development is such a labour-intensive exercise, Western companies are beginning to reduce their overheads by outsourcing their software development requirements to low-wage economies. Countries such as India are particularly attractive. It has a large inexpensive English-speaking computer-literate workforce and as a consequence is beginning to make major incursions into the software market. The ramifications of such a trend have yet to be assessed as financial experts are beginning to realise that software applications are becoming crucial in the global economy.

10

Databases

10.1 INTRODUCTION

The main aim of this chapter is to discuss the purpose as well as the concept of a database and to give an overview of some of the various products and directions of contemporary database technology. Sections 10.2 and 10.3 are concerned with the composition and structure of a modern database system. Sections 10.4 through to 10.8 detail the various ways in which databases are controlled and organised. Sections 10.9 through to 10.12 detail emerging technologies and products whilst section 10.13 gives a snapshot of the current database market.

10.2 MODERN DATABASE SYSTEMS

Entrepreneurs and IT specialists alike know that good quality data is critical to the survival of the modern business. More often than not, this information is provided, directly or indirectly, by a specialist software application known as a database. Because of their success, databases and database technology have now become the dominant automated organiser of business-oriented information.

In the early days of computing a database was often described as a computerised record keeping system. As most early databases were card index type applications containing files of records storing simple data such as text and numbers, this was not such an unreasonable description. However unlike their predecessors the majority of modern commercial databases are much more than just a vehicle for automated filing. They are, because of their sophistication, intricate information systems capable of storing, retrieving and manipulating a host of complex data types ranging from sound, graphics, photo images to moving video. Furthermore modern databases can supply users with a host of ancillary services ranging from conventional transaction processing routines through to the delivery of sophisticated services such as VOD.

However it should be immediately noted that whilst there are converging concepts running through database technology there is a marked difference between the price and complexity of the various products currently available.

10.2.1 Differing products

Simple single-user desktop/PC database applications are usually relatively cheap and cost effective (see 10.11). Furthermore the use of these systems is usually restricted to single-user access. In contrast the establishment of a corporate database system which, for example, operates on multiple PCs or on a mini/mainframe configuration, and which permeates all the activities of a particular organisation, is usually a very expensive affair involving the commitment of substantial resources. Such a system will frequently be designed as a Central Data Store (CDS).

CDS is a term often used to loosely describe that situation where all the data pertaining to a particular database system is, from the point of view of the user, stored in one *logical* location, but where data addresses correspond to the physical position of the data. Although the database may be constructed in such a manner that the user is presented with an interface which integrates with one central data store, the actual data could be saved on a variety of data storage devices all in different physical locations. However what is even more significant is that this type of database will be subjected to multi-user access.

10.2.2 Multi-user access

As its name suggests, multi-user access means that more than one user can access the same database at the same time. Whilst such an attribute is obviously useful it can cause difficulties when users wish to alter the same particular record or data item. This is what is known as a concurrency clash. To preclude such a clash and in order to ensure data consistency it is necessary that the software contains routines which prevent this. These routines are usually contained within the Database Management System (DBMS), a suite of programs which monitor and control the database.

The function and quality of a DBMS differ according to each application. Databases which operate in a mainframe/mini environment usually use DBMS suites which provide full multi-user access capability as a matter of course. In contrast, users of a PC database in a multi-user situation which enables all the users to access the same CDS via a PC LAN will have to ensure that their application provides fully concurrency protection.

It should be pointed out that there are other significant differences between PC-centred databases and the larger systems. However, such differences are starting to blur as mainstream corporate database developers turn out scaleable products designed for the desktop/PC end of the market. Nevertheless, other than those sections which specifically deal with Distributed Databases (DDS) and PC database applications/systems, the reader should assume that the bulk of the text in this chapter is directed at corporate-sized CDS type databases.

10.3 PERCEIVING THE DATABASE

Modern databases often contain millions, if not billions, of bits of data. So that users can navigate and control this data, databases have to be organised in a disciplined and rigorous manner. How this is done does, to a large degree, depend on the technology being employed (see 10.4 and 10.5). However certain themes detailing data organisation and database views are relatively universal to the various systems.

10.3.1 Data organisation

It is best to think of a database as a large collection of data items with links between them. Both the data and any links must be constructed and organised according to formal rules that allow users to manipulate and navigate the data in a controlled manner.

Data can be of several *types*; the most commonly encountered is alphanumeric (letters, numerals, punctuation); logical, sound and video are other data types.

Each data item must be expressed within a specified length (number of bytes), the length depending on the nature of the computer and the database.

A *record* is the basic unit of data stored; it is a collection of data items, usually of mixed data types, each of which is a *field*. For instance, an individual record could be the details of a book held in a library and the fields could be the author's name, the date of publication, etc. One field usually uniquely identifies the record and is called the *key-field*.

A collection of data must be organised inside the computer; certain *data structures* are allowed for this such as lists, tables, strings, arrays and files, each having its own characteristics and use.

Links between data items can allow the user to conduct ordered data searches and retrieval, joining and selecting of data, multi-level searches, depending on the type of data structure.

Files are the most basic of data structures. They are composed of a series of identically structured records and accessed via a file name. The order in which records are stored in a file is a matter for the computer but because computers are designed to optimise their data storage routines, and as files are constantly updated and expanding and contracting in size, so it is unlikely that the user's records appear in a nicely ordered sequence on the storage media. Such data, more often than not, is scattered across the computer's disks/tapes.

A serially ordered file usually refers to a file of records which are stored and accessed in the order they were originally entered. In order, therefore, that the records inside a file might be placed in some form of ordered sequence, databases can create indexes. Sequentially organised files are usually serial files which are accessed in a particular order, alphabetic for example, via an index. In randomly ordered files part of the record contains a unique piece of data which, when processed through a special algorithm, gives the accessing program its physical location address within the database. For more on files, see 12.4.2.

10.3.2 Database views

Database views relate to the composite manner in which the developers actually plan, rationalise and control a database. These views are usually labelled as the conceptual view, the external view and the internal view.

The conceptual view is usually defined as the database's logical perspective and is the view which outlines the various data structures within the database and the manner in which they connect together.

The external view usually relates to that view employed by an outside end user such as an application programmer or any other operator or application which accesses part of the database. The main difference between the external view and the conceptual view is that the external view deals only with a specific part of the database, such as those data structures relevant to the end user's needs, whilst the conceptual view is concerned with the database in its entirety.

In contrast to the conceptual and external view, the internal view is concerned with the physical organisation of the database. The IT professionals concerned with the internal view usually includes programmers specialising in writing the program routines responsible for manipulating and storing the data and organising the data structures within the database.

10.4 ORTHODOX INFRASTRUCTURES

Information requirements differ widely from user to user and application to application. As a consequence the data structures required in customer databases, inventory databases, dating agency databases, police record databases, etc. are likely to be significantly different from each other. Whatever these requirements, it is essential to guarantee operational consistency, data integrity, search facilities appropriate to the application, reliable retrieval, etc. The database infrastructure determines how these requirements are fulfilled and applied in practice. There are three types of database infrastructure, known as hierarchical, network and relational.

(a) Hierarchical databases

In hierarchical databases, records are organised in layers whereby it is possible to penetrate down through the layers, by the links provided, in order to access successively more detailed information. In formal terms, the records in the database are referred to as nodes and each node is affiliated to other nodes by means of a father/son relationship. Each father node may have more than one son but no son node may have more than one father. The node at the top of the database is known as the root record (it could be 'known car thieves'). Because hierarchical databases usually consist of established relationships between the various nodes, and because these relationships must be redefined to handle unplanned queries, they are con-

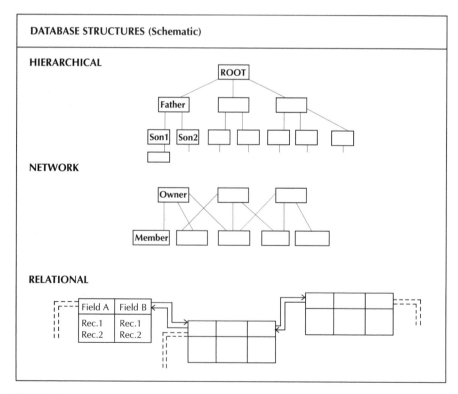

Fig 10.1

sidered to be inflexible. However hierarchical databases enable programmers/users to construct applications for fixed relationships and are considered efficient for large-scale batch processing operations such as payroll. Historically they were the first of the infrastructures.

(b) Network databases

Network databases place the records into sets. These sets consist of a head record known as the owner record plus one or more member records. The main advantage of the network structure over the hierarchical structure is that individual records can belong to more than one set by a network of linkages. Furthermore network databases, like hierarchical databases, contain specific relationships between the various data structures, so enabling programmers/users to produce predetermined applications.

(c) Relational databases

Relational databases are those databases consisting of table-like files. Each table consists of rows, which are in effect the database records, and columns which are in effect the fields within the record structures. The tables are independent of each other and carefully constructed to maximise efficiency and ensure data integrity. Relational databases are very responsive structures enabling programmers/users to create useful linkages between the various tables and discover useful relationships between the records. The majority of modern commercial database systems are currently constituted with relational technology. The DBMS for a relational database is usually designated a Relational Database Management System (RDMS).

10.5 OBJECT ORIENTED DATABASES

In the early days database users and developers soon discovered that flat file structures were suitable for card indexing type routines but were unsuitable for more flexible processsing such as linking or fusing record structures. As a result, more elaborately structured databases as outlined in 10.4 started to appear. However despite certain advantages, conventional database structures were still restricted in the type of data they could manipulate. For example most conventional commercial databases contain data types such as customer address, outstanding balances, payroll listings and so on. However, this type of text-based data is in a format quite unsuited to other types of digitised data such as video images, sound, graphics and other similar data. In order, therefore, to meet the processing demands relating to these new data structures, a different type of database has begun to appear, namely the Object Oriented Database (OOD).

OODs are totally different from conventional databases and are usually constructed using OOL technology. Inside an OOD, various data types, such as a video clip, are defined as an object. Every object is composed of the data relating to the composition of the object as well as a sequence of instructions outlining the conduct, requirements and characteristics of the object. For example, a digitised photo object may contain certain characteristics such as size and colour. In addition, the object which contains the photo could also detail the degree of the projected angle of the photo as well as any magnification/zoom facilities. Object types with identical properties can be clustered together into classes. Furthermore OODs enable the objects within a particular class to pass certain characteristics to other objects. As a result of OOD technology, the database user is provided with a large archive of versatile ready-made objects each of which can be repeatedly utilised in the construction of various database applications. As a consequence, OOD technology has proved particularly successful in reducing the time spent on the database application development life cycle.

The DBMS for an OOD is usually referred to as an Object Oriented Database Management System (OODBMS). Unfortunately OOD technology is not only relatively new but also expensive.

OODs also make considerable processing demands and require a high degree of expertise. Furthermore at the time of writing there is no universal agreement as to OOD standards although it is true to say that most of the major database developers are beginning to co-operate on various protocols to enable various OOD systems to operate in a variety of environments.

In addition as the demand for ever more sophisticated, intelligent, multimedia type software becomes ever more prevalent so it is becoming more obvious that organisations have to pursue OOD type technology in order to satisfy their processing and information requirements.

10.6 THE DATABASE MANAGEMENT SYSTEM (DBMS)

The Database Management System (DBMS) is that term given to a suite of specialist programs which act as the system regulator controlling data updates, user access and the access of other applications.

When the DBMS deals with the read/write requests, it ensures that only those users/applications with appropriate permission can access the data and that any change to the data in the database is consistent. As the DBMS carries out its functions it displays the data in a manner compatible with the user's needs and effectively shields the user from unnecessary complications.

The composition of a DBMS varies from system to system. Nevertheless the DBMS usually contains several regulating core programs. These include a data dictionary, an interrogation language, an application generator, concurrency procedures and security software.

10.6.1 Data dictionary

A data dictionary is a computerised reference manual which gives a detailed view of the data held in the database (or conventional file system). It contains data about data, usually referred to as metadata. Data dictionaries enable database/IS developers to keep track of the data in order to avoid inconsistencies, duplications, and invalid features.

They contain details such as data name, type and size; the various structures, files and tables in which it is held; and what operations can be performed on it during processing. In particular, they can be used to ensure that valid modifications to a data item will be made uniformly throughout the database – in other words, the integrity of the data is preserved.

A data dictionary is a working document which can be deployed throughout the entire development process, certainly in conjunction with the system specification (11.7.3), the logical data flow diagram (12.3.9) and program specification (12.5).

The preparation of a data dictionary is usually automated by the computer.

The manner in which the database structures/relationships are actually modified depends on the type of data dictionary employed by the DBMS. There are three main types of data dictionary: passive, active and dynamic. With passive data dictionaries the user has to program the changes; with an active data dictionary, changes are carried out automatically once they are declared valid; and with a dynamic data dictionary not only are the database structures changed but the modifications are also carried through to any integrating applications. By ensuring that the data structures are unique in name and are consistent in composition, the data dictionary prevents any potential data discrepancies.

10.6.2 Interrogation languages

In order to interrogate or update a database, it is not always necessary for users to utilise specially written programs as such. Most database users wishing to process inquiries or modifications usually employ an interrogation language, otherwise known as a query language. Query languages are normally classified as 4GLs and usually consist of a heavily restricted vocabulary of commands that enable the user to interact directly with the database. The main advantage of query languages is their ease of use as operating the language does not require technical awareness of the more intricate details of the database.

A typical query language command takes the form:

SELECT novels WHERE author-age <40 AND author female Scottish

One query language which has become an industry standard is the Structured Query Language (SQL). However SQL is unusual in that it can be loosely described as being both a database interrogation language and a database data storage format. SQL enables developers to produce independent databases which can, when necessary, use data transferred from other SQL databases. Databases conforming to the SQL standard can also use the applications produced for other SQL databases. The SQL standard is approved by the American National Standards Institute.

Besides being a very user friendly language, SQL has brought a certain degree of homogeneity to the database market. Experienced SQL users know that their skills are transferable to those applications purporting to support SQL features. Such compatibility has proved a strong selling point and as a result many database developers have included SQL technology within their particular product.

10.6.3 Application generators

An application generator is usually a set of program tools which allow the user to turn out applications which are directly compatible with the data structures within the database.

10.6.4 Concurrency procedures

As has already been mentioned (see 10.2.2) concurrency procedures refer to those programs designed to resolve conflicting multiple user access. How this is achieved usually depends on the quality of the software. Some of the more modest DBMS software simply locks those particular files being used by individual users. Unfortunately such a situation usually results in a queue for the more popular files as other users wait for those particular files to be released. In contrast, more sophisticated systems lock particular records or particular fields so enabling more than one user access to the data file that contains them.

10.6.5 Security software

Security software usually includes password control systems, anti-virus programs and stringent backup applications. Because of the strategic and pivotal role of a database there is a particular emphasis on the employment of programs which automatically duplicate the contents of the current database on a regular basis to off-site locations.

10.7 DATABASE ADMINISTRATORS

The strategic and all-pervasive influence of the database within the modern organisation has resulted in an increase in the role and power of IT specialists known as database administrators. These individuals are usually responsible for a whole range of tasks pertaining to the use of the database and the DBMS. These responsibilities frequently involve planning and designing the schema, otherwise known as the internal view, of the database, as well as monitoring the manner in which the database is used. Other duties could include staff training, organising backup procedures and, when necessary, overseeing the commissioning of various end user applications.

Database administrators in large corporate organisations are not only required to possess crucial IT skills but must also be able to act, when necessary, in an authoritative as well as a diplomatic manner. The reason for this is the database operational requirements. For example, organisations operating a fully integrated database means that personnel and departments at every level must pool their own data/information in a manner that is compatible with the rest of the organisation. As a consequence, personnel/departments have to surrender a certain degree of independence with respect to their own data processing requirements. Enforcing such a regime can, as one might imagine, demand strong managerial skills.

10.7.1 Central tasks

A database administrator in control of a DBMS usually has to perform certain central tasks.

(a) Formulation of agreed data structures

A DBMS-driven CDS (see 10.2.1) which is employed by the whole organisation means that data and data structures are shared by multiple users. As a result it is necessary that the users and the database administrator agree on the purpose and type of data and data structures to be stored in the database. A lack of agreement on this particular point can cause chaos if the DBMS posts data modifications to inappropriate records.

In order to minimise such a possibility, details of the data structures are usually stored in the data dictionary (see 10.6.1). In this respect, the data dictionary brings a certain rigour to the formulation of the data structure organisation by preventing the improper duplication of data structures as well as enabling the database administrator to keep track of the overall structure of the database.

(b) Data modification protocols

Data modification protocols are agreed procedures put into place by the database administrator. The essence of such protocols is to govern the manner and rights by which programs can modify the data or data structures stored in the database. For example, personnel applications may be allowed to change an employee's personal details, whereas a payroll program which uses the data for its pay calculations may be disallowed from modifying the employee record without further authority. Given all the different potential points of access to the database, such protocols are vital to maintaining the integrity of a central database system.

(c) Allocation of user access rights

The level of access for the potential users of a CDS type database is usually a very sensitive issue. For example, database administrators not only have to restrict access for reasons of data integrity but also for reasons of data security. Therefore, to minimise inappropriate access or data modification, the database administrator maintains a tight grip on the allocation of user access rights.

User rights may, where necessary, be restricted to simple access. For example, most users of a library information system may only have permission to view certain parts of the database whilst other users, such as library assistants, may have full access to the database so allowing them to modify the data as and when appropriate. The degree of access is usually an issue which is fully discussed between the database administrator and other members of management.

(d) Security procedures

In order to maintain efficient data security the database administrator is also usually in charge of tasks such as regulating passwords and ensuring adequate backup systems.

10.8 DISTRIBUTED DATABASES

A distributed database system (DDS) is significantly different from a CDS type database. With a CDS the database and its ancillary processing equipment are usually all housed in one central physical if not logical location.

However, with a DDS, the organisation could, for example, possess a host of databases stationed at various locations, along with an associated dispersal of computer equipment, all under the control of a computer network. Alternatively, users who download processing tasks from a partitioned central database to local PCs could also be said to be using a DDS.

Within a DDS, an organisation can distribute certain local data traffic such as payroll or stock control or it can assign a particular function of the organisation, such as a personnel system, to locally based or off-site configurations. DDSs are particularly useful to large organisations wishing to relieve pressure on their central processing systems, and can prove extremely economical. For example the organisation does not have to indulge in long and expensive data communication transmissions in order to process local information requirements but its central office can use the DDS to monitor local systems in order to keep a close watch on the company-wide stock situation or financial situation. Furthermore DDSs can provide faster response times when the user's information requirements are based locally. The processing which takes place across a DDS is referred to as distributed data processing.

10.8.1 DDS configuration

Two ways of configuring a DDS are by replicating the database at various sites or by segmenting a database. Replicating databases can prove costly and may result in data inconsistency if changes in the databases are not implemented across the range. However this design does have the advantage of providing the organisation with an excellent backup in the event of system failure.

With a segmented database system, logical parts (e.g. the parts required for stock control) of the organisation's central database are allocated to various sites according to the organisation's needs. The usual routine with a segmented database is that varying amounts of processing are carried out locally and the results are then collated at the centre. This type of distributed processing is cheaper than the replicated database option but it can prove very complicated to organise if users are to avoid inconsistent data.

10.9 FURTHER DATABASE ADVANCES

10.9.1 Data repositories

Data repositories are a relatively new phenomenon in database technology and are usually classified as an advanced type of data dictionary detailing necessary organisational metadata. Metadata is a term used to describe information about data.

In addition to the functions of a data dictionary as described in 10.6.1 the data repository would also usually contain specifications of the various applications that integrate with the database, specifications of the database's users requirements and the overall functionality of various programs.

Data repositories enable the database administrator to gain an overview of the database's entire information provision and enable database developers to integrate different computing resources consistently and reliably. The data repository also enables developers to produce applications for their database in a far shorter time as it provides much of the necessary information pertaining to the specification of a potential application in a readily available format.

10.9.2 Data warehouses

Another new type of database application is the Data Warehouse (DW). As with so many other business computing products there is a range of applications which could be considered or which claim to be a DW but as yet there is no set standard for data warehouses.

DWs are primarily designed to retrieve data from a series of diverse sources. This data is then usually isolated and stored by the DW, in what can be described as a passive information format. The main aim of DWs is to enable an organisation to analyse critical information without affecting the organisation's operational activities. In addition DWs are designed to support the data's end user such as a customer as opposed to an IT expert such as a database designer. A good example of a DW type application is the arrival of customer loyalty cards in the retail sector.

The customer loyalty card not only enables retailers to retain or tempt customers by various discounts or offers but also enables them to build up valuable profiles of their customers' spending habits so allowing them to better target customer requirements.

DWs are usually built around OOD type systems and frequently employ sophisticated features such as metadata archiving files and data marts. Data marts are simply narrow subdivisions of the total data content of the DW. The idea of the data mart is to relieve unnecessary access processing within the DW by supplying users with immediate data relevant to their particular needs although the user may retrieve other information as and when required. Archive files hold data no longer in active use but valuable for certain kinds of analysis like identifying trends.

The need for DWs has arisen as a result of the massive duplication of data within large organisations. Such duplication has usually arisen because of the ad hoc development of the organisation's information systems or because of other activities such as the acquisition mania that has afflicted so many business organisations and which has resulted in an overwhelming plethora of data. Because DWs are basically a summation of organisational activities they are usually considered to be the ideal tool for data mining.

10.9.3 Data mining

Data mining revolves around the employment of those procedures which enable users to quarry into corporate databases in order to extract valuable information. These procedures are very sophisticated interrogation and retrieval techniques. Expert DW users are sometimes referred to as data miners. The arrival of OOD and DW technology appears to indicate to many experts that there will be a certain dislocation in the corporate database market as users seek to take advantage of the new systems. However because most of the corporate sector is so heavily committed to the use of relational database technology, it is expected that such change will not be a sudden event but more a gradual metamorphosis.

10.9.4 Online analytical processing

Online Analytical Processing (OLAP) is a generic title for those software tools which enables a user to extract necessary strategic information from a database. An OLAP application differs from a data warehouse in that a data warehouse stores and retrieves information detailing past and present transactions whereas an OLAP is concerned with future developments. OLAP applications are not so dissimilar from spreadsheet applications other than that they are designed to feed off a database. They can perform complex calculations such as 'what if' scenarios and are used mainly by financial and sales/marketing professionals.

10.10 PC DATABASES

Because of their increasing power and ease of use there has been a significant rise in the use of PC database applications. What is more contemporary PC database applications now contain those features which were previously restricted to the more expensive large-scale computing applications. For example unlike their predecessors top-range PC databases now possess concurrency utilities so enabling multiple users to access the same database.

The bulk of PC database applications can be described as relational type databases. Relational type databases are table-like structures which are saved in indexed files on the PC's various storage media. Industry-standard

211

databases of this type frequently enable users to implement SQL interrogation procedures as well as to run various operations enabling them to link and merge multiple databases.

10.10.1 Popular PC databases

(a) DataEase for Windows

DataEase for Windows from Triangle Software International Inc is a stylish and powerful database system which allows users to produce attractive reports and screen interfaces using clip art images in conjunction with a complete set of drawing tools. The application also supports a central utility program known as the Data Model Manager (DMM). The main purpose of the DMM is to create, validate, compare and review the various data structures within the database. The DMM also enables the user to produce graphical data structure diagrams on the computer screen which are then translated by DataEase into appropriate database tables/relationships all of which may be imported into an appropriate end user application. Another interesting facility is the Live Reports feature which enables users to save on-screen space by allowing detailed groups of information to be compressed into scrollable regions.

(b) Paradox for Windows 95 and Windows NT

At the time of publication, Paradox for Windows 95 is the latest in an elite suite of PC database applications from Borland. Paradox databases from Borland are considered to be market-leading software applications in the corporate sector. A measure of the sophistication of the product can be gauged by the fact that the Paradox 7 table format allows users to store up to two billion records per table. Paradox 7 includes useful tutorial routines such as Quick Start Expert and Quick Tour. It also contains enhanced Object Linking and Embedding (OLE) facilities and useful query routines. For example, Graphical Query by Example is a facility which enables the user to visually join multiple tables. Another example is the Live Query Views facility whereby the user can edit data in query answer tables and have the changes automatically update the source table. In addition Paradox 7 can interrogate up to 32 tables in a single query. Paradox 7 also supports OLE enabling users to store data from other Windows applications such as graphics, sound, video, wordprocessing, spreadsheets or any other similar application. Paradox 7 also includes the ObjectPAL (Paradox Application Language) development language. ObjectPAL is a proprietary high-level OOL enabling users to produce their own database applications. The overall effect of Paradox 7 is to provide potential users with a very powerful integrated database development environment which supports the composition of sophisticated graphical applications.

(c) Microsoft Access

Microsoft Access for Windows 95 is a 32-bit database application designed for use with Microsoft Windows 95 and Windows NT. Access is designed to supply users with a database which is not only sophisticated and powerful but is also easy to use. It is also a product that has been designed to fully integrate with Microsoft Office.

Access uses what has been described as second-generation learning tools for allowing the new user to get familiar with the application. First-generation tools are simple help systems/tutorials. Second-generation learning tools usually refer to applications which try to predict the user's requirements by providing ready-made guides through interface templates known as Wizards or Experts. For example, users wishing to construct a new database will be prompted, when necessary, as to the format and types of field that they can employ in a particular record structure.

Amongst this application's more significant features are its ability to support long field and file names, powerful OLE integration and a performance analyser. The application also includes a Briefcase Replication facility. The advantage of this routine is that the user can take a copy of the database away on a portable computer, make changes to the database and then merge the changes back with the original database so enabling smooth data consistency.

Access is similar to Paradox 7 in that it places a heavy emphasis on the use of QBE. With Access, users accessing the QBE facility employ a grid-like template which enables the interrogation of more than one table. Access users can simply enter appropriate search/calculation criteria within the QBE grid in order to produce reports and process calculations. Access also provides a simpler Query by Form routine. Query by Form enables the user to access another grid layout similar to the QBE set up. However, with the Query by Form routine, users can type the search data into blank cells matching the fields of individual tables whilst simultaneously scanning the contents of the database fields. In addition, Access supports a filter-by-selection function. With filter by selection the user simply selects a record which matches their particular search requirements. Having selected the appropriate record the user activates a filter button and the program retrieves those records identical to the original filter record.

213

10.11 SCALED APPLICATIONS

The success of PC-oriented databases has resulted in a dramatic new direction in database development. Corporate database developers are now propagating scaled-down versions of those database applications which were previously restricted to operating in a mainframe/mini environment. These new scaled versions can normally be supported on PC type systems. Apart from the reduced processing throughput of the PC, there is usually very little difference between the scaled version of these databases and those running on mainframe systems. Both versions usually present a uniform interface as well as a matching range of facilities.

The most significant feature which has been transported with these newly scaled database systems has been the advent of PC-based SQL type applications.

10.11.1 Personal Oracle

Personal Oracle, produced by Oracle, is an excellent illustration of a scaled blue chip database which has been developed to operate on unattached individual PCs. It has been built with a program structure similar to that employed to produce those versions of the Oracle database which run on mini/mainframe configurations.

Personal Oracle has an SQL type structure comparable to that of Oracle, which is a global market leader in Unix-based relational databases. As a result of this design, users of Personal Oracle have the advantage of possessing a PC database whose applications can be ported onto other computers, be they workstations, minicomputers or mainframes using OSs as diverse as Windows, Novell, Unix, VMS and MVS. To be able to employ Personal Oracle in such a diverse environment is a major plus for developers wishing to produce PC-based applications that will run on larger corporate computer systems. In addition, Personal Oracle also provides an alternative access route for those users currently employing Oracle in a mainframe/mini environment and who wish to downsize to smaller PC systems.

10.12 RAPID APPLICATION DEVELOPMENT SYSTEMS

Rapid Application Development Systems (RAD) are usually associated with applications that support specialist software tools which facilitate the expeditious development of database applications. RAD systems usually include certain attributes such as data repositories and can be purchased as independent applications in their own right although they are normally supplied as part of a database package.

RAD systems have tended to be expensive and were usually located on more powerful computer configurations such as minicomputers or workstations. However the facilities supported by applications such as Paradox and Access has resulted in the spread of RAD technology across the PC market. Because of their ability to speed up database application development they have been growing increasingly popular and are expected to make a significant impact on future sales.

10.13 THE DATABASE MARKET

The database market of the late 1990s is a segmented market led by companies such as Informix, Oracle, Sybase, Microsoft, Borland and IBM, all of whom are notably dominant in certain areas of the market. IBM currently still dominate the mainframe market with relational database products such as DB2 and is a market leader with DB2/400, a similar product designed for its best-selling AS/400 minicomputer systems. Oracle leads the world in Unix-based relational databases whilst companies such as Microsoft and Borland are obvious front runners when it comes to PC applications.

Nevertheless despite this current segmentation there is a certain shift occurring within the database market. For example, various database developers are beginning to make major resource commitments in OOD technology mainly because of their suitability in delivering multimedia type services. Furthermore there is the perennial concept of downsizing due to the increased power of the modern desktop computer and the realisation that the battle for the desktop database market is becoming increasingly important to users and developers alike. As a result developers other than the traditional industry players appear to be taking a clearer interest in desktop/PC technology. A good example of this change in direction is Oracle's move into scaled PC versions of its best selling database technology.

However as companies such as Oracle move towards smaller desktop/PC systems so leading PC database suppliers such as Microsoft and Borland are beginning to produce powerful database applications the likes of which were previously the preserve of the mini/mainframe environment. The latest versions of Microsoft's Access and Borland's Paradox are widely recognised as possessing certain critical attributes which make them suitable for traditional mainframe/minicomputer users who are considering migrating to, or at least making more use of, PC configurations.

10.14 CONCLUSION

In view of their overall importance, database applications are undoubtedly pivotal to the success of many businesses and organisations as well as the computing industry as a whole. In addition recent technical advances means that these databases cannot only provide a host of critical services but can also, where appropriate, be supported on smaller, cheaper computers.

Besides the downsizing trend, two other strands appear to be gaining pace in the development of database technology. The first is the emergence of OOD applications, the need for which is being fuelled by the ever-increasing demand for the delivery of multimedia systems, a role for which they are ideally suited. The second strand concerns the development of metadata-centred applications such as DRs and DWs both of which appear to be part of a general trend to enable the user to penetrate the plethora of surrounding data so that they might ascertain that critical information that they are searching for.

11

Information systems: an overview

11.1 INTRODUCTION

This chapter is aimed at providing an overview of the nature of business-oriented Information Systems (IS) and how automated ISs are developed and implemented. Section 11.2 provides a definition of information and data whilst section 11.3 discusses the concept of an IS. Sections 11.4 and 11.5 deal with those ISs employed in a business/commercial context. Sections 11.6 through to 11.8 discuss mainstream approaches used to develop and implement commercial ISs. Section 11.9 and section 11.10 detail IS project management duties and IS staff requirements whilst sections 11.11 through to 11.13 concern the developing trends of outsourcing, business process re-engineering and vapourware.

It should be stressed at this point that the next chapter will concentrate on the actual tools and techniques used to devise and develop a computerised IS.

11.2 INFORMATION AND DATA

Before examining the role and development of an information system it is necessary to distinguish between what is meant by information and what is meant by data.

A pay slip which simply displayed an irregular set of seemingly meaningless numbers would be cause for complaint. However if the pay slip displayed the same set of numbers, processed (sorted and formatted) and presented in an intelligible manner where the meaning of each item was made clear, then the employee may be no happier or sadder but would at least be better informed. In this respect information can be thought of as organised data or, as some IS specialists would put it, information is simply data with direction. Even so, a single piece of data can be informative provided it is seen in the right context.

11.3 THE CONCEPT OF AN INFORMATION SYSTEM

Managers and employers realise that every organisation needs information in order to function and that the type of information required by an organisation depends upon the organisation's activities. To supply, process and communicate this information in an organised and purposeful manner organisations devise or employ a suitable series of routine and non-routine processes collectively referred to as an Information System (IS).

11.3.1 Defining a system

As has already been stated, information is data with a purpose. In turn a system can be defined as an ordered process which performs a particular purpose or function. This process is composed of a sequence of events or activities. A system takes in input (e.g. data), the input is processed, and the result of the processing becomes the output (e.g. information). A change in the nature of the sequence or manner in which the activities are performed could result in a change in the purpose or the function of the system.

So that a process, or series of processes, may be defined as a system, it must have a purpose or objective. Since information is processed organised data, then the purpose of an IS is to provide the means by which the data is processed and organised.

The major objective of any IS must be to supply information which will enable the user/organisation to make better decisions. It is therefore necessary to consider the various types of ISs which are prevalent in the contemporary business environment.

11.4 BUSINESS INFORMATION SYSTEMS

Business ISs are designed to produce information which is of value to the organisation. So that such information is produced, data must be acquired, validated, processed, and stored or dispersed. Activities of this type, be they labour intensive or automated, cost money.

So that the user organisation can be persuaded to invest money in this type of undertaking they must be persuaded of the value of the information produced. The value of this information is in turn dependent on the purpose of the information. For example the system may produce information which enables the user to keep control of the organisation's payroll or enable the management to make better decisions so giving the organisation a competitive edge.

ISs in the business culture fall into three major categories:

(1) Day-to-day or operational systems

ISs of this type concern those operations carried out by the organisation in its normal trading environment. These systems perform necessary routine activities and include applications such as stock control, order processing, retailing systems, share dealing, on-line booking systems and so on. Operational systems can be unexceptional but they are usually critical to the organisation's endeavours.

(2) Tactical systems

Tactical systems are usually associated with those processes which supply information for intermediate decision making within the organisation. Such decisions usually refer to management activities involved with the monitoring of financial budgets, pricing levels, human resourcing, production schedules, stock level planning and so on.

(3) Strategic systems

The users of strategic systems are usually high ranking executive officers of the enterprise. Strategic systems are invariably concerned with those decisions which affect the long-term policy objectives of the organisation. Such decisions usually regard matters like determining the types of products/services supplied by the organisation, the organisation's centre of activities, investment plans in research and development, and issues concerning the financing of the enterprise.

Strategic systems frequently depend on information and data sources that are usually beyond the influence of the individual organisation. For example borrowing requirements and export policies could depend upon national factors such as interest rates and the current level of unemployment or international factors such as currency exchange rates or commodity prices. So useful models such as sophisticated spreadsheet scenarios incorporating data of this type have enabled users to make better decisions than might otherwise have been the case.

The categorisation of information systems is a matter of debate; in particular some regard it as a fruitless debate since change is so rapid, but it can be helpful to sort them broadly into levels according to use. Thus, information systems used predominantly at the tactical and strategic levels are seen as Management Information Systems (MIS).

11.5 COMPUTERISED BUSINESS INFORMATION SYSTEMS

Business and commerce are now fully aware of the computer's capacity to analyse, record, collate and process vast swathes of data with great speed and efficiency. As a result industry has developed a host of sophisticated computer-based ISs.

During the early years, the information system was based on an expensive computer configuration which more often than not was the exclusive domain of management or, even worse, the organisation's data processing or computer section. However the arrival of cost-effective computing power, mainly in the form of the PC, has gone a long way to removing such restrictions. As a result computerised business ISs are now readily accessible as a matter of routine, and are consequently engaged at every level of the modern business organisation.

Modern computerised business ISs also differ from their predecessors in that they are no longer just transaction based. Early business ISs were basic data entry/retrieval systems used for mainstream operational activities such as stock control, booking, accounts and other similar functions. Such systems would usually regurgitate information in a series of standard pre-formatted reports supplying, for instance, current sales, stock levels, price lists, profit and loss details, and other similar output. However professional contemporary business-oriented ISs deal with transactional activity of this kind as a matter of course. Where they fundamentally differ from previous generations is in their additional emphasis on producing information more suited to strategic and tactical decision making.

11.5.1 Advantages and costs

Computerised ISs have demonstrated visible and obvious advantages in maximising revenues whilst simultaneously minimising costs; in general, they promote more effective control over resources. They lead to an improvement in managerial decisions enabling organisations to be more sensitive to pricing and costing as well as to increase product/service differentiation. Other less obvious benefits of a new computerised IS could be a revival in the self-esteem of the organisation's workforce through empowerment and more flexible working practices. Such changes could in turn advance external customer/supplier relationships through improvement in delivery and ordering arrangements.

Unfortunately the expense of developing and establishing a company-wide computerised IS can, in certain situations, be almost, prohibitive. IS costs are not confined to the purchase of the equipment but include system planning (analysis and design), staff training, installation, implementation, monitoring and maintenance.

There is also the problem of the need to continually update the IS as its various users make increasing demands. As far as money is concerned, a fully equipped IS using the latest IT can prove to be a bottomless pit.

11.5.2 Types of computerised IS

Despite their often horrendous expense, the types and nature of computerised ISs are expanding all the time. Among those computerised business ISs in common use are:

(1) Decision support systems

In a way, all ISs, computerised or manual, can be classified as a decision support system, as their purpose is to supply relevant and accurate information to support the decision making process. However recognised Decision Support Systems (DSS) are viewed as having a more specialist use than functional operational applications such as payroll programs. With a DSS program, users are, more often than not, interfacing with a system that can aid if not actually dictate appropriate courses of action at the tactical and strategic levels.

For example, a DSS type application may be a data query program allowing users to interrogate a huge database in order to extract certain critical marketing data. This interrogation may take the form of listing possible relationships between various income groups and modes of transport. A DSS may also be a very sophisticated spreadsheet containing millions of data elements which, when manipulated, provide analytical results which may require the management to take a particular decision or course of action.

It should be emphasised that DSS programs are designed to support user/management decision making, rather than supplant it, although future intelligent systems may reverse this relationship.

(2) Quotation systems

The early to mid 1990s witnessed wholescale changes in the manner in which financial services were supplied. This change was no more apparent than in the insurance sector where massive inroads were made through the introduction of direct telephone selling.

With the development of specialist quotation programs insurers obtain customer details over the phone and give instant and competitive decisions on the required policy's premium. Well known are those dealing with car, home and life insurance. The success of these systems has been such that this type of trading has now been extended to the point where consumers can now use their phone to inquire about and purchase other financial products such as loans, pensions, shares and mortgages.

(3) Human resource management systems

Human resource management deals with the processes used to determine and regulate the individuals which make up the organisation's work force. The object of a computer-based Human Resource Management System (HRMS) is to allow the organisation to employ, appraise, advance, transfer, and educate members of the organisation in a fast and efficient manner. Other functions include the detailing of individual pay structuring, contract of employment, personal details, qualifications, skills, duties and job title.

Systems of this type are usually database applications, which can, when necessary, export data to sophisticated modelling programs in order to assess likely future workforce requirements in terms of quality, quantity and deployment. Two major forces have resulted in a significant increase in demand for HRMS applications. The first is the realisation in contemporary business culture of the need to develop a more responsive workforce in an ever-changing environment. For example, modern managers have discovered that there is a growing need for multi-skilled employees and that they have to be able to call upon employees to perform an ever-increasing and diverse range of roles. Secondly there is the problem of increased legislation. New laws relating to equal opportunities, health and safety, ethnic monitoring and other similar issues can make huge demands on organisations. Fortunately efficient HRMS systems can provide relevant reporting systems enabling management to meet such demands.

(4) Expert systems

Expert systems are computer applications which emulate the decision processes as performed by highly educated professionals such as doctors, accountants and lawyers. These applications are usually designed to act in an advisory role and to supply appropriate and valuable counsel. The advice supplied by an expert system is extracted from a knowledge base which is initially supplied by coordinating the expertise and knowledge of a group of relevant experts.

Expert systems are expensive to develop but they can prove to be very cost effective. A good example is the increasing use of expert systems in the British National Health Service. Consider a junior nurse working in a hospital who may have good clinical experience but is unlikely to have the drug dispensing expertise of a fully trained doctor/pharmacist. The nurse with access to an appropriate medical expert system may, and often does, prove to be a better decision maker as to the drugs appropriate for a patient than a doctor working alone (or even, as has been proved, a team of doctors).

Strictly speaking, expert systems are applications of artificial intelligence (see 13.2). To reach a 'decision', the knowledge base of an expert system is subjected to enquiry by formal rules built integrally into the system. The rules, such as IF ... THEN ... rules, persevere until no further progress can be made and a 'decision' is arrived at.

11.5.3 The balance sheet

Ultimately as has already been stated the main objective of most commercial organisations is to survive and make a profit. In this respect alone, computers and the possible introduction of a new computerised IS can present the organisation with a variety of conflicting factors (see 11.7). Besides being extremely efficient, computers have other well known advantages. They don't strike, they don't go sick, they don't answer back and they are loyal. However they have to be led (programmed), they are often expensive, they can break down, and they don't always do what the user wants them to do.

Ultimately the management will have to make a decision on whether or not to proceed. Before they make such a decision they will have to ask the following questions. Is the change to a new IS and the subsequent hardship really worth it? What are the possible consequences of implementing a new IS? What are the consequences of not introducing a new IS? In order to make such a crucial choice the management will often draw up a simple balance sheet to enable them to get a better picture of the situation. Consider the following example:

Debit	*Credit*
(1) Train staff and persuade management	Automation normally means staff reduction
	Updated systems have positive effect on staff morale/image
(2) Capital outlay on equipment (includes installation and development)	Tax allowances Increased efficiency

	Debit	*Credit*
(3)	Disruption to organisation/ market	Increased control and sensitivity
(4)	Operating costs	Operating savings
(5)	Possible change in organisational ethos	Organisation acquires or develops dynamic structures

Real and potential obstacles to the introduction of a new automated IS can be countered by experienced management. Challenging equipment costs could be dealt with by clever financing such as leasing or rental schemes. Key personnel could provide good inhouse training whilst shrewd planning could minimise potential chaos during any changeover.

When necessary, the management may decide against the idea of introducing a new automated IS. It is an option, and in some cases a sensible one. It must be postulated that this is an increasingly rare event in an ever-increasingly competitive world.

11.6 INFORMATION SYSTEMS STRATEGY

In the event of an organisation deciding to institute or update an IS they will immediately become aware of certain major critical issues. These issues include the cost of the development project and the subsequent impact of the project and the new IS on the organisation's current activities. Other issues include the need to ensure that the organisation is fully cognisant of the new IS's objectives and to ensure that these objectives are compatible with the organisation's objectives.

11.6.1 Why a strategy ?

The current spectacular changes in computing technology are resulting in a proliferation of new and exciting opportunities. These opportunities include the increased use of videoconferencing and other multimedia/communication systems as well as the arrival of sophisticated and intelligent manufacturing and information systems all of which are being delivered on computer platforms which are far less expensive than their predecessors. However if users do not plan the exploitation of these new opportunities in an organised manner they will face chaos.

To rationalise the development of an effective computerised IS users/ management are advised to formalise an information systems strategy in order to harmonise all the various pressures and demands of the organisation. An applicable strategy of this type not only deals with equipment and personnel requirements but also recognises and integrates information in such a manner that appropriate information permeates all corners of the organisation. In an increasingly harsh and competitive economic environment, management of organisations everywhere have realised that it is the ability to supply and manipulate appropriate critical information that allows them to reduce costs, increase efficiency, enhance operational control as well as improve and innovate products and so gain an advantage on other adversaries in the market.

11.6.2 Development and control

When managers and developers set about formulating an appropriate IS strategy they have to give consideration to more than just the processes by which the information is supplied. They also have to ensure that the information supplied is the information that is required by the organisation to fulfil its objectives. If the system fails to supply such information it would probably mean that control of the organisation's IS strategy was being driven by technological imperatives as opposed to the actual needs of the organisation. This is a common pitfall which can only be avoided by designing an IS strategy which follows organisational objectives.

11.6.3 Organisational objectives

In a crude way it might be said that organisations in the business environment usually have one major objective and that objective is profit. However such a view is a little simplistic because whilst profit is essential it can never be a totally overriding objective. If it were to become an overriding objective then it could prove very dangerous to the long-term survival of the organisation. For example the transgression of anti-pollution laws, wholesale and unnecessary redundancies, low wages and other sharp trading practices all in the name of cost reduction and increased profit can result in the organisation becoming a social pariah and being heavily penalised as a consequence.

As a result, the overwhelming majority of business organisations take a more rational and balanced approach when setting objectives. These objectives can usually be divided into short term and long term. Short-term objectives are usually well defined and tangible. They could include a percentage increase in market share over the next two years or the relocation of a factory. Long-term objectives usually contain less tangible goals such as improved customer service or a more attractive product range. What must be understood, however, is that whatever objectives the organisation decides upon it is critical that these objectives should, where possible, complement each other rather than conflict. Another important attribute is that the objectives should permeate the organisation's activities. A good example of permeation through automation is the technique known as JIT (Just In Time).

In order to function properly many organisations such as manufacturers hold large stocks of materials so as to meet operational demands. However large stock inventories tie up the organisation's cash assets and can consequently prove very costly. So, to reduce this idle period many manufacturers are starting to employ the JIT approach. With JIT the output of each step of the production process passes to the next step without an intervening storage period. Similarly, externally sourced components are delivered at the input and in optimally sized and optimally timed batches in order to minimise or eliminate idle-time stockholding. The benefits of JIT are that it removes intermediate inventory storage costs and prevents the organisation's working capital from being tied up in goods waiting in the production process.

The financial advantages of JIT are clear. However so that an organisation might implement a JIT approach it is usually required to operate a fully integrated computerised IS supplying information which is not only accurate and punctual but which effectively flows and controls the day-to-day operations of the organisation.

11.7 INFORMATION SYSTEMS DEVELOPMENT

The development of an information system is, nowadays, a stage-by-stage process. Previously, in the early years, it was something of a haphazard process conducted largely by computing specialists with insufficient regard to business needs and with insufficient consultation with the users. Since then, formalised system development methodologies have appeared which variously lay down a logical sequence of stages, from identifying the business needs through to the actual implementation of the system. The most comprehensive and formal of these systems are what are known as structured systems methodologies whose aim is to bring systems development as near to an engineering discipline as possible.

However, there is a broad pattern running through all these methodologies, as follows.

11.7.1 Perceived need

As indicated in 11.6 the forces which result in organisations giving consideration to the introduction of a new IS can be diverse and complex.

(a) System congestion

The organisation may be facing increased workloads due to an increase in sales activities. As a result users may discover that delivery systems can no longer cope and that delays are having a detrimental effect on customer relations.

(b) Speed and accuracy

Commercial users have recognised the need to supply their organisations with relevant, accurate and timely information. In the furious world of the global market it is more than likely that such information can only be supplied by the latest technology. This is especially the case in the banking and financial markets where literally every second counts.

(c) Market sensitive systems

Users know that modern ISs which monitor changing consumer trends can enable better product differentiation by allowing the company to make more accurate decisions concerning customer requirements. A failure to have such a system in place could result in the organisation missing market opportunities or, worse still, losing market share to the competition.

(d) Financial reporting

Computerised IS systems containing financial/accounting functions mean that users can now instantly produce valuable preformatted reports such as balance sheets and profit and loss accounts with the minimum of delay and without having to constantly refer to expensive professionals.

(e) Increase in external pressures

External pressures due to increased competition could lead to the need to improve customer service. The introduction of a computerised system could have the advantage of doing this whilst simultaneously improving the organisation's perceived status as a modern high tech company.

Other external pressures could be changes in legislation. Such changes could be mandatory compliance to anti-pollution laws by using green-oriented hardware or a requirement to include ethnic monitoring.

11.7.2 Feasibility study

It might be said that given enough time and resources, everything is feasible. However commercial users have to be realistic. The essence of the feasibility study therefore is, for those involved in the development of any new IS, to estimate and recommend to the management optimum possible courses of action.

A critical point is that the main product of the feasibility stage is a report which highlights the broad alternatives, which may include abandonment of any proposed project. The feasibility study is also usually the first stage at which management start thinking about critical choices with respect to the type of IS they wish to have. Such choices concern the complexity, functional levels and benefits of the system options and the associated type of equipment, hardware and software, possible suppliers and a relatively accurate approximation of the proposed costs and date of completion.

Feasibility studies for large organisations can be expensive exercises as big teams of highly paid professionals start to consider the options. Large organisations tend to put such projects out to tender. The tendering technique enables purchasers to transact and deal with specialist suppliers and service providers more conversant with projects of this type. As a result organisations can usually get an overview of possible alternatives with minimal outlay.

Simpler technology

Before going any further into the stages involved in IS development it is useful to consider the fact that there is ample evidence that business users on occasion revert back to simpler technology. This is especially so when users discover that the so-called new technology is either exorbitantly expensive or is inordinately complex. A good example to consider is the technology which enables users to place computer output onto microfilm, otherwise known as COM. COM is particularly favoured by users who need to keep vast amounts of data on a whole range of subjects. Prime users of this technology includes libraries, booksellers, spare-part specialists and so on.

What happens with COM is that users usually supply specialist providers with their information on a conventional data disk. The service providers then take this disk and pass it through a COM recorder which then writes the information to a microfiche, a robust celluloid type slide which users can then access by slotting into a simple microfiche reader. COM is a very basic but nonetheless efficient and inexpensive technology which needs a minimum of user expertise. However because of its apparent simplicity, many contemporary users felt the need to update their COM systems or at least ignore a COM system as a feasible alternative. As a result of this perception COM systems fell out of favour as users turned their attention to more sophisticated systems such as Document Image Processing (DIP).

With a DIP setup, documentation and images are converted into a digital data format which is then stored in a conventional computer system. Users of a DIP system usually employ a handheld or flatbed scanner in order to import and convert the information. This information, text, images, etc. is then displayed on a computer screen in order to allow the user to eliminate any flaws which may have been imported during the scanning process. The information is then usually condensed and written to an optical disk medium in a typically Write Once Read Many (WORM) layout. The disks are then stored in a functional server rack otherwise known as a jukebox.

Unfortunately installing a system such as a DIP configuration can cost tens of thousands if not hundreds of thousands of pounds. In contrast a COM system can be installed for a mere fraction of the price. Operating a DIP system can also prove to be a very complex task the manner of which is often beyond the scope of ordinary untrained users. Because of these two crucial limitations COM technology is currently undergoing something of a resurgence. Some users are even scrapping their more sophisticated technology in order to return to a COM setup.

The point is, users/organisations are gradually realising the extent of the conflicting benefits/opportunity costs posed by various technological solutions, and the fact that their particular needs may be better met by a cheaper lower-grade technology is one they need to be aware of.

Human element

In the final analysis a computerised IS is clearly used and operated by human beings. Nevertheless despite the obvious nature of this statement, business and industry often totally ignore the human element in the development of a new IS. However there is a change of direction in this regard. As a result of recent legal and moral advances, feasibility studies are now having to take full account of the potential impact of a new IS on the human element within an organisation. Issues such as potential redundancies, career progression, stress and the general well being of the workforce is gradually taking centre stage. Any feasibility study that fails to either address or cost the effect of a new IS on the workforce can now result in the organisation facing huge bills for compensation and litigation.

Experienced system designers and users have also begun to realise that in order for the IS to function efficiently it must be acceptable to the workforce which has to actually operate it. A new IS could mean extra responsibilities, especially in the short term when the IS is being installed. It could also mean a radical shake-up in the workforce's otherwise contented work practices. Upheavals in such situations are basically unavoidable. If however the workforce is offered adequate incentives in order to help ensure the success of the new IS then it is obviously more likely to succeed than might otherwise be the case.

11.7.3 Analysis and design

Once the management has examined the feasibility study and made a decision to proceed, so the professionals have to set about accomplishing the development of the proposed IS.

Broadly, systems analysis is concerned with *what* the proposed system does, i.e. the logical aspects, and systems design is concerned with *how* the system does it, i.e. the physical aspects.

Analysis begins with the existing system, if there is one, whether manual or computerised, and identifies what the system is designed to achieve. This is then used by the developers, in full consultation with management and users, as a basis for deriving the specification of a new and improved system. Thus, the output of the analysis stage is a *functional specification* of *what* the system must deliver in order to be judged a success by the management and the organisation.

The functional specification forms the starting point for the systems design stage. First, a fully detailed design is carried out at the logical level to provide a clear picture of the entire data flow through the system and the processing it undergoes. When approved, the logical design is converted into a physical design, showing precisely *how* the system carries out its functions, i.e. how it is to be implemented in terms of data structures, process design, hardware and software platforms, screen designs, network configurations, etc., and how it conforms to expectations in terms of

- Flexibility
- Robustness
- Reliability
- Security

The combined logical and physical design document forms the *system specification*. It provides the starting point for the implementation stage.

It should be pointed out that the description of the analysis and design stages above is particularly applicable to the structured methodologies.

11.7.4 Implementation

The implementation of a new information system involves a number of diverse activities, including, but not necessarily in this order:

- Program development and coding
- User documentation
- Staff training
- Physical installation
- Security

- System testing
- Conversion

(a) Program development and coding

The successful implementation of a system is heavily dependent on the nature and quality of the programs used by the system and of the interface between the computer and the user.

Developers know that well-thought-out interactive programs which enhance user activities will be central to the success of the system. This can be done through due consideration of screen layouts, I/O routines and data validation processes.

Program developers usually require good prototyping facilities as an intermediate stage of development whether they are writing totally new programs or simply tailoring ready-made software packages. Prototyping enables developers to produce simulated models of either the whole IS or parts of it. The advantage of this type of exercise is that developers get an immediate feedback on user requirements.

To complete necessary prototyping tasks within a set time period, developers are starting to use Fourth Generation Languages (4GL). The main advantage of this approach is in employing an application language which accesses ready-made screens and blocks of code and which is usually specifically designed to interface with and/or build database systems. The main disadvantage of employing a 4GL for a prototyping task is that it is less malleable than a 3GL such as Pascal, and requires computers with significantly more processing power.

The final coding of programs can be carried out by code generators, software packages that generate code automatically, usually in association with 4GLs; or by a team of programmers, working with 3GLs or 4GLs, who are experts in the language and perhaps in the selected operating system and who can operate more flexibly than a code generator.

Construction of large-scale programs is known as *software engineering* and it frequently makes use of Computer Aided Software Engineering (CASE) tools (see 12.10); this process is comparable to a large civil engineering project under the control of project software.

(b) User documentation

User documentation outlines the makeup of the IS and provides detailed guidance on how to successfully use the hardware and the software. In the past this type of text was presented in standard paper manuals. However this is changing as more and more developers are supplying modern sophisticated user documentation in the form of intelligent online help screens. Online documentation systems of this type can be expensive to develop but they can, in certain circumstances, also prove to be a long-term saving if the IS user can, as a consequence, minimise training/help costs.

(c) Staff training

This can be done either on or off site, with internal or external trainers. A training course which is off site and run by professional educators can prove very expensive. As a result many organisations are turning more towards an ever-increasing range of computer-based inhouse training systems. Many users also prefer to opt for systems equipped with standard industry hardware/software. By taking this route, organisations are more likely to avoid staff shortages due to unfamiliar or extraordinary equipment.

(d) Physical installation

Developers have to ensure that the IS is adequately housed and fully functioning. The physical installation of a large IS was in the past a complex logistical task which could only be achieved through the application of a reasonable and cogent plan.

However the physical installation of hardware/software is now a relatively short process. Modern computers are much more compact and mobile and do not require the same degree of attention demanded by previous generations of equipment. Software is also significantly easier to install. Setting up the cabling requirements of a LAN and the coordination requirements of the various nodes and servers may well require the greatest attention.

(e) Security

The implementation stage is frequently that stage where the IS's security measures are put into full effect. This stage includes the introduction of IS passwords and site security as well as data backup and data validation procedures. The personnel involved in this stage of IS development should be fully vetted, as they will, more often than not, get a good total view of the organisation's security routines, a fact which poses a security problem in its own right.

(f) System testing

In order to minimise error, the IS should be extensively tested before it is allowed to handle live data. For example, developers can test an IS by processing volumes of different types of transactions over a measured time period. Unfortunately because many ISs are now so complicated, developers have discovered that the complete testing of an IS can be impractical and that many errors are not discovered until the IS is fully implemented.

(g) Conversion

Unless the new IS is in complete disarray, procedures such as staff training and system installation are usually straightforward affairs. However system conversion can make or break any new IS. The conversion period is that time required for the new IS to come fully into operation. If there is no previous system then it is usually simply a matter of turning the key (totally equipped ISs which are supplied and installed from scratch are sometimes referred to as turnkey systems as all the user has to do, in theory, is switch on the system in order to set it in full operation). However, if there is a current system in place, manual or otherwise, then users have to be much more circumspect. The three main approaches to conversion are often referred to as parallel, staged and quick.

With *parallel conversion*, the old system is run alongside the new system. This usually means double the workload for a short length of time and can as a consequence prove to be a costly method. However, despite its expense it is considered to be the best approach to system conversion as it enables transactions passing through the new IS to be checked against results from the old IS. The main advantage of parallel conversion is that it gives developers more time to rectify system mistakes and so avoid possible customer alienation due to inadvertent mishaps.

The *staged approach* is, as its name suggests, a conversion process involving the introduction of the new IS step by step. Unfortunately this technique can prove to be very time consuming. The reason is that developers have to ensure compatibility of data passing between the various stages of the transition. This can be a very complicated process involving intense planning. Its main advantage, as with parallel conversion, is that it provides for a gradual changeover.

The *quick conversion* is where the old system is immediately replaced by the new one. If the new IS is a well designed or simple system or both then a quick conversion is advantageous in time and money. If however the new system is poorly designed or/and complex to operate then users can find themselves in serious difficulties and may have to fall back to the old system or even fully replace the new one.

11.7.5 Maintenance

In order that an IS remains of use to the organisation, systems have to be constantly serviced, corrected and developed. These types of activities are usually referred to as systems maintenance:

(a) Servicing

Servicing usually refers to straightforward mandatory operational procedures. However, even these procedures can be diverse in nature. For example, servicing procedures can involve mundane tasks such as the replacement of printer consumables such as paper and ink cartridges but it can also refer to maintenance programming as users update applications such as the payroll program.

(b) Correction

Developers and users know that it is almost inevitable that their new IS will contain errors or features which are not to their liking. Unfortunately such inadequacies are, more often than not, only discovered after the IS has been installed and implemented. The earlier that such mistakes can be rectified or captured the better.

(c) Development

System development can include activities such as creative computer programming, the inclusion of extra peripheral devices or even an increase in system processing power. However there is often a thin line between what might be construed as maintenance and what might be considered as radical modification. It is all a question of degree.

11.7.6 Feedback

The feedback stage is concerned with evaluating the success or failure of the new IS. The evaluation process itself is usually an investigative routine whereby users determine whether or not the IS functions as it was expected to do. Three critical criteria of this stage are performance, cost and satisfaction.

(a) Performance

A new IS can be considered to be performing successfully if it meets the user's requirements. Unfortunately this can, on occasion, prove to be an elusive goal and experienced developers are all too familiar with users/organisations complaining that even though the new IS fully matches the system specification it does not deliver all the information that they require. Users' demands can heighten during the course of development or installation because they become aware of the possibilities.

In order to reduce this type of IS inadequacy, developers have started to employ structured development methodologies. A chief attribute of this approach is the increased involvement of the user in order to ensure that the IS is producing appropriate information.

(b) Cost

For appraising the cost of a new IS, cost/benefit analysis can be used. This usually involves comparing the total of the IS's capital outlay against the organisation's subsequent change in revenues and decreased costs elsewhere within the organisation. However it must be emphasised that a costing analysis of any new IS must be treated with great caution as there are so many other intangible factors to consider.

(c) Satisfaction

If a new IS is proved to be cost effective and efficient it is likely that the user will be more than satisfied. If a new IS is significantly more expensive than was predicted but still provides sufficient information then the user may still be satisfied. However when the new IS turns out to be rather expensive and rather inefficient then it is more than likely that the user will want the system replaced. In any event, what should be noted is that the development process is a cyclic approach which assumes that all systems are eventually replaced.

11.8 STRUCTURED SYSTEM METHODOLOGIES

The characteristics of structured methodologies were introduced in the previous section. In addition to the rigour they apply, especially at the analysis and design stages, they place particular emphasis on:

- The data requirements of the system
- User participation
- Documentation
- Phase feedback
- Use of diagramming techniques (see Chapter 12)

(a) It is important to distinguish between the data which is input and processed by the system and the actual processing and output requirements of the organisation. The data is likely to remain a constant factor for some time but the processing requirements can change. A structured methodology should result in a system whose data structures are sound but flexible enough to permit changes to the processing in order to meet changing requirements of the organisation (see (d)).

(b) Developers have discovered that increased user participation, especially in the design stage, increases user satisfaction and reduces system error. For example structured system methodologies encourage techniques such as walkthroughs where users and developers pass through the system's processes together in order to ensure that the IS meets the user requirements.

(c) Structured methodologies place a particular emphasis on producing documentation which is useful and straightforward. In order to fulfil this goal, developers are expected to produce documentation text which is written in plain English and which contains clear and uncluttered diagrams and flowcharts.

(d) One major important technique which is common to structured system methodologies is the division of any new IS project into discrete but informative phases. The idea is that these phases are constantly reviewed. This review enables users and developers to adapt to new information and so fulfil the changing user requirements which arise as a result of an ever-changing business environment. Structured system methodology defines the manner in which the information gathered from each phase is allowed to affect the development and direction of the IS.

11.8.1 Structured Systems Analysis and Design Methodology (SSADM)

One of the most important IS development methodologies used in the UK is the Structured Systems Analysis and Design Methodology (SSADM). It was devised by commercial IT consultants in partnership with the UK Government. SSADM decomposes an IS development project into a series of discrete stages. Each stage is further reduced into a number of steps. The steps contain various tasks as well as various input and output requirements.

The following list is an outline of the stages of the SSADM approach:

(1) *Feasibility study*. This phase is concerned with a preliminary investigation into any proposed IS along with a relevant cost benefit report.

(2) *Systems analysis (or Requirements analysis)*. This phase is concerned with analysis of the current system and listing the requirements of the new IS.

(3) *Requirements specification*. This is a detailed and precise specification of requirements of the new IS, and takes the project into the design phase.

(4) *Hardware options (or Technical systems options)*. At this point the developers devise and grade the options as to the computing platform and network configuration.

(5) *Logical data and process design.* The developers design appropriate data structures and processes, including the database, without reference to any particular technical platform.

(6) *Physical design.* The logical design from stage 5 is translated into a physical design based on the technical platform selected from stage 4.

Because the SSADM methodology is such a thorough and prescriptive means of IS development it has to be undertaken by highly trained individuals. SSADM employs a host of different design and analysis tools (see next chapter). It is a methodology which is usually the preserve of the corporate or government sector since it is intended for large-scale systems, often multi-sited, and requires effective structured project management.

11.8.2 Soft Systems Methodology (SSM)

Soft Systems Methodology (SSM) is the name given to a systems methodology developed by Peter Checkland in the 1980s. The main idea behind SSM is to provide a series of techniques to enable developers to analyse people (soft) centred problems. The simple fact is that many problems under examination do not always lend themselves to formal analysis. Many ISs, existing and proposed, can, because of the very nature of the problems they are addressing (e.g. in social services), be both diverse and relatively unstructured. In this respect SSM is a recognition of this reality. When developers employ SSM in the development of an IS they usually follow a strategy composed of the following steps:

(1) *Situation unstructured.* In this step developers build up what is known as a rich picture. The concept of the rich picture is to gain a global view of the problem under analysis, which includes all internal and external influences.

(2) *Situation analysed.* This step involves the formulation of what is known as the root definition. The purpose of the root definition is to outline the properties and purpose of any proposed IS. To ensure that the root definition is clear as well as inclusive developers usually employ those questions as outlined in the mnemonic CATWOE:

- Customers (Clients): The developers identify who the IS will serve, who will benefit, who are affected.
- Actors: The developers identify who will be using and operating the IS.
- Transformation: The developers identify the processes and the changes planned to occur in the system.
- Weltanschauung (worldview): This involves taking an external view of the IS from a number of relevant viewpoints as well as clarifying the point at which it is currently perceived.

- Owners: The developers define who owns the actual IS; the system is answerable to its owners.
- Environment: This involves the developers examining the manner in which the IS interoperates with the current environment.

(3) *Conceptual model.* Having developed the root definition the developers then formulate a conceptual model of what is required of the IS.

(4) *Comparison.* Once the developers have produced a conceptual model(s) they then compare this to the current situation. Any discrepancies are noted and act as feedback to the developers so enabling them to modify the proposed IS.

(5) *Debate and implementation.* By this step it is fair to suggest that the developers have reached a consensus about feasible/desirable changes and formed a working specification of the proposed IS and will usually embark on a more formal system of development.

(6) *Ongoing development.* This step considers any new developments or requirements that need to be incorporated.

The main advantage of an SSM approach is that it it enables the developers to gain a fuller understanding of the problem(s) under review as well as to formalise the actual problem(s) themselves.

11.9 PROJECT MANAGEMENT

The introduction and development of a new sophisticated commercial IS typically requires a considerable degree of effort from the organisation's management. Successful projects of this type require management to ensure that project tasks and activities are completed on time and within the project's overall cost forecast. If the system is being developed by an outside consultancy, then the client organisation should responsibly ensure that the project management team contains members of its own staff and preferably headed up by one.

Large-scale IS projects involving an extensive workforce as well as considerable capital outlay mean that management must introduce strict scheduling systems. These scheduling systems will detail task precedence, task interdependence (e.g. there is no point having new computers delivered until the work area holding them has been fully prepared), task/phase completion dates and staff activities.

Good project management also means that management must, when necessary, be able to formulate and deliver contingency plans to deal with unexpected or exceptional circumstances. Such situations typically include an ability to switch to alternative suppliers or an ability to relocate staff to those tasks requiring extra manpower. IS project managers must also ensure that every completed task is thoroughly evaluated, and, where appropriate, appraised. This type of review provides project managers with critical tactical and operational information enabling them to best direct the project's progress.

11.10 IS PERSONNEL

To develop, implement, maintain and use a computerised commercial IS requires a host of different skills. Unfortunately, because these skills are so multifarious and complex and because there is an ever-increasing global demand for skills of this type, organisations are often required to make huge investments in their human resources in terms of training and pay.

Below is a list of the various types of personnel that appertain to IS development. Personnel that have such skills are usually multi-skilled, that is to say they are usually sufficiently trained and educated to perform more than one of the necessary skills applying to the IS.

(a) System analysts and system designers

The prime task of system analysts and system designers is to investigate and plan the introduction of a new IS. Their efforts usually result in the production of a document known as the system specification. The system specification details the design and operation of a new IS which meets the requirements of the user/organisation. The tasks of the analyst and the designer are such that they are the major roles in the development of any new IS. Because of the actual duties imposed by these roles they are often completed by the same people.

(b) Programmers

Programmers are the front-line technologists in any computerised IS. Their duties fall into two major categories: creative programming and maintenance programming. Creative programming is the more complex and results from work generated by the system specification. The overall task is laid out in 11.7.4. Maintenance programming involves installing, updating or tailoring the programs relating to the IS.

(c) Technical authors

A new computerised IS frequently involves a plethora of user documentation. Until recently the authors of such documentation were usually the actual designers and developers of the IS; however recent years have witnessed the increased use of specialist documentation experts known as technical authors.

(d) Trainers

A new computerised IS usually means new skills and new work patterns and procedures. Such skills are best learnt through adequate training primarily provided through specialist computer-based training systems or expert trainers.

Another popular approach in many large organisations is that of the help desk. The help desk is usually a small team of experts delegated with the purpose of supplying IS users with any necessary technical backup. The help desk can also act as an interface between the user/organisation and the designers/suppliers of the IS.

(e) Project managers

Project managers are usually former senior systems analysts/designers charged with the task of leading the introduction of a new IS. Project management is as much a political role as it is a technical role. Good project management is critical to the success of any new IS (see 11.9).

11.11 OUTSOURCING

In order to take advantage of specialist IS developers and IS service suppliers, many organisations are starting to employ such external agencies. These external agencies provide services ranging from advice on data communications and IS application development to the total provision of an organisation's IS requirements. This is commonly referred to as outsourcing.

The 1990s has witnessed a big explosion in the outsourcing of computing services. In Britain and other parts of the Western world, outsourcing was fuelled by political and economic winds of privatisation, a major consequence of which was the transfer of public sector IS duties to agencies operating in the private sector.

The two main advantages of outsourcing centre on cost reduction and staff deployment:

(a) Cost reduction

What outsourcing does is to enable organisations to tap into competitively priced computing resources and services provided by suppliers who, because they service other organisations, can exploit economies of scale as well as provide necessary expertise as and when required.

For example, the development, implementation and operation of a quality computerised commercial IS is an expensive and potentially risky process. Critical factors such as an overall understanding of the goals and functions of a new IS, a sound estimation of the size, cost and duration of the IS project, and sufficient technical expertise to operate the IS, may quite simply be beyond current management/employee capability. Even when the current workforce has sufficient skills to carry out the necessary tasks pertaining to the introduction of a new IS it is more than likely that IT professionals who specialise in the development of ISs would be more effective.

(b) Redeployment

Outsourcing also allows an organisation to redeploy highly trained staff away from more mundane operational processes to more profitable strategic operations. What this means is that valuable staff can delegate operations such as sales and stock records to an external agency and concentrate instead on more dynamic and creative duties such as devising and improving production systems.

Unfortunately many organisations have discovered that outsourcing has one major drawback. The problem is that, as external agencies take over an organisation's IS responsibilities, so management can lose control of their own organisation. This loss of control can result from the organisation being unwittingly bound into a detrimental service contract, for example a longer-term contract than is prudent. Alternatively if the organisation has dispensed with its own computing expertise it could discover that it is practically totally reliant on the advice of the service provider.

11.12 BUSINESS PROCESS RE-ENGINEERING PRESSURES

It is glaringly apparent that modern technology has resulted in a total change within the global business culture. However whilst business users will always welcome those technologies which deliver new levels of efficiency and economy, the fact is new technology is no longer perceived as being the magic bullet that it once was.

For example, as can be seen from the preceding sections in this chapter, developing, implementing and indeed using a new information system can be fraught with difficulties and its actual benefit is not always immediately, if at all, apparent.

Nevertheless change is a constant force and the fact is that relatively recent computing and technological advances have been so dramatic that users and developers of every type have had to constantly re-engineer their structures and processes in order to stay within mainstream commercial practice. Amongst those directly related pressures are those emanating from the need to constantly re-educate and re-skill and those from what is now euphemistically referred to as technological hype.

11.12.1 Education and re-skilling

The increasing pace of new technology has meant that the IT departments as well the rank and file IT/IS professionals that are present in most corporate companies have to undergo constant re-education. This re-education has included the need to update IT skills to deal with the increasing complexity of new technology as well as to deal with the ever-increasing problem of computer security and social legislation. In addition IT/IS specialists are also having to cope with the growing list of expectations and service requests from other parts of the organisation and to come to terms with ensuring that they provide a value added service and not just a technological bolt-on.

11.12.2 Technological hype

Users and developers are being swamped with information concerning the use and development of IT. This type of phenomena, sometimes referred to as technological hype, is causing stress to organisations and individuals alike. The problem is the computing/communications industry is a dream industry for advertising interests. It is fast-moving, dynamic, exciting and awash with cash. It is also prolific in terms of its output and every week there is a host of new ideas and products all of which have to be promoted in order to establish their particular section of the market. Unfortunately advertisers and marketing departments are also well known for embellishing the performance or attributes of their particular client products, a fact which can have significant consequences for users further down the road. In addition, some of the products are presented in what might be described as an almost menacing manner. This manner often suggests that any failure by the user to purchase their particular product could be detrimental to the user's long-term strategy and well being.

As a result of this often excessive hyperbole, there has been a certain air of panic and confusion amongst business and domestic users, many of whom have been stampeded into purchasing inappropriate systems or products. Sadly, knowing what computer system to buy or use can and has proved as problematical to corporate conglomerates as it has to individual users.

Obviously, decisions concerning the type and cost of equipment/ systems, relating to an individual user or organisation, depend on a host of factors. However, money is central to the business culture and business has had to learn to sift through a plethora of information and promotion material in order to purchase and operate those computer applications which are more likely to suit their profit margins as opposed to the profit margins of the computer/IS developers.

In order, therefore, to bring a certain degree of rationalisation to decisions concerning the investment in and use of the various computing technologies and services currently on offer, more and more users are gradually developing strategies to deal with unsubstantiated technological hype.

Consider the following:

(a) Economic alternatives

Business users are faced with an increasing number of technological alternatives all of which have various advantages/disadvantages. However many successful business users give priority to what is, in essence, the best economic alternative. For example, do employees really need to be equipped with the latest expensive desktop multimedia Internet-linked computers in order to carry out basic report writing activities? Could these employees carry out the same functions with a small electronic organiser or would the organisation be better off just to supply their employees with a range of cheap multicoloured biros along with an endless supply of recycled paper ?

Such questions do not necessarily have clear-cut answers as it could be argued that the latest equipment, despite the expense, will enhance the user's self esteem and so motivate them to generate more profits. However the point is, such a decision or evaluation is best made by the purchaser that is aware of all the relevant economic alternatives.

(b) Budgeting for hidden costs

Users have also started to give greater consideration to what is known as hidden costs. Such costs include those costs incurred in the operation and maintenance of various technologies. For example when potential purchasers are presented with a system's attributes they are rarely given the full picture. Unfortunately, it is not until the system is actually running that users suddenly become aware of critical expenses such as power consumption, consumables and the need to purchase other peripheral devices.

11.13 VAPOURWARE

Experienced users and IT/IS professionals have had to become wary of a somewhat insidious pitfall known as vapourware. This is an expression given over to those prospective technological products which have attracted large publicity and which have had either a very short life span or which do not actually appear. Some products which transpire to be nothing more than vapourware are so as a result of inadvertent circumstances whilst other products which fall into the vapourware category are so because of a deliberate corporate strategy (see below).

Failure to take account of vapourware can result in potential users building their business computing/communication systems on what turns about to be either a non-existent product/service or a technological base which is obsolete long before its initial predicted life span.

Vapourware can materialise because of:

(a) Competition

Numerous computer developers have sought to throw off the opposition by pretending to invest in a new range of expensive innovative products. Developers use this ploy to try and force the competition to either follow suit and thus waste precious resources or, better still, quit that particular section of the market or industry through fear of being unable to match the developer's proposed products.

(b) Cash

Advanced technological research and development (R & D) is horrendously expensive. Unfortunately many computer and communication developers have often found that their visions of the future were bigger than their bank accounts and cash shortages have resulted in some wonderful products failing to be either fully developed or put into production.

(c) Technology

There are, almost inevitably, technological problems encountered with any new product. However, with vapourware, it could be that science or more particularly the organisation's scientists are simply not up to the product's proposed capabilities or it could be that the proposed ideas/products are impractical. The proposed product(s) could even, on arrival, be out of date because of a development in another branch of computing or telecommunication technology.

(d) Marketing

Vapourware is also used as a marketing gimmick. For example, in order to persuade customers to purchase current products it is not unknown for developers to talk about a whole new spread of future compatible products. Potential customers who are under the impression that the product is part of an evolving range will be much more likely to purchase than might otherwise be the case.

11.14 CONCLUSION

It is apparent that every organisations needs an IS. It is also apparent that in order for the IS to be of use to the organisation it must fulfil the organisation's needs. Computerised ISs have proved that they can, when properly developed, be more than adequate in this regard. However a new computerised IS can prove to be a very expensive option so it is imperative that organisations plan their IS development in an organised and methodical manner. Techniques and strategies as outlined by some system methodologies go some way to achieving this goal.

In addition, as ISs become more and more sophisticated, so organisations become increasingly aware as to the pivotal role played by various IT professionals. Unfortunately, permanent full-time personnel of this calibre can prove to be too costly for an organisation to bear. As a result many organisations now outsource their IS processing requirement to external agencies.

12

Information systems: analysis and design

12.1 INTRODUCTION

The analysis and design of information systems requires the application of many formal tools and techniques, of which a selection is given in this chapter, and the design process is nothing if not a choice between the options available.

Section 12.2 outlines the primary objectives of analysis and design. Section 12.3 focuses on the variety of tools and techniques applicable to the analysis stage. Subsequent sections deal with design considerations and options: 12.4 on data design, 12.5 on software design, 12.6 on processing options, 12.7 on hardware options, and 12.8 on input/output considerations. Section 12.9 reiterates the crucial role of user documentation, and 12.10 rounds off the growing significance of CASE tools in the whole development process. Finally section 12.11 looks at expert systems as an alternative to 'conventional' information systems.

12.2 ANALYSIS AND DESIGN OBJECTIVES

The primary objectives of systems analysis and design have been outlined in 11.7.3, and it must be understood that they are crucial to the development of a successful information system.

(a) The tasks of **systems analysis** are to
- *Collect information* – about the business, what information it uses, sources of information, the way in which it is used and processed throughout the business.
- *Record information* – in a clear, unambiguous manner, accessible to all analysts and designers, using diagramming techniques.

- *Utilise information* – the information recorded about the current business is used as a basis to derive the extended requirements of the new system, so that the new system can then be mapped out in the form of a logical data flow diagram (LDFD), which in turn either forms the functional specification or is the basis for it.

(b) Systems design tasks concern the data, the software and the hardware, and can be highly technical in nature.

- *Data*: the LDFD is translated into a physical design which embraces data modelling, file design and database design. Many of the options are given in Chapter 10.
- *Software*: the processing which the data is required to undergo (merging, sorting, updating, etc.) determines the programs needed by the system. The processing requirements are laid out in the functional specification and when they have been firmly established a program specification and design can be developed which almost certainly will involve a suite of programs (for example, a stock control program, payroll program, etc.). Given the program specification and design, the program developers and coders can begin work. Options in software development are outlined in Chapter 9.
- *Hardware*: the importance of the correct choice of hardware platform can hardly be overstated. Many of the considerations and options concerning the computers, networking and data communications are presented in Chapters 2 to 6.
- *Input/Output*: the design of the input/output, or human/computer interface, facilities deserve a special mention because for most users they represent what the system actually is, they are the means by which most users interface with the system. Such facilities involve screen designs, GUIs, WIMPs, modes of input (mouse, keyboard, touch screen, voice, etc.), modes of output (printers, VDU display, etc.).

12.3 ANALYSIS TOOLS AND TECHNIQUES

For the tasks set out in 12.2(a), certain tools and techniques are employed by systems analysts.

12.3.1 Dialogue

The most powerful investigative tool in an analysts's or designer's repertoire is that of human dialogue. It is through dialogue that the goals of the user organisation can be revealed. It is also through dialogue that the analyst is able to converse with personnel that are immediately affected by the IS. Such dialogue usually enables the developers to devise and apportion the processes performed by the IS.

Dialogue is a very effective process which can cover a significant amount of ground in a very short time span. As a result there is a significant emphasis by analysts on interviews, dialogue analysis (such as a taped conversation between a client and a sales representative) and formal as well as informal debates. However human speech and language is riddled with inconsistencies and paradoxes. It is for this reason that human dialogue is supplemented by other techniques.

12.3.2 Surveys

A more discreet form of information gathering is through the use of surveys or questionnaires. They can, if worded correctly, enable the analysts to gather innovative suggestions throughout the organisation. Surveys are also useful for gathering information from groups of employees who happen to be scattered over a wide area.

12.3.3 Observation

The simple observation of the functions performed by personnel in the work place is another extremely useful technique. It can however also cause friction and has to be done with maximum sensitivity. Nevertheless as automation gathers pace so workers of every category are discovering that the observation or shadowing of them in the performance of their duties is becoming an increasingly widespread spectacle within the modern business environment.

12.3.4 Decision grids

Decision grids are useful straightforward lists enabling IS developers to gain a clear understanding of the system's underlying processes. Their unambiguous rule-based style is also particularly well-suited in instructing programmers as to the composition and functions of any programs they are obliged to implement.

12.3.5 Structured English

Structured English, sometimes referred to as pseudo English, is the term used to describe narrative written in a very exact style. The vocabulary used in a structured English narrative is usually severely limited to nouns and simple verbs whilst the text itself is consequently terse and unimaginative. The main advantage with this style of writing is that it minimises communication problems. Complex instructions and descriptions can be conveyed in a meticulous yet unambiguous manner so reducing the possibility of error and conflict. Various methodologies have comparable but differing versions of structured English and, to date, there is no official convention or guideline defining the concept or quality of structured English.

12.3.6 Traditional academic research methods

Traditional academic research methods can also prove invaluable to IS development. Two major categories include archive and statistical research:

(a) Archive

Archive research activity is common to all organisations. The need to refer to various external information sources such as government reports concerning the political and economic climate, legislation, marketing information, press releases is considered almost as a matter of course. Up to date archive research activity has taken on an added dimension with the arrival of the Internet/Intranet and IS developers know that valuable information pertinent to the organisation could be just around the next screen.

(b) Statistical

Statistical methods are becoming increasingly popular in IS development. One reason for this is the relative ease with which developers can operate the new sophisticated statistical computer applications that are now available. Many of these statistical applications are not only friendly to use but are also extremely powerful enabling developers to execute increasingly complex calculations so allowing them to make decisions/forecasts with even greater accuracy.

12.3.7 Graphical analysis tools

The generally accepted role of a graphical analysis tool in IS development is to provide all the parties concerned with a visual representation of the various operations and procedures relating to the proposed new IS. The advantage of such a technique is to reduce the confusion that might result from trying to digest pages of technical text. Such text may be relevant to the IS's designers but could prove meaningless to the actual user if not confusing to the designers themselves. However a well annotated and clear flowchart or diagram is an invaluable device which usually proves extremely useful to the developers and can, for example, highlight possible anomalies.

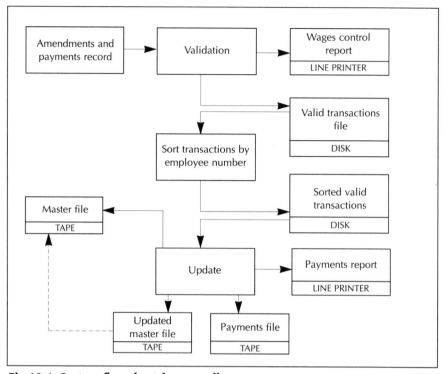

Fig 12.1 System flowchart for payroll process
(Courtesy: *A Glossary of Computing Terms* 8th edn. British Computer Society with Addison Wesley Longman)

12.3.8 System flowcharts

A system flowchart is used to present a comprehensive diagrammatic representation of the physical as well as the functional aspects of an IS. It breaks down the flow of data in the system and displays the tasks, file types and tangible technology as well as the system boundaries with other systems, internal and external. One form of system flowchart is shown in figure 12.1.

This type of flowchart is useful for showing the constituent components of a current IS and is also a useful way of representing the proposed IS. It is the kind of diagram that can be understood by users and managers and can be utilised by analysts throughout their investigation, becoming increasingly more sophisticated.

12.3.9 Logical data flow diagrams

System flowcharts do have certain inadequacies as an actual design tool. Because of their focus on the physical makeup of an individual IS system, flowcharts can actually hinder the development of a new IS. Firstly system flowcharts encourage the former conventional practice of system analysts to simply examine the current processes and functions of the organisation's activities with a view to automating the same activities. Unfortunately, such an approach can result in the inadequacies or errors operating in the current IS being carried over into the new IS. Secondly system flowcharts can fasten the developers to a particular design/configuration at too early a stage in the IS project life cycle, the choice of which they may have cause to regret.

In order to circumvent these errors and constraints, systems analysts employing a structured methodology construct a logical model outlining the passage and transformation of data as it flows through the system. This type of model is often referred to as a Logical Data Flow Diagram (LDFD). It should be noted that an LDFD diagram is not created in isolation from, but in conjunction with, other development tools and techniques. For example the processes which actually transform the data within the IS are not only depicted on the LDFD but are also usually explained within the actual IS functional specification. The explanation of the processes is usually done with the use of decision tables or structured English narrative.

The benefit of the LDFD approach is that it simply presents a diagrammatic representation independent of the IS's physical quality or the IS's physical requirements, which are the responsibility of the systems designers. It would be irrelevant to the quality of a LDFD as to whether staff records were stored in a manual card index or in a sequential database

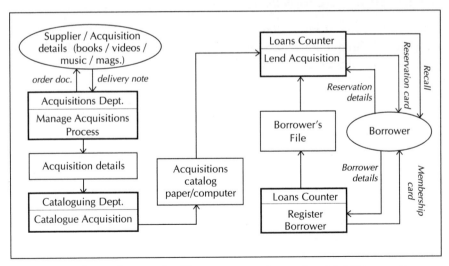

Fig 12.2 High-level LDFD for library system; lower-level LDFDs can then be constructed for Lend Acquisition, Manage Acquisitions Process, etc.

(Adapted from Yeates, Shields and Helmy, *Systems Analysis and Design*, Financial Times Pitman Publishing)

file. By using this method, system analysts can ignore the nature of the technology employed by the current system.

The LDFD representing the current IS is then used as a foundation for a new LDFD representing the new IS. The new LDFD is drawn up in agreement with the user/organisation and is simply a logical representation of the flow and transformation of data in the proposed IS. Using this method means that necessary decisions concerning the actual physical configuration of the new IS can be postponed until the design stage, as already explained.

In a complex system, several LDFDs are required in order to present the system at increasing levels of detail. A high-level LDFD would portray the system at a macro level; the sub-systems would then each have their own LDFD, progressing perhaps down to even lower levels.

Figure 12.2 gives an example of a high-level LDFD.

12.4 DATA DESIGN

At the design stage the proposed new IS starts to become a physical reality and, as with the analysis stage, the design process requires the use of certain tools and techniques. No task of the design stage is more important than data modelling in ensuring that the system's output matches the user's requirements.

12.4.1 Entity relationship diagrams

The construction of Entity Relationship Diagrams (ERDs) is an important graphical technique for analysing and presenting the logical relationships between the various data items required in the IS. ERDs are particularly relevant to designing a database as they make clear the relationships between the different layers of data in a database. They are constructed from the information contained in the logical data flow diagram (LDFD) and aim to identify the key data items fundamental to the design of the database.

An entity, or data entity, is something about which an organisation needs to hold data, for example a book in a library system or a student in a college system. Each entity must be uniquely identifiable and must occur more than once.

An entity has attributes. For example the entity type student could have the attributes: name, sex, address, admission number; the entity type course could have the attributes: course title, course code, cost. These attributes tend to differ from student to student but it is possible that students could have the same name and be on the same course, etc. In order to distinguish one student from another it is necessary for each entity type to contain a

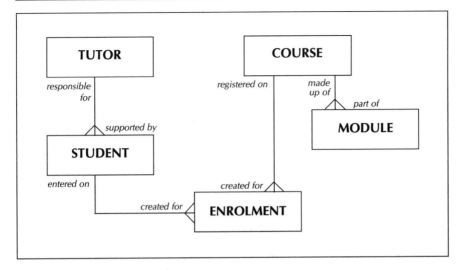

Fig. 12.3 Entity relationship diagram

unique attribute. A good example of a unique attribute for student entity could be the student's enrolment number. This unique attribute is usually referred to as a key attribute.

Along with other entities such as tutor, module, etc., each with their own special attributes, an entity relationship diagram can be constructed. There are many possible relationships between entities but on an ERD only one-to-many relationships are shown, for example a given tutor has many students but a given student has only one tutor. A possible ERD is shown in figure 12.3. and it should be obvious that many ERDs are needed for a college system and that it is not an easy matter to work them out.

The ERDs are then used to construct the data models used in the files or the database.

12.4.2 File design considerations

Despite the popularity of databases, there is frequently a place for conventional files in information systems. They are particularly needed in some real-time systems where searching a database would take an unacceptably long time and also in many batch processing systems. Conventional files are stored on magnetic tape or magnetic disks.

Master files contain records which are critical to the organisation and are of long-term value. Transaction files contain transient data relating to day-to-day activities; they a used to update master files. A combination of a master file (e.g. customer) and transaction file (e.g. daily order) can lead to an output file (e.g. invoice).

253

Files can only be organised in a number of ways, chiefly:

- *Serial organisation*: the records are simply stored one after the other as they arrive, with no regard to sequence; a particular record cannot be accessed directly; to reach the 20th record means going through the first nineteen.
- *Sequential organisation*: records are stored in a sequence determined by a key field, such as alphabetical order or in ascending customer number order.

    Both serial and sequential files can be stored on tape and disk
- *Indexed sequential organisation*: records are stored in sequence within groups where each group is identified by an index; by knowing this index a group can be directly accessed and quickly thereafter the individual record. Suitable only for disk storage.

A number of design considerations apply to files: fixed or variable length, file size, time for accessing data, frequency of inserting, amending or deleting, etc.

The use of files rather than a centralised database can be fraught with danger for a normal business operation. Consider a company where the accounts department may be using a ready-made software application in order to maintain the company's sales and purchase ledgers whilst the company warehouse may be using a totally separate in-house stock control program. It is more than likely that both programs are controlled by different members of staff and that the data is stored in totally different locations. This dispersal gives immediate rise to problems such as data redundancy and data inconsistency.

Another problem with data files being scattered in this manner is the complications encountered by the organisation when it wishes to develop or employ other applications. The consequent inconsistency that can arise regarding the structure and storage of organisational data makes it extremely difficult to produce system-wide compatible applications.

12.4.3 Database design considerations

A collection of files, as described in the last section, can be regarded as a database and indeed many company databases in use take precisely that form and are successful since the search and access requirements are relatively straightforward. They are often known as File Management Systems.

For large collections of data, however, a properly constructed database is more or less essential, particularly if the intention is to create a centralised database. The relational database model is seen as the most advanced and most flexible form of database for 'normal' or conventional data, but there are two qualifications:

- Relational databases can have limitations in regard to on-line processing (e.g. travel agency booking system) because response times can be unsatisfactory. Hierarchical and network databases are fundamentally more suited to such tasks although the more powerful computers are minimising this difference.
- The advent of multimedia and non-conventional data types favours the use of object oriented databases, since these data types are not amenable to the rigid structuring requirements of relational databases.

Relational databases favour situations where data is extensive, where many fields and records need to be established, and where many types of search and access are demanded. They can be located in the central mainframe or minicomputer or distributed throughout a network system. Relational Database Management Systems can now reliably handle distributed database and fast client/server systems.

12.5 SOFTWARE DESIGN OPTIONS

As already explained, the analysis and design stages breaks the system down into functional areas, each of which broadly speaking requires its own program. One problem that arises is that the more programs required, the more interfaces are required between programs to ensure consistent operation. However, object oriented programming can be used to minimise such problems.

The program specification (see 12.2(b)) should, for each program, clearly lay out data input and output requirements, processing requirements, how the program should deal with exceptional conditions, subroutines employable, desirable screen layouts, possibly the operating system and language to be used, etc. A program specification can come in the form of detailed flowcharts and/or so-called data action diagrams based on structured English.

The techniques and considerations surrounding program development have already been outlined in section 9.6 but the higher-level considerations facing an organisation are now expanded upon:

(a) In-house software development

The advantage of producing in-house software is that the organisation is more likely to get an IS suitable to its goals. The reason for this is the user organisation's ability to specify exactly what demands are to be placed upon the IS and the ability of internal development staff to relate directly to the requirements.

The disadvantage of this type of development is the cost. Producing individual IS applications of this type could result in the organisation having to recruit expensive contract programmers as well as having to sustain a staff of permanent technicians/programmers. In addition the time taken to develop such an application can be considerable. In-house IS software development is, for the most part, the exclusive domain of large corporate organisations requiring specialist services.

However it should be noted that there are noticeable success stories where various companies have managed to produce applications suitable to the needs of their particular business and have in turn made substantial profits by then selling the application to other operatives within their particular market.

(b) Ready-made software applications

The majority of users organisations know that ready-made software applications can be a very expeditious and cost effective option. Firstly the user organisation is no longer burdened with the costs arising from the software development life cycle. Secondly ready-made software applications are, as their name suggests, usually ready to use almost as soon as they are installed. This rapid deployment could enable the user organisation to make considerable savings by being able to take advantage of the new efficiencies resulting from the new IS's prompt employment. Thirdly software applications of this type are also generally relatively inexpensive to purchase. The main reason for their competitive pricing is that they are usually created for a much wider market so allowing developers to recover their investment through increased sales.

User organisations have also discovered that market leading titles of this type of application software are typically reasonably robust and well documented. They also tend to have a good support base both in terms of training and user help.

The main disadvantage of these applications is that because they have been designed for the mass market they may not possess those particular attributes required by the user organisation. As a result the user organisation may have to compromise or alternatively invest in underpinning the ready-made application by developing support programs or arrange to have the application *customised* to their requirements.

(c) Software houses

If an organisation cannot afford the cost, or does not possess the capability, of developing an in-house software application and is unable to find a suitable ready-made software application then they usually resort to a software house, especially if the required system is large scale and complex.

Organisations such as software houses frequently undertake projects involving the development of specialist IS computer applications. The software house usually works from a program specification provided by the IS's developers who themselves could be internal or external to the organisation. As well as developing the actual code, software houses usually instruct and train users of the new IS program as well as installing and supporting the application. The main disadvantage of employing a software house or indeed any external service provider is that they are unlikely to fully understand the organisation's requirements. There is also the question of delay as the software house develops the program. However, with the user organisation only paying for services as required this can prove to be an economic approach.

12.6 PROCESSING OPTIONS

In order to focus on the best design alternative it is usual to consider the manner in which the data is processed as it passes through the IS. Three main processing alternatives include batch processing, real time processing and distributed processing. It should stressed that many corporate size organisations usually employ all three alternatives in varying degrees.

12.6.1 Batch processing

Batch processing is a data processing technique which is employed mainly by ISs based on a minicomputer/mainframe configuration. With batch processing, work is collected in a central location and processed at specific times. The idea behind batch processing is to enable users to gain maximum processing efficiency by matching the organisational data processing workload with the organisation's computer processing resources.

A good example of batch processing is with the high street banks. Most European high street banks employ automatic teller machines (ATMs). These ATMs are computer terminals which operate in real time processing mode (see below). They are frequently linked to a central mainframe system at the bank's headquarters. The peak processing requirement period for the bank's mainframe computer in order to service these ATMs is during daylight hours when most of the population is awake. However during the hours of darkness there is an excess of processing capacity on the bank's central computers as they no longer have to respond to the same volume of traffic transmitting from the ATMs. It is during this trough that the bank's carry out their other processing transactions such as updating customer accounts and calculating interest payments.

12.6.2 Real time processing

With real time processing (RTP), the user's input/instructions are effectively processed as they are entered. RTP is suited to those situations where it is necessary for an IS to instantly update the details of a particular record/database or where the output is instantly required in order to influence some situation in the real outside world (e.g. air-traffic control).

The best example of this type of requirement is an airline reservation system. In order to ensure secure seat accommodation, flight customers will usually want their seats reserved as they place their booking. In order to achieve this the airline booking agent usually employs a linked computer terminal which updates a centrally held database as soon as the transaction is successfully communicated. Unlike batch processing, therefore, RTP can require equipment with expensive communication links.

12.6.3 Distributed data processing

The concept behind distributed data processing is for a local computer system (be it a standalone computer or a PC LAN) to process the transactions which are local or which pertain to the duties assigned to that part of the organisation. The results of these transactions are then collated and summarised for transmission to a central computer system.

The main advantages of this type of processing is that it can enhance local control/discretion, reduce communication costs and relieve the workload of any central computer system. Distributed data processing (DDP) has really come to the fore with the massive increase in the use of PC LANS.

12.7 HARDWARE OPTIONS

This section rounds off all the hardware considerations and options provided in Chapters 2 to 6. Given the current plethora of possible computer configurations available to IS developers, users organisations are faced with a complex choice when it comes to equipment provision. Basically IS developers have to ensure that the hardware supporting the new IS is effective and economic. The leasing or purchasing of the latest computer hardware does not always satisfy this criteria.

Three hardware alternatives that developers may consider include the deployment of an in-house computer configuration, the sharing of computer resources with other organisations and the outsourcing of the IS equipment provision to an external service bureau/agency.

(a) In-house hardware

With an in-house computer system, the user organisation has total control over the type of computer equipment employed by the IS as well as the manner in which the equipment is developed. The advantage of this type of control is that it enables the user organisation to rank the tasks to be performed by the IS so enabling them to dictate the allocation of hardware resources.

An in-house computer system also enables the user organisation to determine the choice of software, a choice which is often mandated by the IS's computer configuration. The disadvantage is that the user organisation incurs the total cost of the IS hardware. This total cost includes the purchase of the computer equipment, computer maintenance, computer development and employee education.

(b) Resource sharing

In order to try and reduce costs an increasing number of organisations are beginning to share equipment resources. A good illustration of resource sharing would be the joint purchase of a communications link. For example, organisations inhabiting a city office block could collaborate in the purchase and installation of a satellite dish or ISDN line.

Another example of resource sharing revolves around the use of mainframe computers. Modern mainframes are very useful but their expense is such that they are beyond the means of many users. Organisations wishing to employ the power of a mainframe computer without having to actually acquire one usually contract into a system known as timesharing.

Timesharing involves users literally purchasing processing time on a mainframe computer belonging to another organisation. The client user usually supplies the appropriate terminal(s) and peripheral devices in order to communicate with the mainframe and then pays a fee for that amount of time it uses on the mainframe.

The main advantage of timesharing is that the user organisation doesn't have its money tied up in an asset which they only use as and when required. The main disadvantage is a lack of flexibility as the user may not always be able to access the mainframe and may be unable to secure the type of services/software appropriate to their particular needs.

(c) External agencies

One way of minimising a user organisation's investment in computer hardware is by outsourcing tasks to external agencies. Outsourcing, as mentioned in 11.11, is concerned with the employment of external agencies such as a computer bureau/consultancy for the provision of various IT/IS related services.

The degree to which organisational tasks are externalised varies with the type of IS to be implemented. If the organisation decides to hand over total control of the new IS to an external organisation it is possible that the client organisation has little if any need for computer hardware. However it must be argued that whilst many organisations are taking advantage of this kind of service there is still a need for the organisation to have a certain amount of hardware even if it is only that which is required in order to interface with the IS service provider.

The main advantage of such externalisation is the vast equipment savings, but this must be balanced against the fees charged by the service provider and the organisation's loss of control over its hardware.

12.7.1 Data storage

One issue which is becoming increasingly important to all classes of computer user, and which is critical when designers are allocating an IS's resources, is that of data storage. During the early to mid 1980s a 20 Mb hard disk inside a conventional PC appeared to be more than sufficient for most mainstream small business packages. However the arrival of sophisticated process-intensive GUI programs and other powerful applications has resulted in users demanding far greater data storage capacity. For example, OODs can contain space hungry multimedia data files whilst graphic-intensive Web browsers can download vast amounts of information from the Internet. Complex DTP packages use pictures/images which consume far more storage room than ordinary text files and modern accounting systems can create tens of thousands of ledgers in order to track all the user's various transactions.

Even CD-ROM applications can aggravate data storage space. The problem is that although most of the data is read directly from the CD-ROM, contemporary data access via CD-ROM technology is relatively sluggish. In order to counter this, the majority of CD-ROM applications access parts of the PC's hard disk. This in turn can make considerable demands on the hard disk as it seeks to accommodate all the extra fonts, artwork, photos, sound recordings and whatever else a particular CD-ROM may be designed to deliver.

As a result of these various conflicting data storage requirements, contemporary top of the range PCs in the late 1990s are supplied with 5 Gb hard disks almost as a matter of course. Fortunately, the cost of producing these hard disks is estimated to be decreasing by 20-30% every year. However the downside is that individual data storage requirements are doubling every two years and business users have realised that PC/computing storage needs have the potential to quite literally spin out of control.

In order to try and rationalise their data storage demands, more and more users are beginning to employ inexpensive magnetic tape storage devices. These are particularly favoured by users wishing to back up infrequently used data or that data which does not require fast access. Mainframe and minicomputer system users have always paid particular attention to tape technology and have found that it is significantly cheaper than most disk, optical or magnetic, centred backup systems. Furthermore, PC users are also starting to make greater use of tape technology. The main reason for this sudden uptake has been the arrival of smart magnetic tape systems that can be slotted into unoccupied printer ports. Such devices are not only simple to use but also mean that users of PC configurations are no longer required to purchase expensive magnetic tape drives in order take advantage of the savings that can be enjoyed by using magnetic tape.

12.8 INPUT/OUTPUT CONSIDERATIONS

It is the interface between the human user and the computer system which determines the usability and effectiveness of the whole system and whether it has ultimately fulfilled its purpose. The user must be able to interact meaningfully and comfortably with the system and establish a dialogue with it for conveying necessary instructions.

Input/output design is certainly concerned with the correct choice of device but most particularly it concerns the design of screens for enabling the user to quickly locate the required screen, for enabling the accurate and prompt input or manipulation of information/data (whether forms, spreadsheets, database tables, graphics, etc.), and for enabling the output to be easily understood and interpreted.

12.8.1 Input systems

Command-based keyboard input systems provide a direct way of conveying instructions to the computer and can take the form of single characters, multiple character abbreviations, function keys, etc. Command names should preferably be chosen to indicate the instruction, otherwise they can be difficult to remember. The use of command systems is still very common, frequently in conjunction with a menu-based system once the required screen has been located.

Menu-based systems have become the preferred user input. A menu is a set of options displayed on the screen, usually in the form of icons, i.e. pictographic representations of screens or processes, hopefully self-explanatory. Menu options can be in the form of pull-down menus to provide a cascading menu at multiple levels for accessing progressively detailed menus or screens.

Graphical user interfaces (GUIs) are now the dominant form for most users; they incorporate menu facilities and also the direct manipulation of items or objects on screen, used for example in designing a form or document or constructing a graphical presentation. They also permit several applications to be displayed simultaneously, each with their own window. WIMP environments cater for these requirements.

Voice input (13.3) has certain specific applications at this point in time but is set to spread. Joysticks and tracker-balls are used with CAD systems and animation. Touch screens are used in retail outlets in conjunction with bar code readers and keypads. Digitisers are used for inputting graphics, both photographic and line work, for manipulation by DTP packages or incorporation into any kind of document.

12.8.2 Output systems

For most purposes the alternatives are printers or visual display unit (VDU, the computer screen) or, of course, a combination of these.

Printers are of two types. Impact printers such as dot matrix work in the same way as a typewriter. Non-impact printers are of several kinds and include inkjet printers and laser printers. See 3.15 for more on printers.

A laser printer uses a laser light source to transfer the image stored in the printer's memory on to a special drum. The drum attracts the toner and the paper is pressed against the drum so that the image is transferred to the paper. The image on the paper is fixed by a heater before it emerges. Laser printers print a page at a time. They produce high-quality output, at high speed, almost soundlessly, but relatively expensively. Colour printing is very expensive.

Obviously printing provides a permanent record which can be distributed as required. VDU screens provide a transient image but which, if desired, can be printed out. High-resolution graphics enable the display of highly sophisticated presentations.

Additionally, plotters are used to produce coloured line drawings such as plans and maps. Output can, of course, also be in the form of video images and sound, etc., especially for multimedia presentations.

A special kind of computer language called a page description language has been developed for use with laser printers. They are used to pass instructions to the printer so that the material ready for printing is outputted correctly. Postscript is probably the best known PDL.

12.9 USER DOCUMENTATION

Nowadays increased emphasis is placed on the production of effective and useful documentation. There is a trend towards the use of automated on-line documentation as opposed to paper-oriented documentation. However despite this physical difference, there is a common underlying objective and substance to this particular aspect of IS development. Experience shows that cogent documentation enables IS developers and IS users to engage in an effective exchange of ideas as well as enabling all the parties involved in the IS to have a more comprehensive understanding as to the mechanics and purpose of the IS. Such documentation is usually expensive to produce but it can, and often does, prove to be invaluable.

When IS developers are producing IS documentation they must consider several issues. These issues include the information to be contained in the documentation, the source of the information in the documentation, the objective of the documentation, the users of the documentation, the design of the documentation and the maintenance of the information stored within the documentation.

(a) User manuals

In an ideal world, once the IS developers and trainers have left the scene, users should be able to simply get on and work with the new IS, referring to the user manual as and when necessary. User manuals provide the information necessary to the successful running of the system by giving detailed guidance on all procedural and operational matters and also help sections. These manuals can vary widely in quality, dependent on the care and understanding exercised by the authors.

(b) Input/output documentation

In order to enhance the efficiency of the IS, developers have to give considerable attention to the actual design of the various I/O documents.

Input documents are central to the data capture routines and the content of the various data structures. Consideration must be given to the overall volume and calibre of data passing through the documents as well as their purpose. Overall layout can also have a considerable impact on the quality of the data captured.

Output documents relate to a host of formatted processed data reports such as pay slips, mail merge, screen dialogue and so on. However whilst output documentation is crucial, it is not as perplexing or problematical to IS developers as input documentation. The reason for this is that, once the data is stored in the IS, it is usually a straightforward task to present the information in whatever arrangement the user may require. Corporate IS users are usually familiar with the output routines and are usually well able to adjust and design output documentation.

12.10 CASE TOOLS

CASE tools were mentioned in 11.7.4 in connection with large-scale program development and coding and some CASE tools are restricted to this function only. These are lower-level CASE tools, usually known as code generators.

More sophisticated CASE tools can assist throughout the entire development process. They are computerised support systems used for the production of the various types of diagrams used in structured methods such as SSADM. They can also generate the data dictionary (10.6.1) and assist in certain design tasks such as database design. Sophisticated CASE tools also enable developers not only to adjust individual data elements but, where necessary, to make significant changes to the proposed IS's design without the necessity of completely redrafting the total design. CASE tools can also enforce an ordered work methodology on the developers by ensuring that they follow fixed conventions such as the manner in which data flow charts are constructed and annotated or the manner in which user documentation is produced. Uniformity in these tasks minimises confusion and enables all the developers and users to get a clear understanding of the direction and structure of the IS.

12.11 EXPERT SYSTEMS

The first point to note is that an expert system (ES) (see 11.5.2) provides a user with information just like any other IS. However the information supplied by an ES is, for the most part, specialist and is usually of a totally different character from that supplied from a more conventional commercial IS.

An ES is a complex computer application that simulates the decision-making activities of various professionals such as doctors, lawyers, geologists, and so forth. ESs operate by digesting the particulars of an individual event which is then matched against a template of ready-made knowledge. The ES then produces suitable output the substance of which depends upon the user's initial input, so providing the user with a relevant conclusion and/or course of action.

12.11.1 ES development

In order to create a specific ES the developers must study the routine as well as the functions of the individual expert in great detail. This means that the developers must not only understand the manner in which an individual expert processes information but also have a working understanding of the individual expert's subject. Having obtained this information the developer then has to produce an application which, when confronted with particular information, can apply the same analysis and decision making as that performed by the expert.

Because of their complexity, ESs tend to be very expensive to develop although the actual expense incurred depends on the nature of the particular expertise of the ES and the functions it is expected to perform. ESs can not only be programmed to produce comparatively routine information and conclusions but they can also be programmed to speculate about a conclusion/analysis even when faced with incomplete information. ESs can also be designed to educate novice subject users by providing reports which support and clarify its decisions/conclusions.

Various schema are available for representing the information bank or knowledge base in an ES. The knowledge is organised integrally with the rules used to search it. The structure of the knowledge/rules schema is designed to allow deeper and deeper enquiries, as driven by the input. That is, the ES reasons by 'chaining' through to a conclusion or analysis which is an appropriate 'answer' to the input problem.

The most commonly used rules are IF ... THEN ... rules. A simple example:

IF headache and IF stomach pains
    THEN hangover or illness
IF high temperature and IF sickness
    THEN illness probably

ES developers usually glean requisite expert information from two major sources. These sources are text-based academic references or manuals/books and the experts themselves. Text-based sources are extremely useful but they usually lack that structure which would enable the ES developers to understand how the experts actually perform. In order to obtain this 'reasoning' process, developers have to track the experts themselves.

When the developers are sourcing the actual experts they usually use conventional analysis tools such as interviewing, data flowcharting and observation. Because of the nature of ES development, and the need to formalise the expert's knowledge, there is a particular emphasis on personal interviews. Specialists developers that extract this information are sometimes referred to as knowledge miners.

The degree of accuracy and the quality of the output of the ES are crucial matters which must be resolved appropriate to the function of the ES. For example ESs dealing with financial problems such as taxation can be straightforward mechanical projects and whilst a financial ES may fail to supply the user with an accurate response/analysis, the result may be considered costly but not necessarily life threatening. In contrast a medical ES is a much more contentious application. Such an application must be faultless as well as accurate. Any failure by such an ES can prove to be life threatening and almost certainly a basis for a medical negligence suit. Of course, any ES output is subject to veto or examination by the user.

Despite their dramatic development costs, there has been a spectacular growth in commercial ESs. The reason for this growth has been the perceived successful performance of ES applications. In Singapore the government has started to use ESs to enable motorists to pay for speeding and parking fines whilst in America the courts are starting to use ESs in order to distribute documentation for its convoluted legal system.

The fact is that ESs have several crucial advantages over their human counterparts. They are, on the whole, reliable and consistent. In addition, they can, on occasion, provide superior results to a human counterpart. The reason for this is that professional ESs are usually developed by teams of experts, a consequence of which is an application which sources a combined knowledge base superior to that of a particular individual. ESs also provide an expertise which can be used to train other staff members and which consequently provides a permanent pool of expertise.

13

Emerging technologies

13.1 INTRODUCTION

The main objective of this chapter is to peruse some of the latest computing and communication technologies. To this end the chapter not only details contemporary research but also considers numerous concepts and products which are expected to become mainstream in the next century.

Section 13.2 considers the idea of automated intelligence whilst sections 13.3 through to 13.6 cover various innovative user technologies. Sections 13.7 and 13.8 are concerned with changes within the communications industry whilst section 13.9 discusses the pros and cons of the new multi-function office devices. Finally section 13.10 highlights some of the latest technologies which are expected to emerge in the next century.

13.2 INTELLIGENT INFORMATION SYSTEMS

In some contemporary automated households specially designed domestic computer systems arrange for the TV volume to turn down every time the phone rings. Such systems are undoubtedly sophisticated. However a question that is often asked about this type of application is: is this intelligence? The majority of people would undoubtedly say no because there is an obvious mechanistic movement whereby an incoming signal such as a phone call results in a simple reduction in the TV's volume. It is an event which is easily understood and, for IT specialists, the processes involved in the event would be ones which could be programmed without any great difficulty. However the question that must be asked is what happens when programmers using the same techniques code an application such as a medical expert system, which in turn is able to make a better diagnosis than individual doctors, as is often the case. Is this intelligence ?

As might be expected, defining machine intelligence and putting it into the context of a computer has proved to be a controversial matter.

Nevertheless one computer scientist, an Englishman called Alan Turing, has provided a generally accepted definition of what could be regarded as computer intelligence. In his 1950 paper "Computer Machinery and Intelligence" Turing basically said that a machine/computer could be described as intelligent the day a human being communicating with it did not know whether they were in contact with another human being or a machine.

Nevertheless despite this useful but subtle definition of machine intelligence, the reality is that the massive improvement, intrusion and pervasive influence of computers has resulted, in recent years, in an air of imminent expectancy by the public to the arrival of the fully intelligent, cognisant computer. For some these expectations seemed to be about to be fulfilled when in 1997 IBM provided a purposely constructed chess computer called Deep Blue. What made Deep Blue so special was that it was capable of beating the current world chess champion, something which a computer had never done before. In addition, the statistics pertaining to the computer were astounding. Individual processors inside Deep Blue were capable of evaluating two million moves per second. By arranging these processors in a parallel array it was estimated that Deep Blue could consider somewhere between fifty and one hundred billion alternative permutations in the three minutes given for each move. However, despite these advantages, Deep Blue's human opponent was still able to win games against it. It must be stated that whilst Deep Blue is undoubtedly a good chess player it isn't really designed for anything else. The reality is that whilst contemporary computer systems can appear intelligent within certain domains, the fact is that no system, automated or otherwise, can process information in the same intuitive conscious manner as done by a human being. Yet !

At present, the development of intelligent computer systems comes under the all-embracing term Artificial Intelligence (AI). Although it is a hybrid discipline, AI is basically about producing applications which display reasoning characteristics similar to those found in human beings. AI systems can also be programmed to learn, adapt and self-correct. Successful business applications of AI include expert systems (see 11.5.2(4) and 12.11) and neural networks.

13.2.1 Neural networks

A neural network uses a web of meshed processing units (programs); each unit, or node, in the web initially undergoes a learning process, until the entire web successfully demonstrates that its overall learning task is complete. In other words, a neural network is composed of individual blocks of computer code working towards a mutual goal. A good illustration of this type of neural software in action is that used by banks and other financial institutions to detect possible fraud.

What happens is that neural networks are designed to identify suspicious activities such as unusual spending patterns or the irregular movement of large amounts of cash. They have also been used for visual recognition, particularly in clarifying fuzzy images. The reasoning which underlines a great deal of neural software centres on fuzzy logic.

Fuzzy logic

Fuzzy logic is, as its name implies, a move away from a black-and-white absolutism towards a methodology which recognises degrees of activity or levels of greyness. For instance, there are chemical engineering processes where the chemical inputs need not be in exact amounts but can each be within certain limits; a control program based on fuzzy logic then determines whether the mix of input limits will lead to the correct output.

Another example of applied fuzzy logic is that used in the prevention of credit card fraud. Criminals often use their stolen credit card to purchase tickets or collect cash from automated terminals just to see whether or not the card is still authorised. If they are successful in their transaction the criminal will then, more often than not, try to use the card to make a more audacious purchase or even a cash withdrawal via a bank. In order to counteract this activity, programs designed using principles based on fuzzy logic will, for example, flag those transactions where a card user purchases a local rail ticket and then seeks to make a series of expensive purchases. As a result of this flagging, human monitors will then be alerted to the situation and can act accordingly.

13.2.2 Intelligent agents

One spin-off of neural technology is the concept of the intelligent agent. A major problem with computing technology and modern business procedures in general is the manner in which organisations are being overwhelmed with data.

In order to try and relieve this pressure, software developers have started to produce software programs called intelligent agents. These agents feed off a predefined set of rules, or knowledge base, which then enables them to automate various tasks and procedures demanded by the volumes of data. The sophistication of these agents can be measured by the fact that some can communicate with each other, that is to say exchange information and, where necessary, cooperate in order to carry out more complex tasks, whilst other agents are capable of learning by increasing their knowledge base.

Amongst other functions, intelligent agents are currently used to monitor financial database activity alerting users to significant variations in share prices. They are also employed to provide personalised information digests. For example some ISPs are supplying information-screening applications alerting academic users to any relevant research which may have just been released onto the Internet. Industry pundits believe that intelligent agents will be central to the development of the new innovative tools required to deal with the ever-increasing information mountain confronting users and management. This information, whether scattered across the Internet or throughout a company-wide IS, must be assessed and, where necessary, capitalised on, if the organisation is to succeed.

13.2.3 Intelligent manufacturing systems

Intelligent Manufacturing Systems (IMS) is an innovative manufacturing technology currently being developed by blue chip companies across the world. Its impact is such that industry observers believe that IMS will totally revolutionise current computer-assisted manufacturing technology. Specifically IMS is a process whereby manufacturing systems are streamlined and channelled in order to enable the organisation to function with optimum economic efficiency whilst simultaneously fabricating products that meet individual customer requirements rapidly and as ordered.

One important methodology currently emerging from IMS is the Holonic Manufacturing System (HMS). The idea behind HMS is to provide the customer with a wide product range even if the actual production output is very low. To achieve this, HMS organises the main manufacturing routine to be flexible so that the processes can be adjusted according to prevailing or arising circumstances. With HMS, the emphasis is on any necessary change being executed in a fast and efficient manner whilst simultaneously enabling the organisation to grasp new technologies and overcome potential production/system breakdowns.

Market expectations suggest that future consumer demand will be very dependent on product differentiation, especially for high quality goods. As a result industry observers believe that HMS type structures will eventually dominate the manufacturing of premier priced products.

13.3 VOICE RECOGNITION SYSTEMS

Voice Recognition Systems (VRS) present the user with a hand-free voice-interactive computer interface. In other words users can discard conventional input devices such as a keyboard or a mouse and access the computer system by simply talking to it.

VRS applications were originally designed for the physically disadvantaged. However the recent rise in RSI (Repetitive Strain Injury) claims and the desire by non-typists to access competent voice dictating applications have resulted in a sudden surge by the computing industry in VRS technology. Simple voice command driven applications have proved very effective and are extremely well received by inexperienced users. However although there are numerous applications on the market, the technology is still embryonic and somewhat restricted in use. The problem is that people are irregular in their speech (see VoiceType below). Human conversation is ungrammatical, repetitive and open ended. These characteristics provide programmers with a host of inconsistencies which have proven extremely difficult to accommodate.

Nevertheless, despite the many technical problems which have to be overcome before VRS becomes a mainstream technology there is no doubt that once the technology has been perfected it will revolutionise the use of computers. The possibility of users being able to carry out conventional conversations with intelligent computers in order to elicit various information and services is a distant yet inevitable eventuality.

To date most speech systems are used for text dictation or for single command voice menu options. However contemporary developers are making serious investment into various innovative projects such as context-sensitive voice translation systems. Industry gurus predict that, towards the end of the first decade of the 21st century, users will be able to access intelligent telephones that enable people to converse with each other in their own native language. For example, American users will be able to talk in their broad New York English which when received at the other end of the line will sound like good Parisian French.

It should be pointed out that business users are already employing numerous word processing type packages enabling them to translate text stored documents. Unfortunately they can be expensive and somewhat turgid in their quality. Nonetheless they are relatively successful and usually provide the users with a reasonable translation.

13.3.1 VoiceType

A good example of an effective speech application is IBM's VoiceType. Prior to VoiceType most PC-based speech applications tended to be very slow and could be somewhat inaccurate when translating spoken words or commands. In order to meet these shortcomings IBM developed VoiceType. The main advantage of VoiceType is that it concentrates on the speech patterns of individual users. Users dictate 150 selected sentences to VoiceType which then enables the computer to elicit and recognise the 44 phonetic sounds of the English language as uttered by each particular user. The computer then processes the user's voice data and produces a voice-specific 30,000 word lexicon that it would recognise whenever used by that particular individual.

13.4 HANDWRITING RECOGNITION SOFTWARE

Like speech software systems, Handwriting Recognition Software (HRS) is still in its formative years. However it is beginning to make a serious impact. The two main categories of HRS are those systems where text is written straight onto a computer screen and those where text is replicated via a set source. The former type is that used on PDA/notepad devices such as the Newton from Apple Computers. Although it still has its failings PDA HRS is improving all the time. Present trends suggest that the PDA market will be worth 30 billion dollars by the end of the century. The second type of HRS is concerned with Optical Character Recognition software whereby handwritten text can be scanned directly into the computer ready for editing.

13.5 PHOTOGRAPHIC AND VIDEO ADVANCES

13.5.1 Digital cameras

Prior to the arrival of low-cost digital cameras, users wanting to manipulate photographic images would usually employ either CD-ROM technology, as demonstrated by Kodak's PhotoCD systems, or an image scanner. However with a digital camera, users store their photos in digital files inside the camera. These files can then be ported directly into the computer ready for use, or straight onto a TV/VCR. In addition, most digital cameras enable users to view the photographs stored inside the camera via the viewer or via an LCD colour screen on the back of the camera.

With digital cameras users no longer have the problem of image degradation. Users can simply transfer their photographic images via their modem or ISDN link without any loss of quality. The concept of low-cost digital cameras enabling users to manipulate photographic images with such obvious ease is beginning to have a big effect on the publishing industry as well as the home photography market. The 1996 Olympics is believed to be the first major event where professional photographers made extensive use of digital cameras.

13.5.2 Digital camcorders

Sony, JVC and Panasonic have launched a new and innovative range of digital camcorders. Unlike previous camcorders, they employ a video tape standard known as Digital Video Cassette (DVC). As with other forms of digital technology, these digital camcorders are a step up in calibre in comparison to non-digital devices. Initial users have expressed immense satisfaction with these new cameras as they deliver what may be described as high-quality broadcast-standard picture/sound recordings. However as might be expected, these digital camcorders are still rather costly. This is in part due to the new DVC cassettes, each of which contains an in-built memory chip the purpose of which is to record various data such as the time, date and tape position of particular shots.

13.5.3 Desktop video

Desktop Video (DTV) is a new video-editing technology which can be operated on a suitably equipped multimedia PC. The main objective of DTV is to give the user total control over moving images such as a video recordings. With DTV users can manipulate the individual frames making up the moving image by changing their order, adding text, colours, pictures, photos and other moving images. The results, as with ordinary application files, can be stored and retrieved from the PC's hard disk at will. DTV is still a relatively new idea and has several hurdles to overcome before it becomes mainstream. The main problem, as with most graphic intensive applications, is data storage. Contemporary systems employing DTV can use up to 1 Gb of hard disk space for thirty seconds of compressed video.

NEC have produced a solid-state walkman-sized video playback device whereby the video is held on flash memory cards. It operates MPEG standard video which presents the user with good VHS video images along with excellent sound. Unfortunately, the contemporary product is estimated to store only two minutes of VHS video on a 20 Mb card. Nevertheless, there is an enthusiastic research and development programme centring on the product and it is predicted that memory cards enabling users to play back full-length programs and films will surface at the beginning of the next century.

13.5.4 3D videophone

Another exciting innovation being developed by British Telecom is the 3D Videophone. The 3D Videophone is a realistic one-to-one phone system whereby two cameras record views at a remote location. The recorded

273

images are equivalent to those seen by an observer's left and right eye. These images are then combined and displayed on a flat screen. However, a special surface on the screen enables the user to see separate views with each eye, a result of which means that they are presented with a realistic 3D image.

13.6 TELEPRESENCE SYSTEMS

British Telecom's Camnet is a good example of a telepresence system. Contemporary Camnet users are usually furnished with a lightweight headgear device which in turn is equipped with a camera enabling remote viewers to see the user's surrounding environment. The device also includes an overlapping eyepiece as well as a two-way speaker phone so enabling the user to receive images/instructions from the remote viewers.

With a Camnet system, users can communicate, via the telephone network, with remote viewers who may be experts in their particular field and who can, with the aid of pictures and sound, convey those necessary instructions required by the user in order to perform a particular task or deal with a given situation. The overall effect is to inspire users to perform better as they are, in effect, totally guided in their actions. One major envisioned use of Camnet technology is for paramedics arriving at the scene of accidents. With a Camnet, remote doctors and specialist can give critical life-saving advice.

13.7 DIGITAL TV

The impending arrival of mass interactive TV and High Definition TV (HDTV) is inextricably connected to the fortunes of Digital TV technology. Digital TV is concerned with the broadcast and reception of TV signals which are relayed in a digital format as opposed to the conventional analogue format. What is more, it is this very digital format which gives Digital TV such an advantage. With conventional TV transmissions are broadcast by means of signals travelling along radio waves. However with digital TV, these signals are transmitted as highly compressed streams of digits so enabling the broadcaster to deliver far more information across the same bandwidth.

As a result, commercial broadcasters employing digital TV can transmit a far bigger range of TV channels. This abundance of channels not only enables the broadcasters to provide a wider selection of subject matter but also enables viewers to have more control over their personal scheduling. For example, one interesting service that is beginning to appear on digital

TV is NVOD (Near Video On Demand). NVOD operates when the broadcaster relays a range of films, each of which runs continuously, on numerous TV channels. Each film re-starts at short intervals and the user operates their remote control in order to access the film of their choice. The user is charged for each film they decide to access just as they might for video rental.

Another major benefit of digital broadcast technology is that the quality and substance of the original recording is totally maintained. The composition of the material, from point of formulation through to actual end user reception, is consistent throughout. However, with analogue TV technology, there is always a certain degree of staged degradation as the recording passes from point of production to the final TV/monitor display.

Despite its obvious advantages, Digital TV has certain obstacles to cross before it becomes a mainstream international broadcasting technology. Firstly there is a fierce debate raging in various countries concerning the technological protocols of Digital TV broadcasting. Secondly the TV stations delivering a Digital TV service are required to employ expensive specialist broadcasting equipment such as digital satellite transmitters. Thirdly individual digital TVs, as with digital radios, cost significantly more than their analogue counterparts. As a result the actual take-up of digital TV technology is predicted to be a prolonged process.

However this is all expected to change. Various national TV broadcasters have announced plans to become more involved in Digital TV. In addition, distribution potential is expected to surge as developers increase the Internet bandwidth so fully exploiting its potential transmission role. This increased investment in the industry is expected to have a direct impact on the cost of producing digital TVs as well as fuelling the development of cost-effective set-top digital TV decoding boxes which will allow ordinary analogue TVs to receive digital signals.

13.8 SUPERHIGHWAY RADIO NETWORKS

In 1996 it was announced that three British communication companies, Mercury, Ionica and NTL, were to start building a new web of high-speed radio networks. These radio networks, which are to be based all over Britain, are part of a new breed of wireless communication technology which is specifically designed to provide various Internet/superhighway services directly to the user.

The project is a multi-million pound investment. However if it is successful it could have significant ramifications. The reason for this is the fact that potential users of the system will have access to the Internet and high-speed communications without the need for conventional cabling or special ISDN lines. In order to obtain the service, users will, instead, instal small external reception/transmitter dishes. The economics of this scenario are apparent. The companies concerned will not have to lay expensive cable/lines everywhere on the off chance that they might attract subscribers in a particular area. Their customer investment is basically restricted to those users who actually sign up to the network. Provided these companies can provide a good quality service along with suitably designed and suitably priced reception/transmitter dishes then the new network must have every chance of success.

13.9 MULTIFUNCTION OFFICE DEVICES

Computer users wishing to access various ancillary functions such as linking to external communication systems and networks, faxing, printing, scanning or photocopying, have, until very recently, been obliged to purchase various individual peripheral devices in order to complete each task. Such an array of peripherals is not only expensive but can consume a considerable amount of room – room which can, more often than not, prove to be critical to the conducive working conditions in a small office/domestic environment.

However the need for all these extra devices is gradually beginning to decline. The reason for this is the arrival of multifunction computers and multifunction peripherals. For example, a significant number of PCs/workstations have in-built faxes whilst others employ software packages that emulate the operation of a fax machine. Users of this type of equipment can transmit drawings, photos and text to remote fax machines, without the need for a separate fax machine. Users can also, when necessary, display incoming faxes directly onto the computer's screen so avoiding the need to use a separate printer in order to read the fax.

With respect to dedicated multifunction peripheral devices, the number of various tasks that can be performed by each machine is changing all the time. Simple multifunction peripherals can include modems with answer machine capabilities. Other more complex devices include those currently being produced by leading manufacturers such as Hewlett Packard and Xerox both of which have launched single box machines that can act as a modem, fax, printer, scanner and photocopier. Although these boxes are extremely sophisticated, the developers have designed them so that they operate with the minimum of fuss. For example, these multifunction box peripherals have just three external connections. These include a power lead, a computer connection, either to a network or an individual computer, and a phone link.

Multifunction machines are undoubtedly becoming more popular. Nevertheless there are certain considerations which must be taken into account. The first is what happens if your multifunction machine breaks down. All the activities supported by the device suddenly come to a halt. If you still had a separate device for each function then you could carry on with other activities whilst you were waiting for a particular device to be repaired. The second consideration centres on actual value. A question that is often asked of a multifunction machine is whether or not it is really as good as all the other individual devices which it is supposed to replace. For example does the printing part really perform as well as a machine which happens to be a dedicated printer, and if so, does it do it for the same price ?

The answer to this is a little uncertain at the moment. The problem is multifunction machines are a relatively recent phenomenon and do have a reputation of being expensive and somewhat erratic in both performance and quality. Having said this, they are improving and they are a progressive inroad into the traditional peripheral market.

13.10 ON THE HORIZON

This section is a selection of impending technological developments. Whether these developments have the impact that their protagonists suggest only time will tell.

13.10.1 Advanced miniaturisation

The major reason for the advancement in modern computers has been the ability of computer scientists to continually compress the number of transistors in a confined area of silicon chip. Computer scientists have succeeded in this regard by reducing the size of the tracks which actually link the transistors. In order to fully understand this one should first consider that the critical unit of measurement in contemporary microprocessor technology is the micron (one millionth of a metre). Between 1979 and 1996 the tracks on the surface of the microprocessors have shrunk from about 2 microns in width to about 0.6 micron. Bearing in mind that the original 80086 PC microprocessor had 29,000 transistors and that the Pentium Pro contains 5.5 million then the rate of change is all apparent.

(a) Nanotechnology

However computer scientists are proving even more ambitious in their designs. The latest advances in miniaturisation centre on nanotechnology for which the critical unit of measurement is the nanometre. (A nanometre is one billionth of a metre, one thousand times smaller than a micron.)

Nanotechnology concerns the ability of scientists to manipulate substances at the atomic level. The idea is to eventually construct intelligent cell-sized machines which could evolve into whatever instrument the user required. It is believed that such devices could be self-starting and would absorb whatever necessary matter was required from their surrounding environment. Although it still sounds like science fiction, trends suggest that such devices may not be so far away. For example at the University of Illinois researchers have produced a designer molecule that can act as a secure binary switch. The significance of such a property indicates that it is possible to produce memory systems with incredible storage capacities as each data bit is represented by a single molecule.

Two other complementary advances in this regard are the arrival of the micro machine and the research into Micro Electro Mechanical Systems (MEMS).

(b) Micro machines

Micro machines are small mechanical devices which are created using the same technology used to produce modern microchips. Using blocks of silicon and special photographic processes, developers can carve and tier slivers into fully formed mechanical components. At the time of writing the best known demonstration of a micro machine is the motor developed at Sandia Laboratories in New Mexico in 1995. Barely visible to the naked eye, it is a whole motor which is capable of producing 50 microWatts of power in one square millimetre. Although the motor is simple it is considered to represent a major breakthrough and has made a considerable impact, especially on medical scientists who believe that such machines could be used for essential human medical operations such as clearing blocked veins.

(c) Micro electro mechanical systems

Another example of advanced miniaturisation is the imminent arrival of Micro Electro Mechanical Systems (MEMS), otherwise known as mobile microchips. Contemporary scientists are working on designs that will create robot type devices no bigger than a drawing pin. Such devices are expected to contain integrated wireless transistor technology that will enable them to communicate with each other as well as other computers. Because these MEMS will be built using conventional silicon technology it is expected that they will prove to be cheap as well as useful. However what is interesting is that MEMS and micro machines are expected to make such an impression on the future that a new breed of workers known as imagineers will be required. In other words, it is the people that can produce the most imaginative uses for these new contraptions that are expected to be in high demand.

13.10.2 The new microprocessors

Microprocessors are becoming ever more sophisticated and appear to be on an ever upward performance curve. Their development prospects are also becoming increasingly intriguing. For example there is speculation that the human body could become part of the evolving information superhighway by virtue of specially designed microprocessors becoming part of the human brain (see below).

Two facets of contemporary microprocessor research which is going some way towards fulfilling this type of objective as well as other future processing requirements centre on what are known as Hybrid Optical Microprocessors and Organic Microprocessors.

(a) Hybrid optical microprocessors

The Hitachi Corporation in partnership with the Cavendish Research Laboratory in Cambridge, England is currently undertaking research into a new breed of hybrid optical microprocessors. The idea is to produce a microprocessor which integrates conventional semiconductor technology with optical switches, circuits controlled by bursts of laser light. The belief is that such microprocessors could operate at a million times faster than contemporary processors.

(b) Organic microprocessors

Contemporary research at the University of California has confirmed that it is possible to determine the solution to particular logic problems by means of biomolecular technology. The research itself centres on the manipulation of DNA molecules and the results indicate that it is feasible to construct biological processing systems. Such science is as much controversial as it is revolutionary as society comes to terms with the prospect of technology merging with nature. However the ideas from the computing fraternity are already beginning to storm academic periodicals and developers are already considering the possibility of the human brain linking into the Internet by means of purpose-built microprocessors. Such machine/human interaction is perfectly plausible. At the Sydney University of Technology in Australia researchers have created devices capable of reacting to mind manipulation by enabling users to turn on lights by simply thinking about them.

The real point of biological processing systems is of course the possibility of developing systems with real intelligence. In any event, whatever else organic microprocessors may herald what is apparent is that they, like other computing technologies, are part of a continuing trend towards developing devices that are smart and lifelike as opposed to the relatively unfriendly inflexible machines of contemporary times.

13.10.3 Holographic data storage systems

Holographic Data Storage Systems technology (HDSS) first emerged in the 1960s. Unlike conventional memory storage systems which store data in a serial format, HDDS creates images of the data so storing the binary coded information in large parallel blocks of ones and zeros. How this is done varies from system to system, however the technology is relatively uniform and basically depends upon the use of lasers and photosensitive materials.

One major investor in this technology is IBM. It describes holographic data storage as the recording of an interference pattern resulting from two beams of laser light. One beam holds the data to be recorded whilst the other beam acts as a reference tool. A hologram containing the data is created on the photosensitive material. This hologram in turn is exposed and highlighted by the reference beam whenever it is necessary to retrieve data.

The concept of HDSS is an attractive idea as it enables the almost instant storage and retrieval of large parallel blocks of data. It is also economic in both cost and space. Figures indicate that it is possible to put the entire contents of the British reference library in a space the size of a coffee mug. However current computer architecture is not equipped to deal with data storage in this form. As a result, the amazing gains to be had with HDSS technology is somewhat diminished. Nevertheless despite this current drawback, developers are making considerable investments into HDSS by concentrating efforts on advanced light-driven storage and retrieval methods as current research indicates that the capacity, speed and cost of holographic storage implies that it could supersede conventional storage systems such as magnetic disks, tape and CD-ROM. When this will happen is uncertain but it is believed it will occur towards the end of the decade.

13.10.4 Reusable newspapers

One astonishing innovation expected to dominate the next century is the reusable newspaper/magazine. Although at the time of writing the product has yet to appear, technologists suggest that its arrival is imminent. Press reports suggest that roll-up flat screens constructed from pioneering light-emitting polymers are currently moving from the research laboratory into full-scale manufacturing. The concept of newspapers which do not have to be constantly discarded but which can be refreshed by simply connecting them to appropriate I/O interfaces must revolutionise the print industry.

13.11 CONCLUSION

One of the great things about new technology is that it is just that – new. Because it is new it is usually exciting, innovative and, more often than not, significantly better than the technology which preceded it. However new technology can be expensive in a host of different ways. It can for example, result in the replacement of a whole range of products and industries to say nothing of the people involved in their delivery. On the other hand new technology can and does create new opportunities and is the very life blood of the computing industry.

14

Advancing trends in business technology

14.1 INTRODUCTION

The main objective of this chapter is to discuss some of the ways in which the latest IT is being implemented in contemporary business practice. In order to achieve this sections 14.2 through to 14.4 are centred on the use of that technology which surrounds commercial internetworking. These three sections will consequently consider the Internet, the Intranet and the Extranet. Sections 14.5 and 14.6 are basically about new work practices whilst section 14.7 considers some of the concepts underlying Computer Telephony Integration. Section 14.8 is about the technology underlying the 'Paperless Office' whilst sections 14.9 and 14.10 deal with the new business concept of digital cash. Finally section 14.10 is concerned with Value Added Services (VAS).

14.2 THE INTERNET

Innovative business computing in the mid to late nineties appears to be dominated by Internet technology. The reality is that commerce and industry have finally recognised that the Internet has progressed from being a techie's bulletin board to a serious global trading/information system. By the beginning of 1997 it was estimated that over a trillion US$ passed across the Internet everyday. This is believed to be more money than is possessed by all the governments in the world put together. The current impact of Internet technology on business culture is evidenced by the sudden widespread inclusion of proposed internal Internet development plans in western company annual reports. Such plans have proved to be of such importance that many Wall Street analysts routinely downgrade the stock values of those organisations who do not appear to have an appropriate Internet strategy.

The Internet is also resulting in yet another series of seismic shifts in the technological direction of the computing industry as various organisations seek to exploit the new opportunities. The degree of such movement can be measured by IBM's activities when in 1996 it formed a new Internet division within the company. Famous for its commitment to innovation and development, IBM then allocated the Internet division twenty five per cent of its research budget. Because of this increase in interest, the Internet has undergone, and continues to undergo, considerable growth. In the summer of 1997 it was estimated that Internet membership was increasing at such a rate that, if continued, the whole of the world's population would be linked to the Internet by 2005.

Along with its apparent success the Internet does have some unusual characteristics which makes it more remarkable than might otherwise be understood. For example there is no one government or organisation in control of the Internet. As a result there is no overall design strategy for the Internet. It has, to a large degree, just turned up.

14.2.1 Some main attractions

The number one contemporary killer application on the Internet is e-mail. A good illustration of volume commercial e-mail is the computer company Digital Equipment. In the mid 1990s Digital Equipment had 40,000 internal registered users linked to the Internet who transmitted an average of two million e-mail messages every month with individuals outside the organisation.

E-mail is very cheap, unbelievably fast and incredibly secure. For example, in the aftermath of the Gulf war it was discovered that, because the Internet was able to route and, where necessary, re-route data traffic in the manner that it does, at no time were the US-led forces able to totally eliminate the Iraqi high command's communication systems much of which was based on Internet technology.

Besides being used as a sophisticated communication system users are also using the Internet as a means of accessing various information networks all of which in turn provide services such as news networks, academic bulletin boards as well as chatline and virtual community links.

14.2.2 The World Wide Web

First created in the early 1990s the World Wide Web (WWW) is the fastest developing sector of the Internet. The reason for the WWW's popularity is primarily concerned with its enhanced user-friendly navigation features and the general manner in which information is presented.

Firstly the server computers which support the WWW operate an established protocol known as the Hypertext Transfer Protocol. As a result of this protocol users engage mouse-driven icons or text known as hyperlinks to allow them to pass automatically from one database to another without the need of complex path commands. Secondly the WWW is that part of the Internet which enables information to be displayed in an intuitive and friendly manner through the use of various media such as pictures, photos, video and sound. The information itself is formatted in a data structure usually known as a web page. Web pages are composed with the aid of high-level programming languages/applications such as the Hypertext Markup Language (HPTML). In order to traverse the WWW and download web page information users need a computer application known as a web browser (see 9.10.1(l)).

WWW is currently used by individuals and organisations all over the world as a potent point of contact. With the WWW, communication between the customer and retailer/service provider is not only cheap and efficient but also, because of its multimedia-based technology, seductive and interesting. WWW commercial activity has been of particular benefit to smaller companies. The relative anonymity of the Internet and the overall professional effect of sophisticated web sites enabling users to ponder on a wide range of products/services have led to the birth of the 'Virtual Corporation'. As a result, companies/individuals with the minimum of capital outlay have been able to enjoy the full benefit of trading by connecting with other traders and making deals.

Unfortunately most contemporary users face substantial bottlenecks on the Internet as a result of the processing demands of using multimedia type applications via the WWW. For example, there are reports to suggest that users based in Western Europe which is basically half a working day ahead of the North American continent tend to avoid using the Internet in the afternoon. The reason for this is that as America gradually goes on line for the next working day the Internet is swamped with heavy data traffic so resulting in poor response times.

14.2.3 Economic and social impact

Many economists believe that the Internet is the epitome of the global free market and some intellectuals are beginning to use the term 'frictionless capitalism' as traders make direct and instant contact. Internet trading is, in effect, reducing the role of the middleman. For example financial markets are beginning to feel the full effect of this as traders and investors are beginning to source company information for themselves and so avoiding expensive commissions. In fact there is a general belief that the Internet will level economic opportunities and costs across the globe. For example the spectacular development of countries such as India in programming and IT skills is a good example of the new global competition in the development of software applications. In fact, the success of India has been such that their prices have started to rise and first world investor developers have started to consider poorer regions such as parts of Eastern Europe and Russia.

As a result whilst many view the Internet as an opportunity others are beginning to view the Internet as a threat. In any event what is certain is that the Internet is beginning to have a considerable impact on the business world. Consider the following:

(a) Retailers

Retailers are faced with increasing competition from manufacturers and suppliers as purchasers place direct orders, so eliminating the middleman. Well known retail chains across the world have created large home page sites via the WWW and are subletting sites on their web page sites at premium rates. Software distributors are also using the Internet to distribute their latest products/updates.

(b) Personal stock brokering

The arrival of the Internet has resulted in an explosion in online home-based brokering services. Share analysts and traders can work directly from the home accessing the world's financial markets twenty four hours a day. In order to meet growing demand, stock exchanges all over the world are providing information services so enabling potential users to track and trade irrespective of their physical location.

However because of the sensitivity of much of this type of information and the need to avoid reckless speculation, national governments are beginning to insist on a certain degree of regulation on the manner in which the information is supplied.

(c) Education

Students can access information and courses without the need for physical attendance as universities and colleges across the planet are starting to deliver sophisticated qualifications through cyberspace. In addition, publicly funded research is becoming more transparent in terms of progress and results as researchers effortlessly exchange valuable information.

(d) Virtual communities

The success of e-mail, chat lines and the WWW has resulted in successful virtual communities, business and social, appearing in every quarter. Cyber cafe environments are enabling users to socialise with total strangers and scattered rural communities are able to communicate with their neighbours and gain successful employment by means of contractual arrangements from the local telecottage (see 14.5.4).

Other examples of commercial virtual communities include advanced thinking chambers of commerce scanning the Internet for contracts which they feel they might be able to compete for. Communities are beginning to realise that co-ordinated tendering via the Internet is allowing business interests to mobilise local resources in order to make competitive bids.

(e) Publishing and the media

The Internet is about the provision of virtually instant information irrespective of distance. An instrument such as the Internet is therefore perfectly suited for various dynamic media activities such as hourly national newspapers as well as magazine and book publishing. The Internet is also expected to forefront VOD as well as the development of interactive TV.

(f) Government

The Internet is not only having a direct effect on the manner in which trade is being conducted but is also having a direct impact on the ability of governments to govern. Consider the taxation activities of countries within the European Union, who like most other countries impose Value Added Tax (VAT), a purchase tax on the sale and supply of most goods and services. Obviously, as with other forms of taxation, this is an important source of income. However, traders can illegally bypass this tax by purchasing various products such as software, videos, music and so forth from countries beyond the jurisdiction of their government. For example, users can dial up foreign web sites, place their order and pay via their credit card. The web site is unlikely to charge or collect a foreign tax, whilst the user's government can, for all practical purposes, do little about the delivery of the products in the form of an almost unstoppable stream of ones and zeros pouring down the various transmission media. Such activity is obviously a direct threat and some futurists believe that the ability to avoid government interference will result in the emergence of the cybernation, trans-national communities consisting of a myriad of small but powerful clusters of traders and computer specialists.

However other observers believe that conventional government will eventually restore the balance by adjusting the target of their tax collection base. It is believed that they will, for example, refocus their attention on more tangible products such as property, food and petrol.

14.2.4 Innovative Internet products

The Internet and specifically the WWW is undoubtedly the driving force behind a whole array of new business-centred applications. Below is a sample of recent products:

(a) Voice-sensitive browser applications

Users can now access the WWW without the need for a desktop computer provided they are equipped with a suitable touch tone telephone, mobile phone or a fax machine along with appropriate voice-sensitive browser software (VSBS). VSBS applications employ text to speech routines in order to relay the contents of a web page over a phone. The same software can be used to transmit e-mail and faxes. The main advantage of this type of application is that it enables regular and irregular Internet users to access WWW information but who, for whatever reason, cannot gain access to a suitably equipped desktop computer.

(b) Videoconferencing over the Internet

Videoconferencing over the Internet is one of those applications that is likely to dominate the communication scene well into the next century. Accessing global videoconferencing or services such as video on demand, over the Internet, at local call rates, is extremely attractive to say the least.

One company which supplies a whole range of products for such activity is Cybertec Ltd. Known as the V-COM range, the user can purchase from a variety of upgrade kits. With V-COM technology users can employ inexpensive PC-centred video teleconferencing which supports the transmission of online video as well as voice and data traffic via conventional analogue phone lines, ISDN or cellular telephone systems. V-COM also allows multi-party as well as single-user videoconferencing and is compatible with mainstream products such as Windows, Ethernet, Novell and TCP/IP.

(c) Cheap international phone calls

Web browser developer, Netscape, has included a software application called Cooltalk as part of Navigator 3.0. The advantage of Cooltalk is that it allows users to sidestep conventional telephone routes by relaying voice calls via the Internet. All the user needs for each computer, besides an installed version of Netscape 3.0, is a sound card and a set of speakers. The glaring advantage of this type of activity is that users can place international phone calls at local rates.

14.3 INTRANET TECHNOLOGY

Because of the startling success of the Internet and in particular WWW technology, corporate users have begun to employ web pages and web browsers to operate their own inhouse network information systems. The term Intranet describes those internal corporate computer networks which supply nonpublic company information in a WWW arrangement using Internet protocols. Intranets can connect users to existing corporate databases and enable the pooling of information across the organisation through the medium of an intuitive user-friendly web browser.

Intranets are usually equipped with an Internet gateway; however outside agents are usually restricted by a firewall. External entry to a particular organisation's Intranet usually depends on the organisation's activities. Some organisations enable trading partners a certain degree of access to their Intranet (see 14.4 Extranet). However such intrusion by external parties does raise certain security risks which have to be dealt with accordingly.

Nevertheless the advantages of an Intranet appear very attractive. In addition, because Intranet communication technology is practically identical to the Internet, companies can employ their Intranet for interior messaging/publishing as well as using the Internet as a cost effective communication link.

14.4 THE EXTRANET

The concept of Extranet technology is to enable manufacturers, suppliers and customers to establish a walled-off section of the Internet. This section is in effect a virtual private network which the users can then use in order to streamline their trading activities. For example the suppliers can monitor the manufacturer's work in progress whilst potential customers can feed back on product modifications. Although Extranet technology is still in its early stages of development it is expected to play a leading role in the future manufacture of expensive consumer goods and other more costly high tech products.

14.5 TELEWORKING

Western society is beginning to experience dramatic changes in its work-force. For example current statistics from the Department of Education and Employment indicate that approximately 50% of British workers in 1997 were on either short-term or part-time contracts of employment, double the numbers of the previous decade. Changing labour laws, increased foreign competition and declining traditional industries such as the arms industry, have all had their effect. Nonetheless, employment experts believe that the major cause of this transformation in the workforce is new technology.

Inventions such as digital phones, mobile laptop computers and fibre optic communications have all resulted in the evolution of a new breed of nomadic office worker. Employers can now organise their personnel with optimum efficiency ensuring that they spend the maximum amount of time and effort in carrying out their duties. However even this new breed of worker needs a centre of operations. Teleworker is the term applied to the growing phenomenon of the electronically linked home-based office worker. This is not to say that all teleworkers work exclusively from home but it is a recognition that the home or a base very close to the home is, in effect, their virtual office or centre of operations.

Current technology implies that teleworkers usually communicate with their customers/employers by a variety of techniques such as fax, phone, electronic mail or videoconferencing. Because of the nature of new technology, teleworkers can perform a variety of duties the character of which will depend on the nature of their occupation. Tasks suitable for teleworking include clerical duties such as sales invoicing or payroll, processing insurance claims, document translation and technical authoring. Other more creative activities include desktop publishing, journalism and various design/drafting occupations.

14.5.1 Advantages for commerce

Teleworking can provide massive savings for commerce. For example, any company which downloads clerical duties to a home-based workforce can save money on the following items:

- Office space
- Office equipment
- Heating/lighting bills
- Business rates
- Car parking
- Insurance

- Staff facilities
- Cleaning/maintenance
- Security
- Furnishings

Teleworking also appears to have a positive effect on worker performance and worker stress. Studies indicate that transfer to a teleworking environment usually leads to increased productivity. The main reason for this appears to be the absence of commuting for the teleworker and the ability of the teleworker to organise flexible and productive work schedules. Because of their dispersal, organisations with teleworkers are also less susceptible to natural disasters, transport difficulties and direct and indirect industrial action.

14.5.2 Advantages for the workforce

A teleworking environment is also conducive to workers with family responsibilities, workers with physical disabilities and workers who because of their personal profile or age prefer a more independent routine. Besides the absence of commuting and direct supervision, teleworkers have the extra additional advantage of being able to supply their services to more than one employer. This independence can make teleworkers less susceptible to interruptions to their income due to industrial dispute or redundancy.

14.5.3 Advantages for the community

The obvious reduction in transport pollution means that teleworking is popular with environmentalists. Teleworking also means that it is possible to attract well paid work to the rural community.

A good example of this type of income generation can be seen on the west coast of Ireland. In County Clare there are numerous telecottage villages which have good telecommunication links with big insurance companies in New York. Every day, insurance claims and documentation are transported between New York and Clare via sophisticated ISDN and satellite links. A common language, relatively low costs and instant communications make this ideal for the American insurance companies and a big export earner for the Irish.

14.5.4 The telecottage

The telecottage is the name given to the teleworker's physical workplace. The telecottage can be in the individual's home or, as is becoming increasingly the case, on a communal site within a short walking distance of the teleworker's home.

The degree of technology employed in a telecottage depends on the teleworker's duties and the overall resources. For example, a self-employed teleworking architect could work from an office which has nothing more than a drawing desk and a fax. However whilst the teleworker's paraphernalia can be limited, certain economies can be counterproductive especially if these home-based workers are unable to compete due to shortcomings in their equipment. It is therefore no surprise to learn that the bulk of teleworking is centring on PC-based systems.

14.5.5 The communal telecottage

Communal telecottages can be found in urban as well as rural areas. The crucial feature is their proximity to their workers. They usually contain between 5 and 20 PCs and because of the need to ensure constant workflow they are usually linked in with a major organisation. They are also being perceived as ideal training centres.

14.5.6 Weaknesses

Although there are a lot of advantages to teleworking there are certain weaknesses. For example teleworkers can feel isolated and demoralised due to the absence of social contact, although this lack of contact can be minimised where the telecottage is a communal site.

Teleworkers can also perceive themselves as being disadvantaged with respect to promotion opportunities and can develop hard attitudes to changes in organisational policies. According to a UK Department of Trade and Industry report in 1993 studies indicated that teleworkers that spent at least one day a week in a more formal environment were more likely to be better integrated into the employer organisation. Teleworkers can, it seems, also be exploited. This situation can arise when customers or employers are dealing with isolated communities. Teleworkers in isolated communities may be faced with limited work opportunities and consequently forced to accept less-favourable terms.

Companies can also suffer from teleworking and many have in fact withdrawn from the practice. The reason for this is the loss of personal contact. Various organisations have discovered that teamwork, brainstorming and employer/customer relations become somewhat problematical in a teleworking environment. Managers can consequently find teleworkers difficult to manage. This problem can be exacerbated when managers are required to brief teleworkers who they do not know simply due to lack of contact.

14.5.7 Teleworker profile

There are currently about 500,000 teleworkers in the UK and about 7 million in the US. They are mainly rural based, self-employed and are concentrated in fields such as journalism and the financial services sector.

Because of potential distractions in the home environment organisations employing teleworkers aim to recruit people with strong self-sufficiency skills. Organisations also tend to recruit people with an *au fait* knowledge of their particular industry. Teleworking and nomad style (see below) work routines have brought massive savings to employers and are seen as part of a gradual drift towards the concept of virtual corporations as business and other organisations seek to minimise their costs.

14.6 NOMAD WORKERS

Modern office workers, IT specialists, accountants, lawyers, journalists and other professionals are beginning to evolve into a new class of nomadic worker. Sophisticated portable computers, wireless communication systems, mobile videoconferencing and full Internet connectivity mean that workers can be an integral part of an organisation without necessarily being physically based at a particular site. In essence, modern nomads are skilled mobile workers who follow whoever, whatever or wherever the work is. However, despite this unprecedented mobility workers are, more often than not, still required to make the occasional return to base. A concept which dovetails neatly with this need is hot desking.

14.6.1 Hot desking

Hot desking refers to the temporary physical occupation of a work surface by a particular employee. This work surface could be an actual desk or just a terminal link. In any event the concept of the hot desk is that the employer furnishes a permanent work surface which is available to any worker as and when needed. There is no personal domain pertaining to a particular worker and physical facilities are employed as and when needed. In Scandinavian countries it is now common to find offices with desks and terminals which descend from the ceilings as and when needed.

14.7 COMPUTER TELEPHONY INTEGRATION

Computer Telephony Integration (CTI) concerns the fusion of computer information systems with telephone services. One particular example of this type of technology is Call Line Identification (CLI). For instance a mail order catalogue sales service can arrange for incoming customer calls to immediately retrieve the appropriate customer database record. What this means in effect is that as soon as the operator talks to the customer they will have all the material customer information in front of them. With a CLI application the operator can respond to customer inquiries in a far more efficient manner. Operators employing this type of system are no longer, other than for security, required to glean information from the customer or initiate an appropriate database search routine in order to obtain customer details.

Other CTI applications include:

(a) *Screen dial-up routines.* For example, users can point at a customer account number or a telephone icon, which would activate an appropriate telephone connection.

(b) *Interactive voice response.* Interactive Voice Response (IVR) is simply that technology which enables an organisation to provide a voice-sensitive menu system which articulates selection menus to incoming callers so bypassing the need for a permanent operator.

(c) *Voice/data transfer.* Voice/data transfer involves redirected calls being simultaneously affiliated with any incoming data.

(d) *Screen-directed call routing.* With screen-directed call routing users simply select the icon representing the link or number where they wish to redirect the call.

(e) *Smart routing.* Incoming calls are automatically identified and redirected to the appropriate link/number.

(f) *Internet services.* CTI has advanced with software for enabling users to use the Internet link as a phone service. Its main drawback is that, unlike e-mail, both users, as with videoconferencing, have to be on the line at the same time. However, it also means that users can make international phone calls for the price of a local call. As a result this particular technology is expected to make a major impact.

14.8 PAPERLESS OFFICE SYSTEMS

The paperless office is an expression which refers to the ideal of an office-centred work environment where all necessary information is stored within a computerised IS and where in turn such information can be manipulated, digested and reported without the need for external physical production such as paper printouts. For example, Microsoft is believed to do all its internal report writing via the Excel spreadsheet and e-mail.

However, the expression paperless office is often used as an ironic sideswipe at the apparently unobtainable. The global consumption of office paper in the late nineties is more than five times that consumed in the early eighties. The seemingly overwhelming plethora of computer printouts is obvious to one and all. Nevertheless, trends suggest that there is a gradual change underway and an indication that this type of paper consumption has peaked. Five possible reasons for this trend are:

- E-mail
- Document management systems
- Handwriting recognition systems
- Speech systems
- EDI (electronic data interchange)

(a) *E-mail.* The explosion in e-mail has meant a certain reduction in the use of paper as tens of millions of daily communications are sent and read in electronic format. However there is a counter-argument that such a rate of communication has generated the need for subsequent hard copy. Nevertheless despite this many observers believe it is doubtful that this follow-up output would be as great had there been no such thing as e-mail.

(b) *Document management systems.* Document Management Systems usually refer to those systems whereby organisations both scan incoming physical mail/documentation straight into a digital format and create and store ongoing documentation/information. The data is then manipulated with appropriate document management equipment. This type of system is particularly suited for case type applications and is usually favoured by insurance companies, lawyers, etc. For example lawyers acting in a divorce case could store and track all necessary documentation relating to issues such as the division of property, court orders, maintenance payments and fees without having to constantly refer to a physical filing cabinet. The performance of the individuals responsible for the various stages of the case can be monitored and staff alerted to important dates/appointments.

(c) *Speech systems* – see 13.3

(d) *Handwriting recognition software* – see 13.4

(e) *EDI (electronic data interchange).* Electronic Data Interchange (EDI) is all about the exchange of electronic digital data within a business environment. Specifically, EDI is conducted on those interconnected computers operated by businesses users engaged in a formal trading relationship. However unlike other systems, EDI specialises in the exchange transfer of data which represents that documentation which is central to general commercial trading. These documents usually include sales invoices, purchase invoices, payments, delivery notes and so forth. With an EDI system the actual trading documents are transformed, prior to transmission by the computers, into an agreed message format. This format is usually a well recognised set of EDI protocols, of which there are numerous standards, enabling the communicating computers to interpret and transmit the various documents.

EDI use is believed to be growing at a phenomenal rate and there is no doubt that it has brought about substantial savings for many users. For example there is no need for the production or transportation of the usual regalia of paper. With an EDI system users can place, check and pay for goods/services via the screen and in an instant. In addition errors are reduced as incoming orders do not have to be re-entered into the supplier's computers. Purchasers can also link their ordering systems to their stock control so goods are automatically ordered when their stock falls below certain critical levels. EDI is a favoured strategy of those organisations wishing to streamline or re-engineer their current operations along a JIT type set-up.

However EDI does have its critics. The problem with EDI is that whilst it is popular with those larger commercial organisations wishing to cut down on their overheads it can also be viewed as a burden to smaller organisations. The reason for this concerns the cost of installing an appropriate EDI configuration and the subsequent shift in the burden of overheads. The purchasing of an EDI system which is compatible with that used by a large corporate trading partner can prove somewhat punitive to junior satellite suppliers. Sophisticated EDI applications are notoriously expensive and may necessitate individual users having to totally upgrade their current systems. In addition, many of these smaller suppliers are in a JIT type relationship which means that they must hold sufficient stock in order to meet their customers' immediate needs. Failure by the supplier to meet potential customer requirements can result in the company losing the account or even facing severe contractual penalties. Unfortunately, many smaller companies have discovered that their refusal to enter into an EDI relationship can mean them losing major customer accounts.

14.9 DIGITAL CASH

It has been calculated that about half the transaction costs incurred by high street banks is directly due to their physical cash administration activities. Unfortunately these costs have, for various reasons, been rising in recent years. For example a major contemporary problem for the banks is the manner in which the criminal fraternity is using sophisticated digital technology, such as colour laser printers and industry-standard DTP, to produce counterfeit currency most of which is practically flawless. In fact the only real problem for the counterfeiters is getting the quality of the paper right. In order to combat this, countries such as Australia have introduced plastic notes. Nevertheless in Europe and North America, the major denominations are still paper based. As a consequence, banks and other cash handling businesses have had to instal expensive monitoring equipment in order to combat the increasing use of sophisticated counterfeit money.

Other costs incurred with the physical supervision of money include those concerned with storage, transportation and dispensing. It almost goes without saying that the banks and other similar institutions have passed such costs on to the community. Nevertheless there is an attractive economic alternative to the physical movement of money. The alternative is the relatively effortless exchange of binary coded electronic data. As a result, banking and commerce are currently promoting moves towards a cashless society. This drive is evidenced by the widespread acceptance of credit cards, debit cards and the emergence of digital cash otherwise known as electronic money or e-cash.

Digital cash usually refers to that digital data medium which enables computer-based financial transactions. However it should be pointed out that digital cash is considered to be distinct from the monetary trading which takes place with corporate applications such as EDI systems, share dealings and bank transfers. Two main types of digital cash include digicash and smart cards.

14.9.1 Digicash

Digicash, which is illegal in some juridictions, is a term that is often used to describe those situations where companies effectively distribute their own electronic money. What happens is that users purchase tokens from the company, by conventional means such as cash, cheque or money transfer. These tokens are then stored as customer credits within the company's computer system. Customers can then log on to the supplier company's computer system and spend these tokens by purchasing the company's various goods and services or those goods and services which are provided by other companies who accept trade in the original company's digicash. Although digicash is a relatively recent phenomenon it is expected, eventually, to be a major means of trading on the Internet.

Using digicash has several key advantages to both customer and supplier. The first major advantage is security. Purchasing goods via the

Internet with a credit card usually involves a considerable amount of user as well as transaction detail. This detail must be encrypted in order to secure the integrity of the transaction as well as the customer's privacy. In contrast, with digicash detail is minimal and consequently less vulnerable. In addition unlike a credit card transaction, external observers would not necessarily be able to determine the nature of the digicash transaction. Also, given the possibility of a third party intercepting a digicash transaction it would be very unlikely that they would be able to abuse the user's personal account, something which they can do by obtaining a user's credit card number.

Secondly companies can offer digicash users various incentives if they can persuade them to buy their tokens. The point is that users of digicash can usually only spend this currency in a restricted supplier market. Thirdly digicash users do not have to carry large sums of cash, credit cards or other susceptible sources of money in order to access the supplier's various goods and services.

14.9.2 Smart cards

Smart cards are plastic credit-card-sized devices which contain a small microprocessor. They are in effect the precursor to the eventual arrival of the wallet-sized PC. Smart cards can store vast quantities of data relating to the identity of the smart card user and, when necessary, the smart card user's credit/money.

Smart cards can be filled with data representing what is in effect digital money, but held directly at the bank, and accessed via an ATM or even via a modem. The user presents the smart card in order to purchase various goods and services at the accredited outlets. The supplier can, on receipt of the smart card, usually read off sufficient data to confirm the card holder's authenticity whilst simultaneously deducting the cost of the goods and services from the smart card's digital cash balance.

Ultimately it is home banking which is expected to become the driving force behind smart card technology. The fact is that users can dial up their bank which can in turn relay necessary signals via the telephone, fixed or portable, in order to top up the smart card's money balance. It dramatically reduces the bank's processing and distribution costs as well as providing the user with the ultimate convenience as they will in fact be in possession of their own automatic teller machine.

14.10 VALUE ADDED SERVICES

Because of the increasing sophistication of communication technology, current trends suggest that phone calls and other forms of personal communication will be extremely cheap if not virtually free. As a result it is expected that communication service providers and other IT type business organisations will generate their profits from what is known as Value Added Services (VAS).

A good example of a VAS is the provision of a voice mail option on a mobile phone. Other examples could be the provision of share information or a sports service. Many contemporary Internet providers enable users to browse general information pages for free and only charge user access for those pages providing specialist services.

14.10.1 Help desks

One particular type of VAS which appears to be going from strength to strength is the help desk. Because of the need for computing users to be able to operate their IS/IT in an effective and efficient manner, there has been a massive surge in the provision of phone-linked services of this type. The modern help desk is recognised as a crucial support facility and the fact that phone inquirers can dial help numbers in order to be provided with critical information regarding a particular IT product or service is a potent selling point for any particular company.

The fact that many best-selling computer developers have whole office complexes dedicated to supplying their customers with help desk services is an indication of the importance of this type of facility. Help desks are also popular with the service providers in that they provide useful training experience. Many corporate organisations place junior staff on help desks in order that they might get a thorough understanding of the organisation's products/services. However, if help desks are mismanaged or unstructured they can prove somewhat counter-productive to the organisation providing them. This is especially so if users can't get through or if the actual helpers are inexperienced or badly trained. Such eventualities can lead to the organisation getting a bad reputation and so discouraging potential business.

14.11 CONCLUSION

What is really interesting about the ever-changing world of business IT is the manner in which users and organisations constantly re-engineer their processes and work practices so as to maximise any possible advantage that may materialise from the latest technological breakthroughs. This is no more clearly demonstrated than in the those advances which have arisen from the Internet. The fact is Internet technology and its associated products and services are bringing about such dramatic transformations within commerce and industry that the whole future of world commerce is under review.

What is more, the pervasiveness of this change is demonstrated by the inextricable link that is flowing through all the various technological developments. For example, complementary trend changes such as the increase in the number of teleworkers and the rise in the use of digital cash whilst not always necessarily directly linked to the Internet are nonetheless fuelled by its existence and are as a result providing greater impetus to its overall development. At the end of the day it is this gradual fusion of technology and ideas which usually brings about the greatest advances.

15

Consultation scenarios

15.1 INTRODUCTION

The main purpose of this chapter is to encourage the reader to consider possible solutions to various business IT/IS-centred scenarios. The idea is to reinforce the contents of the book whilst simultaneously enhancing the reasoning processes of the reader with respect to commercial IT/IS issues.

There are twenty six scenarios in this chapter, sixteen of which contain advice. The points of advice given in each of these scenarios is discursive and is in no way definitive. Eight scenarios, namely 15.4, 15.7, 15.10, 15.13, 15.16, 15.19, 15.22 and 15.25, contain no advice and are left as exercises for the reader.

The number(s) in brackets following the heading refer to the chapters in which the subject matter of the scenario largely appears but, of course, the advice as given by the author here or as requested of the reader can be extended to any relevant issue from any chapter.

15.2 GREENCHIP (1, 2)

Greenchip is a select nationwide environmental group made up of IS/IT professionals. The reason why Greenchip was created was to monitor any damage caused to the environment by the use and manufacture of computers and other ancillary equipment/consumables.

The group has a large dynamic and energetic membership. The details of this membership, subscriptions, organisational accounts and so on are held on a large old-fashioned mainframe computer in its London headquarters. The energy requirement of this computer is embarrassingly expensive, a fact which has not gone unnoticed. The group has decided to act. What advice might you give ?

Advice points

The obvious point is that more often than not a large old-fashioned mainframe can be replaced by smaller less-expensive computer(s). Such replacement would normally result in instant conspicuous advantages such as lower power requirements, cheaper software and a release of room space.

However the user's current data processing tasks can prove to be something of an obstacle. If their requirement consists of basic transactions such as mailing lists and subscription fees then one mainstream program or indeed computer system is almost as good as any other. But if the user, i.e. Greenchip, requires certain proprietary applications which are compatible with the current mainframe then there is a problem. A good example would be a specialist computer program processing valuable research data specific to certain environmental projects.

A competent advisor might suggest that the old mainframe be replaced, with a proviso. The proviso would be that any new system should be able to support previous critical applications. However it also possible that the nature of Greenchip has changed or that much of the existing stored data/research was no longer required. In this event, cheaper mainstream equipment would be more than adequate for the organisation's purpose.

15.3 DESIGN-ED (1, 2)

Design-Ed Ltd is a new private school that has evolved from the remains of a local technical college. The idea is that the school will specialise in utilising new technology in training the architects and draughtsmen/women of the future.

Although Design-Ed is a separate legal entity it shares many resources with the old technical college and is in fact physically located inside the main building of the college of which it was once a part. A major shared resource is the minicomputer which is controlled by the old technical college and to which Design-Ed is linked.

As Design-Ed has started to function so it has become apparent that the new generation of CAD software which the school employs is making tremendous demands on this minicomputer. In order to alleviate the situation it has been decided that Design-Ed buy their own minicomputer. Is this necessary ?

Advice points

As we know, workstations were designed to alleviate processing problems in just this kind of situation. It is possible that Design-Ed could purchase

301

cheaper workstations and remain linked to the old minicomputer; after all, contemporary minicomputers are significantly more expensive. However it is possible that Design-Ed is looking for a clean break from its partners and have decided that it would be better to go it alone.

In this situation the school could consider purchasing a cheaper workstation, many of which emulate contemporary minicomputers, or indeed purchase their own minicomputer. However what is of course even more striking is that because of the rate of change in PC technology it could be that contemporary inexpensive PC servers would meet their needs.

15.4 DOWN LOAD (2, 3)

Down Load is a successful London-based second-hand computer shop which has built up a considerable business. The company currently specialises in PC/microcomputers. However, because of its success Down Load is considering the possibility of trading in second-hand mini/mainframe computers. Advise Down Load on the advantages and disadvantages of such a move.

15.5 CHECK BYTE (2, 3)

Check Byte is a small company of accountants specialising in auditing computer accounting systems. Because of the nature of their duties they are constantly moving from site to site analysing data files belonging to various companies. Check Byte has decided to equip their field staff with suitable computers. Your task is to advise them as to their equipment procurement.

Advice points

The most suitable computers for auditors in this line of work would undoubtedly be portable laptop or palmtop PCs. There are however significant differences in the price and performance of these portable computers. For example colour portable computers are usually a third more expensive than their monochrome counterparts. Secondly, as with ordinary desktop PCs there are a range of different microprocessors from which to choose. Thirdly there are significant mobility advantages to be gained from purchasing portable computers incorporating infra red or PCMICA technology. Fourthly, expensive systems usually enable users to access the latest applications as well as upgrade to future hardware developments.

If Check Byte decided that money was no object then colour portable computers equipped with a top of the range microprocessor such as a

Pentium, a large hard disk, PCMICA slots and large RAM capacity could be expected to be more than adequate for the accounting/financial tasks that have to be performed by audit staff.

It could be, for arguments sake, that Check Byte also feels that, as its workers are constantly visiting external organisations, the company's image is enhanced by the sight of their staff porting expensive top of the range computers. However, assuming that Check Byte simply wanted to provide its staff with adequate equipment enabling them to access applications such as cheap but effective spreadsheets or wordprocessors, then a monochrome palmtop portable PC with a low-grade chip such as a 486 may prove to be all that is necessary.

15.6 CHIC EXCESS (3, 4)

Chic Excess is a new dynamic clothes importer that specialises in the latest fashions. Because of the increasingly widespread use of computers in the organisation, Chic Excess has realised the necessity to constantly develop and upgrade the IT skills of its employees.

Realising that Chic Excess is an original and forward thinking organisation, it has been approached by Spartan Mentors, a company offering a totally new computer training concept. It projects the idea that the soundest way to imbue individual workers with a complete and comprehensive set of upgradeable computing skills is by giving individual workers an in-depth understanding of how to use their computer's operating system.

This type of training scheme is an expensive approach as it is in addition to any necessary training that may be required to operate particular applications. Chic Excess is interested. Advise them.

Advice points

Most users usually develop what can be described as a limited working set of procedures when using a particular program or computer. However, the fact is many users are totally confused when they exit the safe confines of a particular application. This lack of control means that such users are unable to perform many relatively routine operations and usually encounter severe difficulty when it comes to manipulating other unknown applications.

If, however, the company's users had a working knowledge of the computer's OS then this would make the users far more productive. They would, for example, be much less inhibited when having to learn about other programs as their knowledge of the OS would usually provide them with certain critical skills which would enable them to move from application to application. Knowledge of the OS would also enable users to have greater control over the computer system's resources. They could, when necessary, reschedule or reconfigure the printers, install new software, make backups and so forth.

Spartan Mentor's idea is radical but logical. Users having a working understanding of the computer's OS are much more independent and self-reliant. In addition, they are unlikely to have to resort to expensive advice/training for what can be described as routine operations.

15.7 SMART SALES (3)

Smart Sales is a subdivision of a multinational personal computer manufacturer called Individual Computers (IC). One of the reasons IC formed Smart Sales was to try and concentrate the innovative personnel within the company in one location so allowing the rest of the organisation to get on with its day-to-day activities. After a substantial brainstorming session Smart Sales have advised IC that they believe that their company would increase their market share if they were to concentrate on the development of ever more sophisticated multifunction personal computers. Advise IC on the usefulness of such advice.

15.8 THE SQUEALER (5)

A satirical magazine called The Squealer has a workforce of six journalists and office staff all of whom are equipped with a standalone PC. The editor has been advised to link these computers in a network. Unfortunately the individual journalists as well as the editor are not convinced of the potential advantage of such a move. Advise them why they should link their machines.

Advice points

LANs enable users to co-ordinate their work in several important ways. Firstly, if the LAN was equipped with suitable desktop publishing software, it would be possible for a group of journalists to all work simultaneously on the same files. Secondly, the data employed by such an application can be passed effortlessly from one user to the another without having to go through repetitive input routines, i.e. stored pictures, stories, etc. can be retrieved at will. Thirdly there are the usual direct economic savings with respect to physical resources such as the employment of shared printer(s), disk space, software and so forth.

15.9 ANCIENT MONUMENTS (5)

Ancient Monuments is a charitable English trust dedicated to the preservation of historical buildings such as castles and old family mansions. However a lot of the buildings that come under the auspices of the trust are used for commercial purposes such as tourism. The trust itself is headquartered in an old keep, the preservation of which is closely controlled by the local authority. The trust has decided to install a LAN in its offices within the keep. Advise them on potential pitfalls.

Advice points

Although an old keep may be an extreme example of a problematic site for a computer network installation, it does nonetheless highlight some of the practical problems encountered when installing a network. For example, because of strict preservation orders which the trust may have helped pass, the trust could well be limited as to the physical nature of the equipment it can install.

Firstly there is room size. If the rooms are huge, then equipment size is likely to be no problem, particularly if the floors are made of stone. However if they are restricted then it is unlikely that the trust can interfere with internal walls in building of this type. Secondly, access to sufficient power points and cabling can be unpredictable and damaging in this type of environment. Excessive wiring may be unacceptable from a health and safety angle as well as being physically challenging. In addition the walls may be so incredibly thick that they interfere with possible wireless solutions. Thirdly there could be aesthetic objections to unsightly, out-of-character equipment configurations on sites of this type.

15.10 COOL COUNSEL (6, 14)

Cool Counsel is an ambitious community-based law centre which is aimed at providing citizens with relevant legal advice with the minimum of cost. Most of the staff at the centre have good computing skills. As result the management are considering the possibility of using the Internet to enhance the service they provide. Advise the centre on the advantages as well as potential disadvantages of such a connection.

15.11 LIFE EXCURSIONS (5, 6)

As a result of the arrival of cost-effective data communication systems, the late 1990s is witnessing a dramatic rise in the number of people working from home.

Joe Doe, a former travel writer specialising in safari holidays, has decided to set up his own travel agency called Life Excursions. His aim is to sell all-inclusive holidays to people interested in safari style wild life trips. These holidays are somewhat expensive and are consequently unlikely to attract ordinary tourists. Joe has decided to work from home using a PC. Advise him as to some of the advantages to his business in connecting his computer to an appropriate WAN system.

Advice points

As a small travel agency cost-effective links are crucial in order to communicate with other organisations and individuals. If Life Excursions was connected to a WAN this would enable it to deal with distant computers/ databases ensuring immediate and accurate bookings. Given the distance of many exotic locations, such a communication system would be crucial to the organisation's existence. Tourists arriving in faraway places without proper support and accommodation would be a marketing and possible financial disaster for the company.

Assuming that Life Excursions was targeted at an elite customer base, a WAN connection would also enable the organisation to gain access to national as well as global customer contacts by way of specialist bulletin boards or by using e-mail systems to implement advertising mail shots. It is suggested that other than specialist WANs such as airline booking systems Life Excursions would undoubtedly do most of its work via the biggest and most probably cheapest WAN, namely the Internet.

15.12 LOCAL NEWS (5, 6)

A regional office of a national newspaper has decided to install a WAN connection to the organisation's main headquarters. The reason for this connection is to ensure the speedy transmission of copy. Advise the office management as to a cost effective means of doing this.

Advice points

If the management decided on a digital transmission connection as provided by ISDN networks or dedicated digital cable links, then they would have opted for the most technically secure and efficient means of transmitting data. However, digital data transmission is a more expensive solution. With dedicated digital cables, the cost of the line is exorbitant and only suitable for organisations with heavy data traffic. It is fairly unlikely that regional newspaper articles would fall into this category. Employing services as provided by a standard ISDN network is more economic. However in order for the computers at the regional office to connect to a digital network via the telephone link, it is necessary for the computer to be fitted with a special adapter. This adapter is usually the same price as an expensive modem. If the newspaper decided to use a standard modem, dial-up transmission charges can be higher because of the slower transmission speeds. However it is unlikely that even very large articles, or even whole newspapers, would be expensive to transmit. It might, therefore, be more suitable for the newspaper to simply purchase a standard modem with its supporting communication software. Ultimately, the system which the management chooses will depend upon the volume of data that it wishes to transmit.

15.13 CAPITAL HIGH (7, 9)

Capital High is a large secondary school in a deprived part of London. So as to try and raise academic standards the management have persuaded the local authority to invest in a high technology learning centre within the school. As one of the school's educational advisors you have been asked to indicate which software you think would be of most benefit to the student's education. Include in your advice relevant information concerning the software's actual attributes and how you think such applications would motivate the students.

15.14 VIDTECH (6, 7)

VidTech is a private training school which has been set up by a team of newly redundant college lecturers. Because of the school's reputation for high quality teaching it has been franchised by a top American university to present its long distance learning Masters in Business Administration (MBA) qualification. The course is targeted at executive personnel working in different companies all over Europe. Given that the school is delivering to such a dispersed market what multimedia techniques would you suggest to deliver the MBA program?

Advice points

The means by which VidTech can deliver the MBA or indeed any other qualification or training program will ultimately depend on the fees which students/companies are willing to pay.

Given that the scenario is an MBA program in the corporate sector it might be reasonable to assume that money is not such a problem. The best solution therefore would be videoconferencing. It is well established that good interaction between lecturers and students is crucial to the learning process. With videoconferencing lecturers can deliver to students from a central point to classrooms scattered across Europe and simultaneously deal with student inquiries and problems as and when they arise.

From a student/employer angle, travel and absence from work is minimised without due loss of tutoring. With respect to VidTech, the school can make massive savings on overheads such as office/classroom rents/costs.

15.15 LOOKATHAT (7)

LookAthat is a mail order concept catalogue specialising in new ideas for the home and office. It has just received details of an expensive market survey stratifying the makeup and needs of its customer base. The survey indicates that their customers are mainly highly educated, professional, discerning and well paid. The survey also suggests that their customers would be more prone to purchase LookAthat products if they could glean more information about individual items. Suggest a new approach that LookAthat might employ so as to encourage more sales.

Advice points

The first point to note is that the customer base is well educated and well heeled. Given that modern education includes (or should include) a reasonable understanding of how to access a computer-based information system and that a vast swathe of the Western middle class now possesses a domestic PC then LookAthat may consider delivering new catalogues on CD-ROM.

CD-ROM has several advantages for this type of retail. Firstly, more often than not, people make casual purchases of this type just from the look of a product. With CD-ROM, LookAthat can supply high quality digitised photographic/video images giving the potential purchaser an all-round feel for the item on offer. The products themselves, when they are accessed by CD-ROM, could trigger a "seductive" sound track so adding to LookAthat's selling pitch.

A CD-ROM catalogue whilst possibly being expensive to produce can also bring about direct savings. Two major savings to be considered would be post since a light CD is far cheaper to mail than big heavy catalogues and a reduction in staff time dealing with customer product inquiries as hopefully a CD-ROM catalogue would give clearer product details and reduce potential misunderstanding as to what the purchaser may be buying.

15.16 BRIGHT PEOPLE (8)

Bright People is an elite personnel agency specialising in the recruitment of management calibre IS/IT staff. As part of its repertoire the company keeps a conventional but nonetheless comprehensive database detailing their potential employees' personal and professional attributes. Advise Bright People as to their responsibilities under the Data Protection Act and the type of strategies they might pursue in order to ensure that they comply with the spirit of the legislation.

15.17 EU-OIL (8)

Eu-Oil is a new European company that has been offered a contract by the Russian government. The contract concerns the drilling and transport of oil from the Transcaucus. In order to achieve this objective, Eu-Oil will have to make a considerable investment in a new high tech complex. This complex will house sophisticated and expensive computer systems which will monitor and control the whole venture. Part of the deal includes a considerable rent payable to the Russian government by Eu-Oil for the use of large nineteenth century palaces that were in fact the former offices of the communist party. It is proposed that these palaces are used as housing for the new computer complex. Advise Eu-Oil.

Advice points

The first thing that Eu-Oil must do is to assess the surrounding political and physical environment. Unfortunately the Transcaucus of the late 1990s is a politically volatile region. This is a man-made threat and given certain reasonable safeguards and assuming that former offices of the communist party are reasonably fortified, it may be one which Eu-Oil can ignore.

However there is another threat which is not man-made and for which the region is equally famous. This is the threat of earthquakes. As a result of the catastrophe which occurred in Kobe in Japan in January 1995, it became apparent that the only large office buildings which were capable of with-standing significant earthquake tremors were those of recent construction. Computer complexes housed in older buildings were completely des-troyed. Given this backdrop and assuming that these palaces are relatively simple in construction, it could be that the overall deal has an unacceptable element of risk.

15.18 TRAFFIC CONGESTION (8)

Statistics in the late 1990s indicate that Britain is experiencing a significant increase in road traffic congestion. In order to relieve this congestion the government is spending huge amounts of money developing detour routes. However a lot of these detours are being built through sites of outstanding natural beauty. Such construction is somewhat controversial and no more so than that of a proposed new road which will run through Maids Meadow which is on the outskirts of the hamlet of Uppertweed (a previous winner of the national tidy village competition).

In order to organise protests against this development a pressure group called the 'Hedgehog Marauders' has been formed. The leadership of the Hedgehog Marauders has decided to place all their membership on a PC database in order to keep the organisation informed via automated mail shots. However some members think this may not be such a good idea. Advise the leadership.

Advice points

The first point to consider is that the database will contain the details of living individuals. As a result, the database will immediately come under the auspices of the Data Protection Act.

The next point that must be considered is whether or not the database needs to be registered. This would really depend on the nature of the data and the way in which it is used. If the data is simply a mailing list used for the distribution of leaflets explaining details of forthcoming events of what is in effect a private club, then it would appear that registration is unlikely. If however the database has commercial connotations whereby Hedgehog Marauders could profit from the information, either through direct retail or by selling the list to interested parties, then the database would most certainly have to be registered.

15.19 EASTERN PROMISE (9)

Eastern Promise is a software house based in India. The significance of this company is that it 'promises' to produce stable and useful computing applications for a fraction of the time/cost that the same applications would take to produce in the West. The main reason for their ability to perform in such an efficient manner is their access to the vast pool of cheap but highly educated Indian software developers. Advise local British companies on the pros and cons of contracting Eastern Promise.

15.20 TROLLEY STOP (2, 3, 9)

Thanks to the increase in home shopping computer systems, there has been a sudden demand for door-to-door delivery services. In order to meet this demand, a new nationwide company called Trolley Stop has suddenly appeared. Trolley Stop is an organisation which is composed of a fleet of vehicles based at various transport depots around the country. However, because Trolley Stop is a relatively low technology concept, there is fierce competition for delivery contracts. So Trolley Stop can compete they have decided to invest in suitable computing technology such as a sophisticated cost/schedule application. Unfortunately, Trolley Stop cannot find a program suitable to their current needs. Advise Them.

Advice points

The management at Trolley Stop has three basic alternatives. Firstly, they can commission developers to produce a suitable piece of software. The advantage of this approach is that Trolley Stop is more likely to get a computing application that is appropriate to their particular needs. However such an approach can prove very expensive and very time consuming. In addition, software development projects can prove somewhat capricious. For example, finishing dates for software development projects are notoriously difficult to predict. As a consequence, Trolley Stop, for whatever reason, may face a considerable delay before the program is actually completed. Commercially speaking, such a delay could be detrimental to the organisation's ability to compete for particular contracts.

With the second alternative, Trolley Stop can purchase ready-made applications such as a spreadsheet/accounting system and then tailor the application to their own particular needs. A ready-made application may not be the ideal solution, given the user's requirements. However generic tools such as spreadsheets will usually provide a platform to enable users to process most of their information requirements. The main advantage of this approach is that the organisation can be provided with relatively cost effective systems which can be up and running as soon as they are installed. Ready-made applications can also act as a short-term stop-gap until a more suitable remedy is produced.

Thirdly, Trolley Stop could recruit and equip computer-literate management capable of using 4GL programming languages. Such an approach could result in Trolley Stop being supplied with sophisticated suitable applications in a reasonably short period. The disadvantage of such an approach is that it could be expensive and may result in the organisation having a fractured information strategy as individual managers create their own applications.

15.21 TAXBASE (9, 10)

TaxBase is a local firm of specialist tax consultants located in Nottingham. As a result of the new tax assessment reforms, and the consequent expected rise in business, their chief accountant, Mr Hood, has decided to place all their customer details on an office-wide database system. Although the organisation is profitable, it is small and Mr Hood has a limited budget. However the company has ambitions and is hoping to attract some of the area's blue chip companies. Mr Hood has been informed that he should purchase an SQL type system. Advise him.

Advice points

SQL type database systems have several critical advantages. Firstly, they are usually compatible with other SQL systems. Compatibility of this nature usually means that users can use applications developed for other SQL databases. Secondly, users can, if necessary, integrate/merge the data between various SQL databases as well as other applications. Thirdly, there is a skill cross-over as users realise that their knowledge is transferable to other SQL systems. Fourthly, the SQL format is a common standard for corporate-sized database systems, a fact which would enable users to talk to larger database users in their own language so to speak.

The major disadvantage of SQL systems/applications is that they can be expensive to purchase and are usually very demanding on the computer's processing facilities. However as ever, these drawbacks are being countered by the arrival of ever increasingly powerful PCs as well as the arrival of cost effective sophisticated PC/scaled SQL database applications.

15.22 JOHN STRESS (9, 10)

John Stress is an overworked accountant working in a local bank. What is more the bank is undergoing a major reorganisation. and management are making more and more demands. As a result of all this pressure John is finding it increasingly difficult to produce his hitherto regular financial reports. In order to try and alleviate the situation John is considering the possibility of using a purpose-written report writing software application.

Unfortunately John has discovered that the type of application he is looking for is not available on the open market. The bank's IT section which is also under considerable pressure has informed John that they haven't got time to produce it. As a result of these shortcomings John who possesses modest computing skills has decided to employ a 4GL programming language to produce the required application. Advise John.

15.23 WORLD ADVANCED SYSTEMS (9, 10)

World Advanced Systems (WAD) is an international trading company specialising in the supply of various electronic components. The company is very successful and makes extensive use of a centralised mainframe database. Unfortunately because of the size of the company, management has discovered that it is becoming overwhelmed with information and that the organisation of their database is not alleviating the problem. Advise them.

Advice points

Sadly information overload is a common phenomenon of the modern business. In this respect alone, colossal corporate databases can prove more of a hindrance to an organisation than a help. However two new products in database technology, namely Data Repositories and Data Warehouses, appear to be going some way to relieve the problem.

Data Repositories are usually aimed at IT professionals. They provide readily available metadata detailing the relationship between the database's various structures as well as the database's uses and user details. Such information enables users to minimise their search routines as they seek to elicit certain critical details in order to carry out various activities such as the creation of new database applications or any necessary modification of the data structure(s) within the existing database.

In contrast Data Warehouses are directed at the end user. The idea of the Data Warehouse is to sweep through the organisation's IS with a view to enabling users to summarise critical data items without affecting the organisation's operational activities.

15.24 LAST BELL (11, 12)

Last Bell is a furniture company specialising in producing fixtures and fittings for the licensed trade. The company produces good quality wooden benching, tables, shelves and counters. The main reason for the quality of the company's products is its use of highly skilled craftsmen and the utilisation of expensive materials.

Unfortunately Last Bell is facing increased competition from similar manufacturers as well as a sharp rise in production costs. In order to meet these challenges Last Bell has been advised, by a team of highly paid consultants, to introduce a JIT system. Explain some of the advantages and disadvantages of such a move.

Advice points

A properly instituted JIT system is ideal for a manufacturing organisation. For example with a JIT system, idle stock levels and work in progress inventories are minimised as the requisition for raw materials and labour requirements are timed to coincide with sales orders. This can lead to massive savings as the company's finances are no longer bound up in inactive assets.

The disadvantage of introducing a JIT system is the expense and effort incurred in developing and implementing it. If it is to be successful it must be done in a professional manner. This means that the organisation's IS must dovetail the organisation's means of operation and production. In addition it is more than likely that the organisation will have to develop a closer link with its supplier chain in order to optimise the flow of raw materials.

15.25 UTILITY INFORMATION SYSTEMS (11, 12, 14)

Utility Information Systems (UIS) is a high tech consultancy specialising in the development of ISs for small to medium sized enterprises. Because of their success UIS is considering entering the servicing sector of the outsourcing market. In other words, not only will UIS create individual company ISs, but they will, when requested, operate and maintain them as well. Advise UIS as to the various strategies they might pursue so as to make a success of this type of operation.

15.26 PUTTING FUN (11, 12, 14)

Putting Fun is a very small private computer manufacturer based in Tipperary. However despite its size, the company has proved to be spectacularly successful in providing applications and equipment for corporate entertainment. The reason for its success has been its development of a PC-based 'virtual golf course' system. As a result Putting Fun's management have decided to employ a computerised IS in order to keep track of the organisation's finances.

Unfortunately, whilst the workforce of Putting Fun are highly skilled and talented in the development of computerised entertainment systems they are less experienced when it comes to producing a useful organisational IS. As a consequence Putting Fun is considering whether or not to 'outsource' such a project. Discuss.

Advice points

Outsourcing usually involves the hiring of an outside agency to perform certain critical services. These services can range from the design of an externally controlled payroll/accounting infrastructure to the provision of a total IS.

The first issue to be considered by Putting Fun is the services that the organisation may wish to outsource. It should be noted that many diminutive computer-oriented organisations such as Putting Fun are often made up of small teams of 'enthusiasts'. These enthusiasts can be very talented but do have a tendency to be a little anarchic in nature. Such an ethos, necessary for an organisation with a creative spirit, is not always conducive for those commercial operations of a more pedestrian nature. It could, therefore, be reasonable to suggest that Putting Fun outsources tasks such as the payroll or stock control so enabling the company to concentrate on what it is good at.

The second issue that Putting Fun must consider is control. If Putting Fun outsources certain tasks it will lose a certain degree of operational control. If the tasks are relatively minor or routine, then Putting Fun is unlikely to be seriously affected. However if major tasks are outsourced then Putting Fun could be putting itself at risk.

Bibliography

Andersen, R. *Computer Studies*, Blackwell 1990.

Avison, D. and Shah, H. *The Information Systems Development Life Cycle*, McGraw Hill 1997.

Barnatt, C. *Cyber Business*, Wiley 1995.

Clifton, H. and Sutcliffe, A. *Business Information Systems*, Prentice Hall 1994.

Combs, M. *Information Systems for Business Management*, Financial Times Pitman Publishing 1995.

Cringley R. *Accidental Empires*, Penguin 1992.

Curtis, G. *Business Information Systems*, Addison Wesley Longman 1995.

Fidler, C. and Rogerson, S. *Strategic Management Support Systems*, Financial Times Pitman Publishing 1996.

French, C. S. *Computer Science*, DP Publications 1991.

Fulcher, J. *Introduction to Microcomputer Systems*, Addison Wesley Longman 1989.

Gates, B. *The Road Ahead*, Viking 1995.

Harry, M. *Information Systems in Business*, Financial Times Pitman Publishing 1997.

Huws, U. *Teleworking in Britain*, Research Series No. 18, Dept. of Employment Oct. 1993.

Lemay, L., Perkins, C. and Morrison, M. *Teach Yourself Java in 21 Days*, Sams. Net Publishing 1996.

Maney, K. *Megamedia Shakeout*, Wiley 1995.

Martin, J. *Principles of Database Management*, Prentice Hall 1976.

Meyer, B. *Object-Oriented Software Construction*, Prentice Hall 1988.

Negroponte, N. *Being Digital*, Hodder and Stoughton 1996.

Norton, P. and Mueller, J. *Peter Norton's Complete Guide to Windows 95*, Sams 1997.

Peppard, J. *IT Strategy for Business*, Financial Times Pitman Publishing 1993.

Robson, W. *Strategic Management and Information Systems*, Financial Times Pitman Publishing 1997.

Schultheis, R. and Sumner, M. *Management Information Systems: the Manager's View*, Irwin 1995.

Thomas, R. and Ballard, M. *Business Information*, Stanley Thornes 1995.

Weaver, P. and Lambrou, M. *Practical SSADM Version 4+*, Financial Times Pitman Publishing 1998.

Yeates, D., Shields, M. and Helmy, D. *Systems Analysis and Design*, Financial Times Pitman Publishing 1994.

Zorkoczy, P. and Heap, N. *Information Technology: an Introduction*, Financial Times Pitman Publishing 1995.

Index